The practice of rights

RICHARD E. FLATHMAN

Professor of Political Science
The John Hopkins University

CAMBRIDGE UNIVERSITY PRESS

CAMBRIDGE

LONDON · NEW YORK · MELBOURNE

Published by the Syndics of the Cambridge University Press
The Pitt Building, Trumpington Street, Cambridge CB2 1RP
Bentley House, 200 Euston Road, London NW1 2DB
32 East 57th Street, New York, NY 10022, USA
296 Beaconsfield Parade, Middle Park, Melbourne 3206, Australia

Printed in the United States of America

Typeset, printed, and bound by
Vail-Ballou Press, Inc., Binghamton, New York

Library of Congress Cataloging in Publication Data

Flathman, Richard E
The practice of rights.

Includes bibliographical references and index.

1. Civil rights. I. Title.
JC571.F52 323.4 75-38185
ISBN 0 521 21170 0

CONTENTS

For
NANCY, KRISTY, KARIE, AND JENNY

PREFACE

The present work represents a continuation of my effort to analyze concepts that are prominent in politics and in political philosophy. Both the importance of the topic of rights and the assumptions from which the work proceeds suggest that the analysis should be able to stand alone as an attempt to contribute to clarity and critical reflection concerning a dimension of political life. One hopes, of course, that studies of this sort will accumulate toward an integrated understanding of major features of politics. The recurrence of certain themes and topics – for example, *rules, action, practices, the social* – in the analysis of a number of major political concepts offers some encouragement in this regard. The more apparent of these continuities, however, tend to be at what might be called the metatheoretical level. It remains to be seen whether they foreshadow coherencies of a more substantive character. But substantive coherence of the sort sought by political philosophy can be forced only at the cost of losing contact with the political realities putatively under analysis. Hence patience (sustained by belief in the value of particular studies) is required. Unfortunately, substantive discontinuities and disjunctions are less difficult to come by.

Work on the present study began in 1970–1, when I had the pleasure of a year's residence at the Centre Universitaire International in Paris. My thanks to the staff of that excellent facility for their many kindnesses and to the University of Chicago for research leave and generous financial support. Most of the writing was done between 1972 and 1975 under the distinctive conditions that obtained in the Department of Political Science of the University of Washington at Seattle. Whatever range of effects the experiences of those years may have had on it, there is no doubt that this study benefited from the able research assistance of Susan Hekman and Craig Carr, from the comments of Arthur DiQuattro, Selvin Eisen, Margaret Levi, Joel Rosch and Stuart Scheingold, and from my many conversations with Paul Brass, Morton Kroll, and especially Ruth Horowitz. My thanks also to Phillip Abbott, Nannerl Keohane, Paul Peterson, and Melvin Richter, all of whom commented critically and helpfully on the manuscript.

London, 1975   R. E. F.

Introduction

Individual rights are a familiar part of the experience of the members of many contemporary societies. Having and exercising, respecting and violating such rights are actions that a great many of us regularly take and encounter. Responses to this experience, moreover, tend to be favorable. Having rights is widely counted among the advantageous, the beneficial aspects of life. Efforts are recurrent to lengthen the list of rights, to deal with additional dimensions of social and political affairs under this apparently comfortable rubric. Societies that accord and generally respect individual rights thereby win a degree of respect and approbation, whereas those that deny or regularly violate them earn disapproval and disrespect.

The aim of this work is to present a systematic account of this familiar aspect of human affairs and an assessment of some of its most salient features. We attempt here to identify, analyze, and assess the patterns of thought and action that make up what we call the *practice* of rights. A number of moderately specialized issues about the grounding and objectives of such a project – that is, issues concerning theorizing about social practices – are discussed in Chapter 1. The primary aim of this brief introduction is to anticipate some of the main substantive questions and themes that figure in Chapters 2 through 10.

A right provides the agent who holds it with a warrant for taking or refusing to take an action or range of actions that he conceives to be in his interest or otherwise to advantage him. Once accorded or otherwise obtained, what we will call the administration of the right (and hence the acting) is in large measure at the discretion of the person who holds it. It is for that person to decide whether, when, and how to exercise it, whether to alienate it, how vigorously to defend it, and so forth. The actions the right warrants are commonly viewed by other persons as contrary to their interests, as limiting their freedom, or as in other ways disadvantaging them personally or as members of the society in which the right is held.

Despite the approbation it receives, the immediate, one might even say the primitive, question that arises about this arrangement is how it can be justified. Contrary to the impression often given by natural rights theorists from Locke to Robert Nozick,[1] rights are not natural, divine, primitive, or brute facts. Nor are they somehow self-justifying or self-evidently justified. Those who hold particular rights can perhaps be expected to favor the arrangement in respect to the rights they hold. But on what grounds can a society or polity expect those who are disadvantaged by those rights to accept the restrictions and interferences that they entail? How can a society or polity justify imposing those restrictions when the persons affected by them are unwilling to accept them?

As we have formulated them thus far, however, these questions are primitive not only in the sense of being elemental and inescapable but in the sense of being crudely stated. To begin with, there are many distinct types of rights and a large and diverse set of instances of each of the major types. In Chapter 2 we develop some of the important distinctions, a process that indicates why no one justification (or disjustification) can be expected to cover all the cases. It is hoped that this discussion will help to explain why the explicitly normative and prescriptive arguments of the last three chapters are directed primarily to a limited set of rights.

A second respect in which the preceding statements require elaboration concerns the individual and individual action and the relationship between them and the settings in which the individual acts. A brief glance at some familiar moments in modern social and political theory should help to identify the substantive issues and themes that will be of concern in this regard.

The idea of rights, and particularly the idea of rights of the individual, is commonly associated with the various forms of liberal individualism as they developed in the West (particularly in England, France, and America) in the seventeenth and eighteenth centuries. Although at odds with most versions of liberalism in arguing for a sovereign with all but unlimited authority, the most powerful statement of the theoretical underpinnings of this position was provided by Thomas Hobbes. In Hobbes' view nature herself had supplied the individual not only with the physical attributes that are a necessary condition of the sort of directed, purposive action that exercising rights involves, but with something very close to the sufficient conditions of such action. Moved by powerful inborn passions and desires and guided by powers of reason that owe little or nothing to history, social relationships, or cultural experience, the individual appears not as shaped and formed by his place or role in a social or political order but as an all but self-subsistent agent.

Despite his often acerbic remarks concerning it, Hobbes had no desire to alter man's nature. Man's passionate, self-directed actions are in themselves no bad thing. To have, to act upon, and to satisfy passions and desires, so far from being evil or even unseemly, is the condition Hobbes called felicity – that is, the best condition to which man can aspire. So long as his natural condition remains unaltered, every individual is justified in pursuing the satisfaction of his passions and desires exactly as he sees fit. Indeed every individual has what Hobbes chose to call a right – the "right of nature" – to pursue the satisfaction of his passions without other than prudential regard for the consequences of his actions for other persons.

The difficulty as Hobbes saw it was that exercising the right of nature is self-defeating. In addition to according men the capacity and the right to act in a self-actuated and self-directed manner, nature cast them into circumstances in which they have no choice but to act in company with one another. Because all men have the same capacity and the same right, the result is destructive, indeed deadly, conflict. Because it is impossible (and would be undesirable if it were possible) to alter man's passionate nature, this result can be avoided only if each person will give up the right of nature and submit to such restrictions and prohibitions as are necessary to allow individuals to "keep company" with one another and yet to satisfy their passions and desires to the greatest possible degree.

Some of the numerous and powerful objections to Hobbes' theory will concern us just below. But there are at least two aspects of his argument that any theory of individual rights must take very seriously indeed. First, it is difficult to imagine any defender of individual rights giving up altogether Hobbes' understanding that (1) individual holders of rights are capable of self-directed action and (2) there are at least some respects in which such action is a good or at least an innocent thing. As we will see in detail as we proceed, the practice of rights pre-supposes point 1 and institutionalizes forms of point 2. Second, Hobbes sees clearly the other-regarding as well as the self-regarding consequences of having a right. As important as it is to Smith himself, Smith's having a right has substantial conse-quences for Jones. That Hobbes deliberately exaggerates these consequences in order to discredit the notion of a right does not invalidate the point made by his argument – a point not sufficiently appreciated in much later liberal and individualist theory.[2]

As any number of critics have observed, however, there are powerful objections to be made against Hobbes' contentions, objections that have regularly been brought to bear on later formulations of liberalism as well as on the stark and often illiberal pronouncements of Hobbes himself. From Sir Robert Filmer to Peter Winch,[3] commentators on Hobbes have con-tended that his theory renders the individual incomprehensible. It so abstracts individual persons from a historical, social, or cultural context that, to mention only one point, the passions that are said to animate human action are and must be empty categories, purely formal placeholders. Some of these same com-mentators have objected that Hobbes' moral latitudinarianism – his insistence on accepting, as far as is consistent with achiev-ing a reasonable degree of security of life, each person's passions and objectives as that person formulates them – yields a "liberty to do as one lists" in respect to all matters not specifically regulated by the sovereign. Thus life in a society modeled on Hobbes' theory would alternate between all but unquestioning submission to authority and sheer license.

Edmund Burke's polemics against the "metaphysical individualism" of the natural rights theorists of the eighteenth century[4] involve closely analogous objections, as do the charges that T. H. Green, F. H. Bradley, and Bernard Bosanquet leveled against Hume, Bentham, and the two Mills.[5] Slightly later, Emile Durkheim and G. H. Mead put similar contentions at the foundation of the new disciplines of sociology and social psychology.[6] For these theorists Hobbes' all but self-subsistent individual is a meaningless abstraction unknown in the real world of human affairs. The individual is the set of statuses, roles, and other intrinsically social positions and relationships that devolve upon a mere biological entity in the course of the more or less patterned interactions that make up social life. The individual's rights (if any) and duties, indeed his interests and desires, objectives and purposes, are incomprehensible apart from the language, the norms and beliefs, the institutions and arrangements that make up a social order. Bradley's formulation that "man is a social being; he is real only because he is social. . . . The mere individual is a delusion of theory"[7] is only the most unqualified of any number of statements that could be drawn from late nineteenth-century and early twentieth-century theorists.

In our view it would be out of the question to defend liberalism and its commitment to individual rights without taking account of the great force of these objections and the alternative understandings of society and human action on which they rest. At the same time these latter understandings seem to exclude or make it very difficult to comprehend features of individual action that are in fact a prominent part of our experience and that have much to be said for them on normative grounds. It is impossible to study rights without being impressed by the extent to which they presuppose, encourage, and in fact instantiate *both* an elaborate skein of concepts, norms, rules, institutions, and arrangements that must be called social as a Bradley or a Durkheim would use that term *and* self-directed individual actions that cannot be completely conceptualized as social.

In this perspective the problem is to evolve a conceptualization that (1) is responsive to the genuine difficulties in the theory that has dominated sympathetic discussion of rights, namely, liberal theory as it comes down to us from Hobbes and his successors; (2) accounts for the sort of individual action that in fact is involved in the exercise of rights; (3) provides optimum reasons for thinking that such action and the device of rights that encourages and protects it are desirable features of our social, political, and moral lives. We conclude this introduction by commenting briefly on three features of the conceptualization that we have arrived at in pursuing these objectives.

The first of these is the concept of a practice, the notion of treating rights as forming a social practice. As explained in the following chapter, the concept of a practice is drawn from such ordinary language expressions as "the practice of law or medicine," "we have always made it a practice to . . . ," "I felt I had to do it in the circumstances but I don't intend to make a practice of it." But the notion of the practice of rights is not established in ordinary language. We have adopted it here because its properties as a unit of analysis concept are promising as a way of recognizing and reconciling both the individual and the social dimensions of rights. Rights arise out of and are accorded within a rule-governed social practice. But they are accorded to and exercised by individuals whose actions cannot be analyzed without significant remainder in terms of properties of the practice or the society more generally. We add only that the present use of the concept of a practice is informed by work in the philosophy of language and the philosophy of action, particularly that of Wittgenstein and those influenced by him. Languages are social, rule-governed, and highly traditional phenomena that deeply influence individual thought and action. Yet languages are constantly put to distinctive, unprecedented uses by those who make up a linguistic community. Thus one can look to the shared, rule-governed, persisting features of a language as a grounding for generalizations about social life and at the same time retain a basis – particularly in the analysis of concepts such as *intention, purpose, reason for action* – for accounting for the kinds of individuated conduct involved in the exercise of rights.

The second is the *liberal principle,* a normative principle according to which it is a prima facie good for individuals to have and be in a position to act upon and satisfy their interests and desires, objectives and purposes. *If* there is a historical antecedent for this principle (and we certainly do not claim that it is common to or characteristic of all liberal thought), it is what we earlier called Hobbes' latitudinarianism. Unlike Hobbes (and natural rights theorists in respect to alleged natural rights), however, we will attempt to derive this principle not from unmediated nature but from conceptualizations that are well established in ordinary language. We will defend it in part in terms of its derivation and in part in terms of the advantages of reasoning from it to conclusions about various questions concerning the practice of rights. The latter part of this task will be implicitly and sometimes explicitly comparative in character. It will concern the advantages of reasoning from the liberal principle as compared with reasoning from various alternatives to it – especially principles generated by natural rights and contractarian theorists. It might be added that we do not view this principle as merely negative. As the place of the term *good* in the principle might suggest, actions and arrangements that accord with the principle are a positive achievement for which liberals should work and from which they can and should take satisfaction. Contrary to numerous critics, liberalism need not be "essentially negative," need not be limited to "a series of denials."[8]

Derived in part from analysis of the practice, the liberal principle will also form a vital part of our attempt to assess that practice and to justify certain aspects of it. But the liberal principle is by no means a sufficient basis for an assessment and

justification that can meet the objections to liberalism and to
individual rights. Owing to the encouragement and protection
that the practice of rights affords individual action, anyone who
accepts the liberal principle will have grounds on which to be
favorably disposed to the practice. But these grounds must be
supplemented by reasoning that takes account of the wider
consequences of establishing and maintaining the practice, particularly the consequences for other persons who are directly
or indirectly affected by rights and their exercise. A justificatory
theory of rights is part of political and moral theory. The liberal
principle, as important as we think it is, is not a sufficient basis
for such a theory.

We hasten to add that this work does not pretend to offer a
fully developed political or moral theory. It does attempt to
use the study of rights as a vehicle for presenting elements of
such a theory. To this end the final chapters make use of three
encompassing concepts or understandings of political society,
concepts that yield contrasting perspectives on the practice of
rights. The three are private individualism, communitarianism,
and public or civic individualism.[9]

Theorists of the first two of these models agree that liberal
individualism in general and individual rights in particular
divert the members of a society from shared activities, values,
and concerns, particularly those that theorists of civic individualism have thought to be the essence of the specifically
political role known as citizenship. Private individualists, however, welcome this result and have defended individual rights
precisely or at least largely on the ground that they constitute
limitations upon and offer protections against the collective
aspects of social life. The rights of citizenship are valued in
large part as a way of limiting the scope and significance of the
role of citizenship. We will suggest that this construct cannot
yield a satisfactory answer to the primitive question about rights
that we noted at the outset of this introduction.

Communitarians are typically no great defenders of citizenship. But in this case skepticism about citizenship and the
rights associated with it stems from a desire to maximize the

scope and the intensity of other commonalities of social existence (together with the belief that the practice of rights privatizes the individual and diverts him from those commonalities). The construct is not a promising source of justifications for the practice. We take it up primarily because it poses a challenge that any defense of the practice of rights must meet and in order to argue that the most valuable aspects of that practice are in fact compatible with achievement of the defensible objectives of a communitarian understanding.

Civic individualism is the conception in terms of which we will develop a positive argument for crucial aspects of the practice of rights. This choice is rooted in three considerations: first, the conception is genuinely a form of individualism and can be formulated so as to be consistent with the liberal principle; second, it is capable of locating the individual and individual actions in the sociopolitical context in which we in fact find them; and third, it gives suitable emphasis to those aspects of the practice of rights that we have found to be the most important and the most defensible, namely, those that bear directly on the role of the citizen and the citizen's place in what has traditionally been known as the *vivere civile*. In this last regard use of this concept contributes importantly to an objective of this work: to restore to theorizing about rights a primary concern for their political value and significance.

This last objective is a part of the explanation for some of the significant limitations on the present effort. Chapters 2 through 7 attempt to analyze the distinctive characteristics of the major types of rights. But the more explicitly and insistently normative arguments of Chapters 8 through 10 bear primarily on rights of citizenship such as freedom of speech, the press, and association. The justifiability of a host of important and highly controverted rights or alleged rights – such as to welfare, to various forms of compensatory preference, to protection when accused of a crime – is not explicitly addressed in the present work.

We hope to take up some of the latter topics in future work. But given that practicalities dictated inclusions and exclusions, a focus on rights of citizenship was suggested by a growing (and understandable) uncertainty whether, or if so why, citizenship can or should be a meaningful and valued role or dimension of life in contemporary societies. For reasons central to the notion that rights form a social practice (see Chapter 1), such uncertainty all but necessarily foreshadows a further weakening of the commitment to those rights that warrant and protect the activities of which citizenship consists. Hence there seemed to be more than a theoretical point to an attempt to fashion, or rather to contribute to the effort to revive and adapt to present circumstances, a conception of human society that gives us reasons to value those activities and the rights that protect them. Such a conception leaves many important questions about rights unanswered. But its acceptance would contribute to a society in which the answers to them could be pursued in a manner worthy of us all.

1

The Practice of Rights

Central to the approach to the study of rights that predominates in much of this work is the concept of a *practice;* we will treat rights as forming a practice, and our study will be an attempt to analyze and assess the major features of that practice. In this chapter we explicate the assumptions that underlie our use of this concept and identify the implications of employing it as an orienting and organizing concept in the study of rights. Because of the prominence and importance of the contrast between *practice* and *theory,* much of this explication concerns the complex relationship between *practice* as we use it and several dimensions of the concept of theory.

I.   The concept of a practice

Although a technical, philosophical, and social-scientific concept in some respects that we will identify as we proceed, the present concept of a practice is rooted in ordinary language. Expressions such as "the practice of law," "the commercial practices of the modern farmer," and "Williams makes it a practice to" indicate the standing of the concept in nontechnical discourse and provide us with the foundation on which the present use of the term is built. Our first step, accordingly, is to discuss several of the leading features of the ordinary use of the concept. We then develop and refine these features, doing so primarily by pursuing the contrast between practice and theory.

The most prominent aspect of the ordinary language notion of a practice is that it concerns things that people do, actions that they take. The practice of medicine consists of those modes of conduct – *making* diagnosis, *performing* operations, *prescribing* drugs, *contributing* to the AMA – in which doctors of medicine qua practitioners engage. *Commercial practices* of the modern farmer refers to such actions as taking out loans to finance crops, holding acreage out of production to keep prices up, forming marketing cooperatives, and so on. This aspect of the notion of a practice is the most common point of contrast with such notions as theory or the theoretical, speculation or the speculative, contemplation or the contemplative. We discuss it from this perspective in the following pages. In philosophical contexts the connection between practice and action also invites a contrast between things people do and events they experience or suffer, between actions that people take intentionally, knowingly, for reasons and things that happen to them, that they undergo unknowingly, unintentionally or even despite their efforts to avoid them. As the phrase *for a reason* already begins to suggest, this contrast is closely related to the practice-theory dichotomy. It is a contrast that is particularly important to understanding the exercise of rights.

Second, the notion of a practice is most commonly applied to *sets* of actions that recur over time and that are thought to be interrelated or to cohere together in some significant degree. Once again, applications such as the practice of law or medicine provide accessible examples. Practicing law or medicine is not the same thing as working on an assembly line or marching in a platoon. There is no fixed repertory of all but invariant behaviors that are repeated in more or less uniform sequences. Timing, style, emphasis, and much more are in considerable (though variable) measure for the practitioner to determine. The actions that make up the practice vary significantly from one specialization to another and from locality to locality and they change substantially over time.

For all their variability, open texture, and permeability, however, these practices present distinct, recognizable modes of activity marked by recurrent and interconnected characteristics. Practitioners are readily identifiable and those of their actions that are part of the practice can usually be distinguished from other actions they take. There is no single type of action that is necessary to or invariably a part of the practice, but there is a configuration or pattern of actions that is characteristic of the practice and by which it is in fact identified. The elements of this configuration, moreover, are interconnected both in fact and in understandings of practitioners and reasonably knowledgeable observers. Very often these interconnections are so close that it is difficult to understand one action apart from an understanding of its relationship to others in the configuration. Sometimes it is possible to predict action A on the basis of observation of other actions with which A is commonly associated in the pattern. For example, it would be difficult to understand the prescription of a medicine, regimen, or other remedy apart from the making of a diagnosis; it is often possible to predict the objection a defense counsel will make on the basis of the line of questioning followed by the prosecution.

This second set of characteristics might encourage us to view *practice* as primarily an observer's concept, as a concept used to discuss observer-detected regularities in human affairs. The parallels between *practice* as it emerges from the second set of characteristics and the concept *system* as it is commonly employed in contemporary social science could easily lend support to this inclination.[1] Nor is the inclination altogether inappropriate. Use of *practice* to refer to sets of human actions is by no means restricted to participants. Although it happens that the present writer (and presumably most readers of this work) is a participant in the practice of rights, nonparticipants are hardly debarred from analyzing and assessing that practice as such. Moreover, participants, observers, and participant-observers all use the concept of a practice to identify and otherwise to talk about observed regularities.

The ordinary language concept of a practice, however, cannot be reduced to the status of a device for analyzing observer-detected regularities, nor do we so use the concept here. The key to the differences between *practice* and such observer concepts as *system* (and the key to our reasons for wanting to preserve those differences here) lies in the conjunction of two points, first, that practices consist of actions that people take, and second, that they involve rules and rule-guided conduct.[2]

The most important point in the present context is that the recurrent actions and patterned interconnections characteristic of practices can be best (though not completely) understood in terms of the acceptance, by participants in the practice, of rules according to which it is right, obligatory, proper, prudent, or simply expected that they act in certain ways and refrain from certain other actions. An example of such a rule from the practices to which we have been referring is the requirement that the doctor-patient and lawyer-client relationship be treated as confidential. An example from the practice of rights would be the rule that we should not expect gratitude for respecting the established rights of others, that holders of the rights are entitled to such respect. Learning and coming to accept and act upon such rules is an integral part of learning to practice medicine and law. The processes of transmitting knowledge and acceptance of such rules to new generations of practitioners is one of the chief means by which continuity is maintained in these practices.

These rules neither result from nor create natural, physical, or logical necessities.[3] It is possible for the participants in a practice to violate and even simply to disregard the rules governing it, and in most practices violations are not in fact uncommon. It is also possible to change the rules, and such changes, although typically slow, are commonplace and a primary means of changing the practice.

For these reasons, to state the rules is rarely, if ever, equivalent to stating a scientific law in the sense of a regularity that holds without exception or with a definite and predictable frequency of exceptions under specifiable conditions. Thus statements of such rules do not explain regularities in the conduct of participants in the sense in which an event has been "explained" when its occurrence has been subsumed under a scientific law that is part of a so-called nomothetic theory. As ordered, regular, patterned as it often is, rule-governed conduct involves human *action;* it involves reflection, intention, and decision on the part of the agents in question. Above all it involves having reasons for what one does. Following a rule requires discriminations among correct and incorrect, defensible and indefensible interpretations and applications of the rule to sets of circumstances. It also requires that the agent accept the rule, or at least acting on it, as a right, good, useful, or prudent thing to do in the circumstances. (A person's behavior might accord with the requirements of a rule without satisfying these conditions. But then it would not be conduct guided by the rule in question.)

Conduct that satisfies the conditions just iterated, however orderly, patterned, and even predictable, must be understood and explained, at least in part, in terms of models that accommodate both its regularity and interconnectedness, on the one hand, and the significance of individual and often highly individuated reasons for action, on the other; models that take cognizance of individual interests and desires, objectives, purposes, intentions, and other reasons for action, on the one hand, and rules, institutions, understandings, and values shared among and exercising an influence upon the conduct of numbers of people, on the other. The notion of a practice is put to this use in ordinary language and we attempt here to use it for the same purpose in analyzing and assessing rights. By treating rights as forming a practice, we try to capture the ways in which they can be devices for warranting highly diverse and individuated action and, at the same time, one of the means through which individuals have been incorporated in sociopolitical orders marked by patterned coherence and considerable stability and even predictability.

II. Practices and theory

Practice and *theory* are very far indeed from being univocal terms. There is, accordingly, no single relationship between them. The major uses of each, moreover, are neither tightly delineated nor clearly discriminated one from the other; hence, the relationships among them are complex and difficult to specify. Without attempting a systematic clearing of these muddy waters, we are aiming here to identify three more or less distinct (though hardly unrelated) kinds of theory in which the latter is significantly involved with practices and the study thereof. Very roughly, the three are (A) The body of assumptions and propositions that underlies use of the notion of a practice as an orienting and organizing concept in the study of human affairs. Some of these assumptions and propositions fall into what is conventionally called social theory; some form a part of the philosophy of social science and epistemology. (B) The body of ideas, beliefs, attitudes, values, and so forth, held by participants in a practice and forming a part of the (at least implicit) basis on which they act. (C) The body of descriptive and normative propositions about political society that one hopes will emerge out of the study of particular practices and that will contribute to the larger theoretical enterprise traditionally known as political philosophy. Each of these kinds of theory is prefigured in the foregoing discussion in this chapter. In this respect what follows is a further elaboration of the notion of a practice as we have delineated it thus far and as it will figure in this study of rights.

A.   *Theory and the "social practice" approach to the study of human affairs*

Systematic study of human affairs involves and depends upon at least implicit assumptions and propositions concerning the general characteristics of that phenomenon. Such assumptions and propositions influence the investigator's choices as to the appropriate methods to be employed, the kinds of evidence available and relevant, the objectives that can properly and reasonably be pursued. At least since Aristotle distinguished between the practical and the theoretical sciences,[4] numerous investigators into human affairs have attempted to identify the distinctive characteristics, if any, of this subject matter and to identify and refine the methods and objectives appropriate to systematic inquiry concerning it. Now commonly designated by such labels as the philosophy and methodology of social science (with vital relationships to epistemology), these reflections have produced a rich variety of conceptions and theories that compete for the allegiance of social scientists and theorists. Investigations focusing on practices are theory infected at least in the sense that they involve choices among the assumptions and commitments out of which theories about inquiry have been and (could be) formed.

It is part of the very notion of a systematic inquiry that it seeks to identify and understand regularities, orders, patterns in the phenomenon it studies. (It is not part of the notion of such an inquiry that it find regularities, orders, etc.) In the study of human affairs there is continuing controversy as to where and how investigators will most properly and profitably seek to satisfy these objectives. As understood here the study of practices searches for patterns and an understanding of them primarily (though not exclusively) in those aspects and dimensions of human affairs that are known by and meaningful to the actors who participate in them. Its aim is not to ferret out some previously hidden or veiled reality, some set of forces unknown to participants, but to identify and give a systematic account and assessment of the assumptions, beliefs, ideas, values, expectations, and modes of action that are prominent in the practice as its participants understand it and engage in it. The enterprise of analyzing a practice is in large measure dependent upon, one might say responsible to, the understandings and activities of the participants in it.

The strategy of focusing on participant meaning is common to a number of schools of thought concerning the study of human affairs, including phenomenology, pragmatism, and linguistic or conceptual analysis as it has developed out of the philosophical work of Wittgenstein. The present effort is influenced most heavily by the last of these sources. The concept of a practice as here used is analogous to Wittgensteinian notions such as *language-game* and *form of life* – that is, to notions that refer to clusters, nodes, or foci of meaningful activity that form more or less distinct aspects of the life of a society or subsocietal social group.[5]

A key element in this mode of analyzing such clusters of meaningfulness is the notion of *rule* and *rule-governed conduct*. The notion of a rule (or a convention) first enters Wittgenstein's later philosophy as part of his effort to analyze the phenomenon of meaning or meaningfulness in what deserves to be thought of as its most fundamental sense or form; that is, in the fact that human beings are able to use language in a mutually intelligible manner. Wittgenstein argued, very roughly, that intelligible use of a language depends on the fact that the proper use of its units is governed by rules and conventions of various types (e.g., semantic and syntactic) shared among those who speak it. *A* can know the meaning of *B*'s statements because both *A* and *B* know and follow the same rules in using the concepts and other linguistic units of which *B*'s statements consist.

On this view the investigator who seeks to give an account of meaningful discourse in a particular aspect of human affairs will seek to identify the rules and conventions that are operative in communications that take place in that discourse. In Wittgenstein's understanding, however, meaningfulness in the fundamental sense of the meaning of words, logical, arithmetic, or musical notations, and so forth, is not somehow unrelated or irrelevant to meaningfulness in wider senses of the term. The idea that investigations into language and its uses are concerned with words or "mere words" and nothing more is totally foreign to his thinking. To begin with, to speak, write, or otherwise communicate is to act. There is a tradition that goes back to at least Aristotle according to which speech is the mode of action that is distinctively human. Communication, moreover, is rarely for its own sake. One speaks or writes intentionally, for a purpose, to achieve some objective, to bring about some desired effect or outcome. The act of speaking or writing is almost always some further act as well. If I say, "I have a right to do *X*," it is unlikely that I am merely displaying my capacity to form cor-

rect sentences. Indeed practices such as rights consist in large
measure of such statements as the one just presented. These
statements are meaningful to the actors in question not only in
the sense in which *meaningful* contrasts with *nonsensical* but in
the wider sense in which it contrasts with such adjectives as
trivial, insignificant, or *unimportant.*

There is, however, a broader point here, a point that lies at
the very foundation of the social practices approach to the study
of human affairs as here understood. We can explore this point
by examining aspects of Wittgenstein's notion of a language-
game.

It is characteristic of the activities in which statements such
as "I have a right to do *X*" figure that they depend upon a more
or less definite set of conditions or circumstances, the setting of
particular institutions and arrangements, and the presence of
delimited groups or classes of persons that have shared certain
experiences. The actions, assumptions, procedures, and understandings characteristic of the activity are readily comprehensible within those conditions and among those persons. But if the
same actions are taken, the same procedures followed, outside of
the usual context they are surprising, they seem odd or even
bizarre, and we have difficulty comprehending and responding
to them. In the context of the auction house and surrounded by
items to sell and experienced auction goers to purchase them,
the agitated manner, the loud, rapid-fire speech and technical
terminology of the auctioneer pose no problem for us. The
same conduct and terminology on the part of a salesclerk in a
department store or the corner grocer behind his counter, to say
nothing of the lawyer meeting clients in his office, would leave
auditors puzzled and perhaps dismayed. The anxious pacing,
repeated inquiries, stories and concerns exchanged that are
commonplace among "expectant fathers" in the precincts of
hospital delivery rooms would be incomprehensible in a barber
shop, a ticket agency, or even an employment office. Those present might know all the words spoken, might have seen all the
physical movements and gestures, and yet be mystified by both.
Auctioneering, we might say, is a language-game (or a practice)

and various concepts, gestures, and so on, that have a clear meaning within the game are puzzling outside of its limits.

The intimate relationship between meaning, on the one hand, and the things we do and the contexts in which we typically do them, on the other, is at the heart of Wittgenstein's notion of language-games. "But how many kinds of sentences are there?" A common grammatical answer might be, "Assertion, question, and command." But this is woefully inadequate. In fact there "are countless kinds: countless different kinds of use of what we call 'symbols,' 'words,' 'sentences.' And this multiplicity is not something fixed, given once for all; but new types of language, new language-games, we might say, come into existence, and others become obsolete and forgotten." And "the term language-game," he goes on to say, "is meant to bring into prominence the fact that the speaking of language is part of an activity, or of a form of life."[6]

Language-games sometimes involve terminology confined to the activities in question. The technical terminology of physicists, football players, and fraternity members exemplifies words with such a restricted use. But distinct terminology is not the key to understanding the concept of a language-game or to distinguishing one language-game or one practice from another. The key, rather, is the role that the words (and gestures, facial expression, and other means of communication) actually play in the activities we perform in playing the language-games, activities that, in various ways, we distinguish one from another as a part of engaging in them. What role do the technical terms, gestures, and rapid speech play in the auction? What role do the pacing, repeated inquiries, and so forth, play in the activity of expectant fatherhood? Of course these roles are determined in part by the rules, techniques, purposes, and so forth, of the actions and concepts that are part of activity. But at least a part of the point of talking about language-games, of adding that concept to such terms as *rule,* is that there is more to meaning than can be encompassed in any one of the notions discussed earlier or in a mere adding up of what is conveyed by each of them alone. We get closer to Wittgenstein's idea by saying that there is the combination of, the connections among, particular rules, techniques, and purposes. Some rules, purposes, and techniques seldom, if ever, appear apart from one another. And the distinctive combination formed by them, the particular ways they connect up in our use of them, may be thought of as forming a language-game. But there is more: "it is our *acting*, which lies at the bottom of the language-game."[7]

What, over and above rules, purposes, and techniques, and combinations thereof, does Wittgenstein have in mind when he says that acting is at the bottom of language-games? Perhaps something like the following. Children who have never played card games might learn rules of poker, such as the rank order of hands, might see their purpose in the game, and might be able to apply them to decide who had won a particular hand. But knowledge of such rules, purposes, and techniques of application would not be sufficient for them to grasp the meaning of many of the things that are said and done around poker tables. Even adults experienced with other card games and well instructed in the rules of poker are at first awkward in their own play and slow to comprehend many of the remarks, gestures, facial expressions, and so on, of experienced players. Indeed seasoned poker players often have the same experience on their first encounter with a group of players. Or to use one of Wittgenstein's examples (he is talking about someone doing geometry): "What tells us that someone is seeing the drawing three-dimensionally is a certain kind of 'knowing one's way about.' Certain gestures, for instance, which indicate the three-dimensional relations: fine shades of behavior."[8] These fine shades of behavior are never entirely uniform among all those who participate in an activity and they are rarely if ever covered by rules governing the activity. Hence we cannot adequately explain them or the learning of them in terms of rules or rule application and following. Yet regular participants in and observers of such activities will know their place in them. They will readily be able to distinguish between their own capacity to participate in activities in which they "know their way about" and those in which they do not, and they will be able to distinguish between others who do and who do not. Such persons, we might say, have not only mastered the rules, purposes, and techniques involved, they have mastered the language-game.

There is nothing mysterious, nothing tacit in any specialized sense, implied in this notion of a language-game. Wittgenstein often omits the term and simply talks of the context, the customs, the surroundings, the characteristic features, and so forth, of particular activities and uses of language. Far from being hidden or tacit, these features are known to and perpetuated by experienced participants in the activity. If they are seldom discussed or iterated explicitly, this is because they are taken for granted in the conduct of participants. They are among the most important things new participants learn from those who are experienced in the activity, and they are among the most important things that observers must learn if they are to understand the meaning of what participants say and do. Philosophers of language, social scientists, and all others who wish to understand meaning must look to see how the activity in question forms a "pattern which recurs, with different variations, in the weave of our life." They must look to see how the uses of this or that concept fit into and contribute to that pattern and that weave. Such is our objective in the present study of the practice of rights.[9]

B.   *Theory and the actions of participants in social practices*

The assumptions and propositions discussed in section A apply to the study of human affairs only insofar as such affairs in fact include the more or less distinct, internally cohesive clusters of rule-guided, purposive conduct that we are calling practices. Theories in the sense of a coherent set of assumptions and propositions in the realm of the philosophy of social science are significant as guides to the study of human affairs only insofar as the empirical conditions and circumstances they posit are in fact instantiated in societies and social groups. In this respect the relationship between theory and practice is one of dependence of theory on practice.

At the same time, to the extent that the empirical conditions posited by a social practices approach to human affairs are in fact instantiated, there is a sense in which theory and theorizing, or something with important parallels and analogues to them, is intimately involved in the workings of a practice. Practice is dependent upon a kind of theory and theorizing.

A social practice, we have suggested, consists of a distinguishable and more or less internally cohesive cluster or set of rule-guided, purposive actions. The shared ideas, values, and rules that figure in such a set, the concepts in which those ideas, values, and rules are embodied and through the use of which they are expressed and otherwise acted upon, supply participants with their way of making sense of the world in which they live and act, their way of understanding, organizing, and giving verbal and other modes of expression to those understandings. There is an important sense in which, as Peter Winch has said, the world in which participants in such a set or practice live and act is *what* it is by virtue of the concepts by which they make sense of it.[10] In the absence of a set of concepts the "world" would be that "blooming buzzing confusion" of which numerous psychologists and philosophers have spoken. Rational, purposive action in or upon such a world would be impossible. Using a different set of concepts than the one any given group of participants now has, their world and their actions would be other than they now are.

The set of shared ideas, values, rules, and concepts by which participants make sense of a practice and their place in it might be viewed as constituting a sort of theory; and their development, application, and interpretation of it might be viewed as a sort of theorizing. Our willingness to use this terminology will presumably depend upon such factors as the coherence that obtains among the elements of the set in question, the degree of self-consciousness concerning that set among participants, and the willingness to modify the set in the light of thinking about and acting in and upon it. These factors vary from participant to participant and from one practice to another. Little would be gained by stipulating that they must be present in a particular form or degree in order to justify use of *theory* and *theorizing* in discourse about them.

What is more important than whether to use *theory* or weaker terms such as *belief system, ideational dimensions,* or *ideology* is that we recognize the ways in which the patterns of meaningful conduct that are the hallmarks of a practice involve the sorts of activity of which theorizing in the fullest sense (say, the sense in which we would agree that Kant or Plato theorized) is the most systematic form. Consider an example from the practice of rights. Assume that *A* claims a right to strike and picket the plant at which he works. To formulate and advance such a claim *A* must know and know how to apply a number of rules. There are, first, the rules governing the use of the several concepts of which his formulation consists. And some of these linguistic rules double in brass as legal, moral, or prudential rules of conduct. To claim a right to strike and picket is to allege that the concept of a right in general, and this right in particular, has meaningful application to the proposed action, that the question of whether there is such a right arises in a meaningful way in the circumstances at hand. It is also to allege that the rules that establish rights in the society do in fact accord the right claimed. Further, to advance such a claim involves a judgment, perhaps moral, perhaps exclusively prudential, that some interest or objective that *A* has, whether purely personal or shared with some number of people, will be effectively served by this particular mode of conduct. These several judgments are likely to be challenged by others. And challenges dramatize the extent to which such judgments involve interpretations and applications of general statements; the extent to which they require the individual to identify, select from, and organize the facts and other considerations that support the conclusion he wishes to defend. However we choose to label them, these features of a practice are at the heart of the approach we are attempting to delineate. Much of the present work is devoted to identifying and analyzing the theory of the practice of rights in this sense of *theory*.

C. *Political philosophy and the study of political practices*

Theory in the third sense we examine is both about and an attempt at further development and assessment of those elements of practices we have just discussed. In the respects in which it is about the latter it can be viewed as dependent upon but external to the practice. In the respects in which it is a further development and assessment of elements of practices it *may* be internal to those practices and the political society of which they form a part.

To begin with the respects in which political philosophy is about practices, this can be said because political philosophy has claimed to be descriptive of political reality, has claimed to give an accurate, albeit abstract, systematic, and hence severely selective, account of political life. Even in its most insistently normative and prescriptive moments, political philosophy assesses and prescribes to something, not to anything whatever; it evaluates politics as it is or has been in time and space. Even those of its proposals judged to be the most utopian have been built upon, have projected from (however accurately), features of human beings and human affairs. To suggest, as Talcott Parsons and Edward Shils have done, that, "What has traditionally been called political theory has contained more of philosophical and ethical explication of the problems of government than of empirical analysis of its processes and determinants,"[11] is to suggest that political philosophers have been great fools. It is to suggest that they have presumed to give advice about matters that they have not first troubled to know or understand.

To the extent that social and political life includes practices with the features we have been discussing, a political philosophy that aims to be about political life will be about (among other things) those features. By giving an account of the assumptions, ideas, beliefs, concepts, rules that figure in the practices it wishes to assess, it avoids the charge that political philosophy misses its mark, that it is (or may well be) irrelevant to the understanding and assessment of political life because there is no reason (or it has given us no reason) to think that it is about political life as it has been, is, or could be.

As we see it here, however, the relationship between political philosophy and the features of practices discussed in section **B** is not simply the same as the relationship between empirical political science and political reality. This is partly because of the sense in which those features are themselves an example of the same genre of activity of which political philosophy is a more abstract, more systematic example. It is partly for this reason that political philosophy is not only about but a further development of the sort of theorizing that is a part of practices such as rights.

Political philosophy attempts to render the world comprehensible in a sense going beyond that which is involved in day-to-day conduct. It does so (among other ways) by evolving concepts and conceptual sets by which to identify and chart the relationships among the elements of the world as understood and acted in by participants in the practices it studies. The conceptual sets that are part of a practice serve a related purpose. Indeed sometimes participants have developed these sets so fully, so well, that there is little for political philosophy to contribute. Philosophers who have been impressed with the extent to which participants do this – for example, Wittgenstein in his later work – have accordingly argued that the only contribution that philosophy could make is to "issue reminders" of what human beings as participants already know. On this view the theory contained in practice is (truistically) complete and the notion of developing it further is a misunderstanding.

This view seems to us to be inadequate. First, participants in a practice typically display their command of the rules, concepts, and so on, of which it consists in the course of acting in that practice. But it is one thing to know how to do something, another to be able to give a systematic account of what one does in the course of that activity. Competent speakers of a language are able to formulate grammatically correct sentences, but it is by no means the case that they can therefore perform even such simple analytic tasks as parsing sentences and conjugating verbs. These tasks, to say nothing of the vastly more complicated tasks of linguists and philosophers of language, require special training concerning what competent speakers of a language do when they speak. Similarly, most members of societies that include rights are familiar with and able to assert, defend, exercise, and violate them. Possession of these capacities, however, aside from being unevenly distributed in society, is not itself a sufficient condition of being able to give a detailed statement of what a right is, of what rights one has, and of how rights relate to other attributes and practices of the society in question. If one requires detailed information about such matters, one goes to a specialist – a grammarian, a lawyer, and so on – whose concern it is to be able to provide it.

Even grammarians and lawyers, however, are not as such likely to be prepared to give a genuinely systematic account of a language or a practice such as rights. The relationship between the ordinary man, the lawyer, and the legal theorist in respect to the practice of rights illustrates this point and, thereby, a second reason why the Wittgensteinian view about philosophizing is inadequate. The lawyer is expected to have a clearer and more detailed understanding of at least the legal aspects of the practice of rights. He is expected to know what rights people have and what is and is not legally implied in having them. He is also expected to have a better-developed understanding of the rules establishing and defining rights and of the sorts of reasoning appropriate to interpreting and applying those rules. In short, the lawyer is in many respects the most skilled and knowledgeable participant in the legal aspects of the practice.

The knowledge and skills of the lawyer, however, are not a sufficient basis for the kind of comprehensive, systematic account that legal theorists aim to give. The latter attempt to abstract from the details of day-to-day practice and identify higher-order rules and principles under which that detail can be subsumed, comprehended, and viewed in relationship to other aspects of the legal system. Once these higher-order rules and principles have been stated it may be tempting to say that they were always implicit in the workings of the practice. If we choose to speak in this (rather Hegelian) manner, however, we must at least recognize that the rules and principles had not previously been among the features of the practice in the sense of being items that would appear, in their own name as it were, in statements by practitioners. (They might become part of the practice in this sense after the legal theorist has enunciated them.) *At least* in this sense the propositions advanced by the legal theorist involve additions to the account of the practice provided by practioners. At least in this sense legal theory involves theorizing in a sense going beyond those we have discussed heretofore.

Political philosophizing in the full descriptive-normative sense that we are trying to develop is an enlarged and extended version of the kind of theorizing exemplified here by legal theory. (Recognizing, of course, that legal theorists have often also been political philosophers in the wider sense.) Grounded in and responsive to theory in the sense of the conceptual and ideational patterns that are part of practices themselves, it seeks a systematic and (hence at least implicitly) comparative understanding of practices and their place in political societies. It adds to theory in the sense discussed in section B in a manner analogous to ways that the lawyer adds to ideas of the common man and legal theorists to the accounts of lawyers. It develops its theory yet further in that it seeks to place (in this case) the ideas explicit and implicit in the practice of rights in the context not only of the wider legal system but of an entire sociopolitical order and indeed of generic types of sociopolitical order.

Political philosophy is dependent upon practices and the theories explicit or implicit in them because the latter provide a starting point for the former. Is there any significant relationship in the other direction? Can, should, practices – and hence practice – be influenced by political philosophy?

At least a part of the answer to this question is implicit in the view that political philosophy is a more abstract and systematic example of the kind of theorizing we found to be intrinsic to practices. Although at too abstract a level to answer the questions that typically arise in the day-to-day working of a practice – that is, questions that assume the practice – political philosophy is at one with the conceptual and ideational aspects intrinsic to practices in that it seeks to understand, to assess, and hence often to influence the latter. From the perspective of a study such as this one, perhaps the distinctive contribution it has made and can be expected to make is to offer understandings and critical judgments concerning entire practices, the connections among them, and the contributions they make to political life. Although hardly necessary to the emergence, operation, alternation, or demise of practices, the perspective that political philosophy seeks to provide may contribute to critically reflective participation in them The practice of rights as we analyze it here might well have developed to just its present form even if political philosophers such as Hobbes and Locke, Burke and Paine, Rousseau and Kant, Hegel and Marx had never presented elaborate reflections that, among other things, placed rights in the larger context of the social, political, and economic arrangements of modern societies. Whatever influence these thinkers may have had or may yet have – and there is evidence that it was and is considerable – their constructs have been and remain available to anyone seeking an inclusive understanding of a prominent and obviously significant dimension of human affairs. Because such an understanding is not a sufficient basis on which to act concerning any particular example of the practice of rights, and because it is no guarantee that anyone will in fact so act, political philosophy can be neither a necessary nor a sufficient condition of practice. It has been and can continue to be a factor contributing importantly to the quality of practice.

III.   Concluding remarks

Theory in each of the three senses we have discussed figures importantly in the present study of the practice of rights. The notion of a practice collects a number of assumptions about human affairs that fall under *theory* in the sense discussed in section A. In the course of doing the study it has been a working assumption that the conditions referenced by those assumptions are in fact instantiated in respect to rights. The results reported here constitute a claim, among other things, that the assumption has been justified. Justifying that assumption, moreover, involves showing that theory and theorizing in the sense discussed in section B are in fact present and operative in societies that include the practice of rights. Much of the present work, particularly Chapters 2 through 7, is an attempt to show what the theory is, to identify and analyze the major concepts, beliefs, rules, and so forth, that inform the thought and action of participants in the practice of rights. Finally, *theory* and *theorizing* in the third sense discussed here are present in the two closely related forms already examined. First, the account given of *theory* and *theorizing* in sense B is selective and attempts to be more orderly and systematic than one finds such theorizing to be in the practice itself. Second, parts of the present discussion (especially the final three chapters) seek to develop a normative and prescriptive theory grounded in the practice but going beyond existing features thereof in an attempt to provide an optimal justification for it.

Complementary as they are in certain respects, there is more than a little tension involved in trying to bring these three kinds of theorizing together to form a single interpretation and argument. The assumptions of *theory* in our sense A are only imperfectly satisfied by empirical materials. Working from those assumptions therefore serves to distort as well as (we hope) to illuminate *theory* in sense B and other features of the practice. Similarly, the very attempt to give an orderly and systematic account of the practice strains the linkages – demanded by the assumptions of A – between empirical instances of the practice and the account thereof. Finally and most important, the search for an optimal justification may break those linkages altogether, may render *theory* in sense C utopian or applicable to the practice only by persons willing to manipulate or simply impose upon the understandings and patterns of action of participants.

The first two of these tensions are inescapable. There is no such thing as an investigation that makes no use (with whatever degree of self-consciousness) of orienting and organizing assumptions and there are no investigations that do not select and attempt to order and systematize. Tension between these features of an investigation and respect for the phenomena investigated cannot be eliminated; one can only work at keeping it within intuitively acceptable limits and remain open to the objection that it is not within such limits in this way or that.

One could, however, eschew search for an optimal pattern of justificatory (or disjustificatory) reasoning about the practice under investigation. One could take the view that the *only* modes of reasoning relevant to assessing a practice are those that constitute the theory of a practice in sense B. As noted, some of the Wittgensteinian facets underlying the present social practices approach seem to require this view.

The argument of the last three chapters of this book aims to be faithful to the Wittgensteinian elements of its inspiration by maintaining roots in features fundamental to the practice of rights as it emerges from the present analysis. The foundation of that argument is the liberal principle and that principle is derived from aspects of the conceptual-cum-ideational scheme that the author has found at the center of the instances of the practice he has examined. If participants find the argumentation presented in the last chapters relevant to thinking about their rights, this is because the root assumptions of the argumentation are a part of their day-to-day experience with those rights.

The preceding contention implies, of course, that the argument of the last chapters would not be intelligible to persons whose experience with what they call rights literally did not include the assumptions referred to. This might be the case with persons whose experience with rights was limited to corporate rights in a feudal system. The contention also implies that the argumentation would properly be judged irrelevant (not just unsatisfactory) to thinking about rights by persons who are familiar with but who categorically reject the liberal principle. This might be the judgment of someone holding an extreme collectivist or communitarian position. Thus the present argumentation can claim to be optimal only under certain conditions. (It is of course tempting to suggest that persons such as we have just speculated about are not in fact participants in a practice of rights. But to take this line would be to guarantee the intelligibility and relevance of our justificatory argument by the unsatisfactory device of conceptual fiat.)

It would be impossible, however, to show that the liberal principle, whatever the validity of the present derivation of it may be, is in fact viewed as the exclusive or best foundation of proper arguments for or against the practice of rights or for or against particular rights. The fact that a principle is somehow implicit in a conceptual-cum-ideational scheme does not establish that it is recognized, accepted, or acted upon by those whose thought and action takes place in that scheme. Our claim is not that the pattern of reasoning we have proposed is unanimously accepted and employed, but that it carries advantages that make it preferable to other patterns we have encountered or devised. Although rooted in practice in various ways, the argument seeks a kind of intellectual purchase on practice that is not afforded by argumentation established, in its own name as it were, in existing forms of practice.

2

Types of rights

Few concepts are as prominent in contemporary moral and political discourse as *rights*. It is positively ubiquitous in political speeches, in the law, in the media, and indeed in the workplace and the marketplace. The right to work and to strike, the rights of consumers, of women, of children, of the accused and of the convicted, of homosexuals, of professors and students, the right to walk safely on the streets, the right to know what one's government is doing and why, the right to privacy, to medical care, to vacations with pay, to a good education, to free child care centers, to serve on juries and to refuse to do so, to travel, to citizenship, to refuse to do military service – all these and many more have been asserted and denied, exercised and waived, interpreted, violated, and respected, and above all extensively discussed and disputed in numerous contemporary societies. A considerable part of the controversy and conflict in our politics takes place under the rubric of rights. If we include the large number of well-established and little-controverted rights and the many actions and interactions that their exercise involves, it is evident that in concerning ourselves with rights we take up a practice of great prominence in the moral and political life of contemporary societies.

A number of explanations for the prominence of rights lie ready at hand in the literature of political philosophy. In ways and for reasons that we will explore as we proceed, *rights is a legalistic concept.* It may be that its prominence, at least in the United States, is to be understood as part of the American tendency, emphasized by commentators from Tocqueville to Shklar, to transmute moral and political questions into legal ones.[1] A second, somewhat broader explanatory argument, ad-

vanced by Leo Stauss among others, contends that *rights* is one
of the central concepts in the political philosophies that set the
dominant tendency of modern moral and political thinking and
practice in the West.[2] The philosophies in question are those of
Hobbes and Locke, and the dominant tendency is liberalism –
a set of beliefs and practices that accepts the individual's understanding of himself and his interests and objectives and seeks to
arrange moral and political life so as to allow him to act on that
understanding and successfully to pursue those interests and objectives. From this perspective, rights are devices for guaranteeing the freedom to act against the incursions both of political
authority and of private persons and groups. Rights became
increasingly prominent as the liberal understanding that rec-
ommended them was adopted by an ever larger part of the
populace of Western societies.

A third, yet less favorable, explanation is provided by Marxism. Liberal theorists are said by Marx and Engels to have
emphasized rights as part of their rationale for the emerging
capitalist system and the entrepreneurial activities of the bourgeoisie.[3] Initially intended to free the bourgeoisie from the
restricting remnants of feudal structures, they then served a
progressive purpose. Later they came to be used primarily to
protect the now exploitative practices of the property-owning
class against the threats and demands of the emergent proletariat. The continued, indeed increasing, prominence of *rights*
is due in part to the surprising (in terms of the expectations
created by Marxist theory) tenacity and even growth of capitalism and the bourgeoisie. It is also due in part to the associated failure of the proletariat to realize that *rights* is a concept
tied to the capitalist system; that rights are granted to members
of the working class only in name, not in fact, and only to buy
off any inclinations to revolution that develop among them.

I.   Types of rights

These accounts and assessments, which are at the level of political philosophy, are highly suggestive and provide alternative

perspectives from which to view the particulars of the practice of rights that we will be examining. We return to this level of analysis in the final chapters. As we suggested in Chapter 1, however, we cannot assess the merits of such explanations and assessments of a practice until we identify more clearly the explanandum, the that which (or more technically the sentences describing the that which) the explanations (explanans) are said to explain. In the case at hand, the that which we have thus far identified is little more than the fact that the words *right* and *rights* are prominent in moral, political, and legal discourse. Very little examination of this discourse suffices to convince that this fact constitutes a single explanandum only (if at all) in an uninteresting sense. We are concerned not with words (symbols, markers) but with concepts. As with many other words, *right* and *rights* are used to mark a large number of concepts distinct from one another in important respects. A couple of obvious examples: In the statement "We had him dead to rights" the word *rights* does not mark the same concept that it marks in the statement "My rights as a U.S. citizen include. . . ." Nor does the word *right* mark the same concept in any two of the following statements: "I have a right to telephone my lawyer"; "He carried his briefcase in his right hand"; "The base is at right angles with the axis"; "He did the right thing in voting against credits for the SST."

This list of examples of the different concepts marked by *right* and *rights* could be substantially enlarged merely by noting more of the well-established dictionary distinctions among *right* as a noun, an adjective, and a verb; the distinctions within each of these grammatical categories; and the commonplace distinctions between *right* and *rights*. But it is by no means the case that the distinctions among all the concepts marked by *rights* and *right* are as clear or as well-established as those mentioned in standard dictionaries. Nor will dictionaries or any mere list of examples give us the details of the rules governing the several concepts that the words mark; they will not, for example, identify the conditions that must be satisfied in order that any one of the concepts be available for use and they will not tell us what moves can and cannot be made after a concept has been properly used. Put another way, they will not tell us whether the conceptual differences to which they point are deep or superficial; whether the several concepts marked by *right* and *rights* form a closely interrelated family across which significant generalizations can be made or a heterogeneous collection sharing little more than orthography. For these reasons dictionaries and lists of examples, as valuable as they can be, are insufficient even in respect to the limited number of distinctions they provide.

We can begin the process of adding to the distinctions the dictionary provides by examining and building on the best-developed literature concerning *rights* and *right,* namely, the recent literature of jurisprudence. Although primarily taxonomic and schematic – that is, not attempting a full analysis of the logic of the concepts it distinguishes – this jurisprudential tradition goes well beyond dictionary treatments of *rights* and *right.* The largest parts of this body of analysis concern the use of *right* and *rights* in and in direct connection with the law. It is an attempt to distinguish the several main concepts marked by *right* and *rights* in statutes, court decisions and opinions, commentaries on the law, and other legal materials. Because we are much concerned with legal rights and because there is a good deal of overlap between legal and extralegal uses of *rights,* these analyses are directly relevant to our purposes. We begin with them in order to establish some major distinctions and then proceed to a more detailed analysis of those categories that emerge as most important to understanding and assessing the practice.

The following sentences exhibit the main uses of (the nouns) *right* and *rights* that legal theorists have been anxious to distinguish. (Throughout this work we employ the following abbreviations: A = the subject, possessor, holder of a right; X = the right A holds [i.e., the things that he is entitled to do and/or have by virtue of having the right]; B = the person or persons, not in public authority, who have obligations to A in respect to A's right to X; Y = the obligation B has vis-à-vis A's right to X; C = persons in public authority who have obligations in respect to A's rights to X; $Z =$ the obligations C has vis-à-vis A's right to X; $D =$ the person or persons, not in public authority, who, although not having obligations to A in respect to A's right to X, have an interest, a concern, perhaps responsibilities in respect to A's right to X.)

1(a) A (to C, a policeman who is ordering A to stop giving a speech to a group of people gathered on a secret corner): "I will not stop. Haven't you ever heard of the right to free speech? Go read the First Amendment!"

(b) B: "Why on earth are you buying peppermint fudge? It's the worst flavor they have!"

A: "Mind your own business! I have a right to buy whatever flavor I like."

2 A: "Our agreement gives me a right to payment within three days after delivery of the merchandise."

3(a) A: "I warn you, young man; I have a right to disinherit you and if you continue to see that girl I am going to do so."

(b) A: (the president of the United States): "I am aware that Congress has appropriated funds for child care centers. But as president it is my right to authorize expenditure of those funds or not as I judge appropriate."

4 A: "With all due respect to the committee, I choose to exercise my right under the Fifth Amendment to refuse to answer this question on the ground that doing so might tend to incriminate me."

In all these cases the As are using *right* to advance a claim that, despite any objection that B or C has made or might make, they are legally or morally warranted in having some thing or doing (or refusing to do) some action, and they are claiming that their warrant is strong and well established such that, despite the possible adverse effects for them, B and C are legally, morally, or in some other way bound to respect the right. The As are not saying merely that it would be desirable or good or beneficial if they had or did what they wished. Nor are they merely urging B and C to consider whether they might perhaps accede to the claims. They are asserting that their claims are legally or morally warranted and that it would clearly be legally or morally wrong for B or C to refuse to honor them. (Later we deal with statements in which A is urging that a certain right, not as yet clearly established in law, morality, or some other system of rules, ought to be so established.)

Understanding the features common to the preceding uses of *right* requires an examination of the relationships between *right* and various kinds of moral, legal, and semantic rules. This will be a major item on the agenda of later chapters. At this juncture the important point is to notice the differences among the claims that A is advancing. We begin by labeling the various statements in the manner that has, since the work of Wesley N. Hohfeld, became more or less standard in jurisprudence.[4] We then work out the distinctive features of the four main types or categories of rights and comment on some of the normative questions that arise concerning each of them. From a descriptive-analytic standpoint, all four types will remain before us in the chapters that follow. As brief as they are, the comments in this chapter on the normative issues surrounding three of the types of rights constitute the bulk of our treatment of those issues. We suggest, however, that the first type of right, which we call liberties, is particularly important from a normative and political perspective and our discussion of it in this chapter will be elaborated in later chapters (especially Chapters 8 to 10).

II.   Rights in the sense of liberties

1(a) and 1(b) are examples of uses of *rights* in the sense that Hohfeld labeled *privileges* and which followers of Hohfeld's analysis have most commonly preferred to call *liberties*. Hohfeld's analysis of rights is cast largely in terms of what he called the *opposites* and *correlates* of each of the main uses of the concept that he identified. The *opposite* of a right refers to that which is the opposite of what A has if he has a right in a particular sense. In the case of liberties the opposite is a duty; the opposite of A's having a liberty to do X is for him to have a duty to do X. The term *correlate* refers to a moral or jural attribute that characterizes some B by virtue of the fact that A has some species of right. In the case before us if A has a liberty to do X, some B has a *no-right Y* that is the correlate of A's X. (In the case of rights in what Hohfeld called the *strict sense,* to anticipate in order to draw a contrast, the opposite of a right is a no-right and the correlate is a duty.)

As noted, all types of rights provide A with a warrant for doing or having some X but the specific characteristics and consequences of the warrant vary from one type to the next. As is suggested by its opposite, a liberty provides a warrant in the sense that it signifies that there is no duty, obligation, or any other moral or legal restriction that stands in the way of A's doing or having X. The point here is probably best rendered as follows: A showing that there is a right in the sense of a liberty is, at least, a showing that having or doing X is morally and legally innocent.

Much of the difficulty, but also much of the interest, in understanding liberties resides in the notion marked by the neologism *no-right*. What exactly are the consequences for the Bs and Cs of the fact that they have (?) a no-right correlating with A's liberty? (One of the puzzling features of *no-right* is that an apparently privative term is used as a substantive that predicates something of or attributes something to the Bs.) When liberties are compared with rights in the strict sense, it appears that the difference between them lies in the fact that there is no obligatory act that falls upon the Bs or Cs by virtue of A's liberty. Moreover, it is clear from Hohfeld's discussion that the no-rights of the Bs and Cs do not in themselves forbid the latter from actions that might in fact render A's attempt to do or have X unsuccessful. In example 1(b), the fact that A has a liberty to buy peppermint fudge is no bar to B's buying the same flavor. If it happens that there is only one portion of peppermint fudge left in stock (and if B is first in line), B's decision to buy it will make it impossible for A to do so. In example 1(a) the fact that A has a liberty to give a speech is no bar to B attempting to give a speech at the same time and place. Nor is A's liberty in itself any bar to B's roaring the engine of a motorcycle while A attempts to speak. Of course the Bs and Cs may be prohibited from various acts that would hinder A's doing X. In the race to be first in line at the ice cream shop B cannot use force against A, cannot deceive A as to whether peppermint fudge is in stock, cannot bribe the clerk into selling him the last portion if A is ahead in the line, and so on. But limitations such as these are not conceptualized as obligations that correlate specifically with A's liberty; if there are such obligations, the right is not a liberty, it is a right in the strict sense.

There is, however, one kind of action that is ruled out by the conceptual union created by A's liberty and the correlative no-right of the Bs and Cs. As is implied by the preceding account of the warrant that a liberty provides, the Bs and Cs are debarred from contending that A's doing or having X would be other than innocent. B and C can compete in various ways with A for a portion of peppermint fudge; but they cannot properly tell A that it would be morally or legally wrong for A to have peppermint fudge if that is what A wants. In example 1(a) the Bs can try to shout A down but they cannot contend that it is wrong for A to give the speech. Most important, the policeman, and the legislature and judges that stand behind the policeman, have no right to act so as to make A's action illegal and hence no right to punish A for such actions.

On this interpretation of the notion of a no-right, a serious question can be raised as to whether liberties that correlate with them should be thought of as a type of right. X may be a right action, a good action, or, at least, an innocent action, but little, if anything, is gained by saying that A has a right to do X. To say that A has a right to do X implies more by way of protection for doing X than is provided by a no-right. Indeed there is serious question whether the liberty – no-right pair constitutes a moral or jural relationship of any significance to those who participate in it. Having a liberty in this sense does so little *for A* and so little *to B* and C that it might seem that it should be dismissed as insignificant.

We can explore these possibilities by considering Thomas Hobbes' discussion of a right that seems to have just the properties that characterize liberties and no-rights in the Hohfeldian sense. As noted in the introduction, Hobbes calls the right in question the *right of nature* and he says that all men have this right in the state of nature. In Hobbes' words this right is the "liberty each man hath, to use his own power, as he will himself, for the preservation of his own nature; that is to say, of his own life, and consequently, of doing any thing, which in his own judgment, and reason, he shall conceive to be the aptest means thereunto."[5] In the state of nature – that is in circumstances in which there are no rules or laws – the right of nature is unlimited; it gives "every man a right to every thing; even to one another's body."[6] It is crucial to Hobbes' purpose in incorporating this right in his theory that it carries no moral or jural implications for other persons. This is because the right is indeed equal and substantively unlimited; all men have it and all men have a "right to everything." Thus to renounce the right "giveth not to any other man a right which he had not before."[7] The only moral or jural effect that the right can have is to make it impossible for other persons to argue that I am less than innocent in doing anything that I do. Because they all have the same right they are all warranted in doing whatever they want to do, and as a practical matter their actions and mine are very likely to conflict. Neither they nor I have any obligation to avoid such conflicts or any consequences that may follow from them. The only restriction upon us is that none of us can claim that the other was unwarranted in doing what he wished to do.

It is of course Hobbes' point that such an arrangement is, as a practical matter, utterly unworkable. As a practical matter the right of nature is useless (indeed counterproductive) because one can rarely, if ever, exercise it effectively. Thus it is essential that moral and especially legal rules be established, accepted, and enforced. If Hobbes' right of nature has the same logic as rights in the sense of liberties, it would seem that Hobbes' reflections on this subject provide cogent support for the view that such attributes should not be called rights at all and that they are, at least as a practical matter, not to be numbered among our valuable moral or legal possessions.

In fact, however, the larger pattern of Hobbes' thought presents us with a line of reasoning that makes what he calls the rights of nature valuable and important. We referred to the fundamental point in this reasoning in the introduction. The fact that a person has an interest or desire to do or to have X, that he makes it his objective or purpose to do X or have X, is itself a reason that he should not be denied X. Hobbes calls this principle the right of nature and argues that a society based exclusively on it would be unworkable. But this argument shows only that A's wanting X is not always, indeed is often not, a *sufficient* or *conclusive* reason that X should not be denied. It is not and cannot be a sufficient reason if only because it provides no way to adjudicate the conflicts that arise when two or more persons want to do or have an X that only one person can do or have. But first, it is not always the case that desires conflict. Sometimes I am the only person who wants the X. And sometimes several persons want to have or do X but circumstances are such that they can *all* do or have it without conflict. Happily, social life is not a zero-sum game in all respects! The important point, however, is as follows: Very often people object to A's doing or having X not because it harms or deprives other persons in definite ways but because it is contrary to A's own "true" interests, because it is "wrong in itself," "unnatural," in violation of some moral, religious, or other code not concerned to prevent identifiable harms and deprivations. Hobbes' right of nature is important at least because it excludes these kinds of moralistic meddling in our lives and affairs. It requires that those who object to A doing or having what he wants specify concretely the ill consequences thereof and show why those consequences should outweigh the good that is involved in A's proposed action.

Such a right, if that is what it should be called, is also important in respect to cases in which, as a practical matter, the desires of two or more persons *do* conflict. For it debars B from

contending that his desires ought to be satisfied in preference to
A's because those desires are "intrinsically," or perhaps "naturally," more important, more worthy of satisfaction, and so on.
Commitment to the notion that it is a good that each person's
interests and desires, objectives and purposes, as that person conceives them, be satisfied, requires that *B* show specifically and
concretely why satisfaction of this and that desire of his should
take precedence in the circumstances at hand. It may indeed
be possible to show this; hence it may be possible to show
that it is right or that there is a right to act so as to prevent *A*
from acting to satisfy his desires, that *A* has an obligation to
allow *B* to satisfy his desires, and so on. But this has to be
shown; it cannot simply be assumed on the basis of some posited
intrinsic or generalized superiority of *B* or of *B*'s interests.

The least we can say, then, is that moral and political life
that includes what Hobbes calls the right of nature can be substantially different from moral and political life that lacks it.
But these reflections also lend support to an argument that the
case for Hobbes' right of nature is the proper foundation for
the entire practice of rights. The argument in question harks
back to points that we mentioned in discussing possible explanations for the prominence of the concept *rights*. We suggested that this concept is especially prominent in the theory
and practice of liberalism because of the commitment of many
liberal theorists to the understanding that each person's conception of himself and his purposes should be accepted unless actions based upon that conception significantly conflict with the
self-conception and purposes of others. Rights are prominent in
liberalism in part because they provide a means of protecting
individual self-assertion and action; and the various types of
rights that Hohfeld distinguished provide several distinct sorts
of protections that are adaptable to diverse classes of actions and
threats thereto. But Hobbes' right of nature should be at the
foundation of the scheme because it establishes the basic notion
that action in pursuit of the satisfaction of individual interests
and desires, achievement of individual purposes and objectives,
is a prima facie good that a liberal society will encourage and

protect *at least* to the extent of not giving credence to categorical or undefended restrictions upon it. As Hobbes teaches us, this understanding, this commitment, leaves many questions unanswered and many problems unresolved. But the commitment is fundamental because it affects the definition of further questions and problems and limits the kinds of answers and solutions that will be entertained. Additional principles and arrangements may prove to be necessary in order to give more substantial protection to certain modes of action and certain objectives thought to be especially important. But the obligations for other persons that these further arrangements involve will have to be justified in a manner that meets the arguments grounded in the understanding on which the right of nature is based. Again, legal and other limitations may have to be placed on the manner in which this right is exercised, but these will be viewed as limitations on the fundamental right and to this extent an evil in need of defense, not an unqualified good.

In the perspective that emerges from this discussion, Hobbes' right of nature is not a right at all – whether in the Hohfeldian sense of a liberty or any other. It is a principle or precept that can be employed in reasoning about rights of the several kinds that have developed in our moral and legal practice. (As indicated earlier, we call it the liberal principle. It should be emphasized, however, that we do not intend to suggest by this usage that the principle as we have formulated it has in fact been accepted by all liberal theorists. As Professor Melvin Richter has rightly insisted in this connection, historically speaking, *liberalism* refers to a family of ideas that permits of no essentialist definition.) If this principle is accepted, rights in the various Hohfeldian senses can be accorded in order to provide further warrants and more elaborate protections for particular Xs judged to be especially important and/or in need of stronger forms of protection than the liberal principle, taken alone, provides.

This conclusion brings us back to the question of whether there is an interpretation of *liberties* in the technical Hohfeldian sense that identifies a distinct and significant species of rights.

The strongest case for a positive answer to this question concerns the kinds of liberties exemplified by our 1(a), namely, liberties held against state authority. In a number of countries freedom of speech, press, association, and other civil liberties are identified and established in public law with a specificity going well beyond the liberal principle as we have discussed it. Establishing them involves placing limitations on one of the most salient features of these societies, namely, the formal authority of government to regulate conduct. Because they are formally established, involve specific limitations on an especially salient agent, and hence protect definite actions from an important source of interferences, there is a case for treating these liberties as going beyond the more general liberal principle. Also, there is no doubt that in a number of countries such liberties as freedom of speech, the press, and association are widely regarded not only as rights but as among the most important rights. The respect (or lack thereof) accorded them by governments, to mention only one indication, is a primary consideration in evaluating the latter. Indeed, discussion of these rights has been prominent in controversy concerning the practice of rights from the seventeenth century to the present. For these reasons, to treat liberties held against public authority as equivalent to the liberal principle would be to underemphasize to the point of distortion a salient aspect of that practice.

(We should not, however, err in the opposite direction and put civil liberties in the category of rights in Hohfeld's "strict sense." It is tempting to do so because there is a sense in which these liberties impose correlative duties on the Cs, namely, duties not to legislate against the actions that constitute the liberties and not to interfere with those actions under color of law. Strictly speaking, however, the duty that the Cs are under is not a specific correlate of these liberties but the perfectly general duty not to exceed the authority granted to them. Even the latter statement of the situation is misleading. If C – whether the policeman of our initial example, the executive, or the legislature, acts in a manner that exceeds his authority, there is a sense in which, jurally speaking, he simply fails to take the action he apparently intends to take. The order, law, decree, or whatever that *C* issues is not in fact an order or law but a mere expression of personal preference or opinion. In the eyes of the law it is properly null and void, no one can be punished for failure to conform with it, and in some circumstances the *C* in question is subject to punishment for acting ultra vires. Thus to say that the *A*s have a right to do *X* means, strictly speaking, that they are at liberty to do *X* and that the *C*s have no right (i.e., no authority) to say them nay. As noted earlier, however, these ways of talking about civil liberties, although valuable for purposes of analytic jurisprudence, partake of what is perhaps an excess of jural formalism.)

There is also a case for treating some applications of the liberal principle to interactions among private persons as assertions of a species of right. Statement 1(b) is a possible example. *A* has a desire for peppermint fudge ice cream. Under the liberal principle the fact that *A* has this desire is itself a reason that he should be in a position, morally and jurally speaking, to act to satisfy it. But this fact alone is not yet enough to bring the strong, even abrasive, language of rights into play. We do not speak of rights to all those myriad actions we take to satisfy desires, pursue interests, and so on. If acting on a desire is not challenged we simply *do* the appropriate action – in its own name as it were. And if the action is challenged by someone who, for any one of a very large number of reasons, has a justifiable concern with it, we warrant the action not by claiming a right to do it but simply by defending the value or merits of the action.

Rights comes into such exchanges, at least in the first instance, not to justify the action itself but rather to deny that *B* has any proper concern with it. Hohfeld's language does seem apt here: *A* uses *right* primarily to assert that *B* has a no-right to meddle in what *A* is doing. Though perhaps less than the most agreeable feature of our interactions with one another, such exchanges are common enough. As used in such exchanges, *right* and *rights* add less to the liberal principle itself than do any of the other common uses of those concepts; they are in effect a way of giving vigorous expression to that principle. As such they are important from an analytic perspective because they testify to the intimate relationship between rights and the liberal principle. They are important from a normative perspective because, however uncomplicated they may be logically or structurally, their availability does offer a measure of protection for that principle and actions taken under it.[8]

III.   Rights in the strict sense

The liberal principle demands respect for individuals and their efforts to pursue and satisfy interests and desires, objectives and purposes. A society in which this principle is widely accepted is at once less in need of and better prepared for rights than societies in which the principle has little or no standing. It is less in need of rights because acceptance of and respect for the principle already reduces unwarranted interferences with individual action and hence reduces the need for more elaborate moral and jural protection devices. It is better prepared for rights because the idea is established that individual pursuit of interests and desires, objectives and purposes is a good. The idea then provides a basis for accepting such more elaborate forms of protection as prove necessary to ensure realization of that good. It is difficult to see how a society with no commitment to the liberal principle (or some analogous notion such as Hart's natural right to equal freedom could sustain or benefit from the practice of rights.

Liberties (in the Hohfeldian sense) held against authority and, to a lesser extent, asserted against other private persons are the type of rights that are built most directly upon, that add the least to, the liberal principle. To say this is by no means to suggest that they are insignificant. We will argue, rather, that certain liberties held against authority are both the most defensible and the most important of rights. It remains the case, however, that taken alone they leave the individual without protection against numerous and important sources of threats to the autonomy of action to which the liberal principle accords

such an important place. In turning to rights in the other senses
Hohfeld identified we turn to types of rights that, in the
language we used earlier, do more *for* A's autonomy of action
than do liberties. Inevitably, however, we also turn to types of
rights that do more *to* the autonomy of action of the Bs, Cs,
and Ds.

   In example 2, A is using *right* in what is called the strict
sense (hereafter, *right s.s.*). A is not only advancing a claim
about his own jural or moral situation, namely, that he is
warranted in doing or having X, but also a very substantial
claim about the situation of some other person or persons,
namely, that he or they have a definite duty or obligation Y in
respect to A's right to X. If A's right is a legal one, the Y is a
legal obligation that is properly enforced by the state. In our
example if B does not pay for the merchandise within three
days of its delivery, A can bring suit to require specific performance and perhaps payment of damages by B. If A's right is
a moral one B has a moral obligation and is subject to moral
disapproval and other forms of moral sanction if he fails to
discharge it. The content of the obligation will of course vary
with the content of the right and with other factors. Sometimes
it can be inferred from the description of the right itself; sometimes it is specified by the legal or moral rules that identify the
right and determine the duties that go with it. The manner in
which performance of the duty is enforced also varies with the
content of the right and with other features of the legal and/or
moral system under which the right and duty exist. In the terms
of Hohfeld's taxonomy of opposites and correlates, the opposite
of A's having a right s.s. is for him to have a no-right to X, and
the correlate of A's having a right in this sense is for some B
to have a duty or obligation. It is a point about the conceptualization that the latter is invariable: to show that there is no
B with a definite duty in respect to A's alleged right is to show
that the right s.s. that A claims is not in fact established in the
legal or moral system in question.[9]

   The logic of this, perhaps the most widespread, use of *rights*
is quite well specified and quite exacting; the rules governing

it lay down a number of conditions that must exist in order that the concept properly be used and they specify a number of consequents of its proper use. There can be a duty that correlates with a right only if the content of the latter, the X, is closely enough specified and clearly enough established to allow a determination of what the duty is and what would count as discharging it or not. Put another way, the semantic rules governing this use of *right* require the existence of legal or moral rules that are specific and well established, that are capable of governing human interaction in considerable detail. Thus use of *rights* in this sense is usually indicative of especially settled, well-established patterns of action and interaction among the participants in the practice.

As is evident from the strictness of their logic, having rights s.s. puts the As in a position, jurally or morally speaking, to exercise a very considerable degree of control over their relationships with the Bs and Cs. If A has such a right it is for him to decide whether to exercise it in a particular circumstance. If A so decides, there is an important sense in which that decision leaves B no choice but to act in the manner that accords with the obligation that correlates with A's right. If A's right is a legal right to a certain payment, B must, legally speaking, pay A on demand – even if doing so has severely disadvantageous consequences for him. If A's right is a legal right to strike B's firm, B must respect A's decision to strike even if doing so puts B into bankruptcy.

In this perspective rights s.s. are a device by which the As can, as it were, tie down their futures in a manner that they regard as advantageous to themselves. Having reason to think that they will have a certain continuing interest or objective, and also having reason to expect that the Bs or Cs might be inclined to prevent the satisfaction of that interest or the achievement of that purpose, the availability of the device of rights s.s. provides the As with a means of assuring, so far as jural or moral arrangements can do so, that they will be able to serve their interests and achieve their purposes.

Of course the As cannot create or otherwise obtain rights s.s.

by unilateral decision or action. The Bs- and Cs-to-be must in some manner agree or accede to the establishment of the kind or type of right in question and to the assignment of an instance of that kind of right to a particular A. Perhaps the most common type of rights s.s. are rights to private property, and they illustrate both the respects in which such rights allow As to control their future relationships with Bs and Cs and the ways in which Bs and Cs must agree to A's rights and hence to A's being in a position to control the conduct of the Bs and Cs. In most societies the institution of property is, in part, established by law. Most members of these societies, it is true, accede to this institution only in the exceedingly indirect ways in which they accede to the structures of authority through which law is made. But the law also establishes devices such as contracts by which rights to particular pieces of property can be obtained, exchanged, terminated, and so on. Such contracts require the agreement of all parties thereto, and hence A cannot use them to acquire a right without gaining B's assent to the right in question.

The fact that the Bs must agree to A's rights s.s. in these ways has been an important part of the defense for them. Their value to A is tolerably obvious, and any disadvantages that may result for B are accepted, presumably knowingly, by the latter. (As noted earlier, in Hart's view this is the sole justification for special rights.) It nevertheless remains the case that, once obtained, the rights s.s. of the As allow them to control, largely at their discretion and as a matter of right, aspects of the lives of the Bs. This latter fact has been a focal point for criticism of such rights. Critics have questioned whether the Bs can in fact adequately anticipate the future consequences, for them, of acceding to A's rights. They have called attention to the fact that, because of various inequalities, some members of a society are much better placed to make such anticipations than others. Insofar as societies make devices that create rights s.s. available to their members they almost certainly accentuate and augment such inequalities and their consequences. Finally, critics have argued that the actions of A that are authorized by rights s.s.

have consequences beyond those that impinge directly on those
*B*s who are most directly affected by them. As we will see in
Chapter 9, writers of a communitarian persuasion argue that
rights s.s. (indeed rights of all kinds) encourage an individualistic, even an egoistic, ethos that is destructive of the most
valuable kinds of human relationships and productive of an
anomic and politically vulnerable society. Others have argued
that rights s.s. leave a society too much at the mercy of individual choice and action and render difficult, if not impossible,
effective development and equitable use of societal resources.
This last criticism in particular has found an increasingly sympathetic response in recent years, and nonsocialist as well as
socialist governments have placed significant limitation on
rights s.s. to forms of property (both real and moveable) that are
judged to constitute significant public resources. We take up
some of these normative views and questions at various junctures, particularly in the final chapters and in a brief appendix.
As already suggested, however, we do not attempt a systematic
justification or disjustification of rights s.s. as such. (We do
attempt such a justification of liberties held against the state.)
There are an enormous number and range of such rights, and
arguments for and against them must take their particular
characteristics into account. Because this last enterprise is well
beyond the scope of this work, the most that we can do is hope
that the present analysis of the features common to rights of
this type will be useful to those who attempt an assessment of
particular examples of them.

IV.   Rights in the sense of powers

We now return to our list of examples of uses of *right* and
rights and take up 3(a) and 3(b). These sentences exemplify
rights in the sense that Hohfeld called powers. To begin with
3(a), it would be *too much* to say that the fact that *A* has a
right to exclude *B* from his will puts *B* under a legal or moral
obligation vis-à-vis *A*. (It might *oblige B* to stop seeing the girl.)
But neither is it *enough* to say that *A* is at liberty to disinherit

B and that *B* has a no-right vis-à-vis *A*'s liberty. So far as we have sketched the situation, *A* is at liberty to disinherit *B* and *B* does lack any warrant for saying that it would be other than legally innocent for *A* to do so. But in the case of powers, the law (and the moral code, in some cases sufficiently analogous to legal powers that it might be said to create moral powers) is involved in a more direct and substantial manner than in liberties. The law does not require that *A* use his powers and the fact that *A* has a power itself places *B* under a liability, not an obligation. But *A* has the power and *B* the liability under or by virtue of specific provisions of the law, not by virtue of the silence of the law. There are no powers or liabilities in this sense apart from specific provisions of a legal (or moral) system or code. Moreover, the legal authorities commit themselves to making *A*'s use of his powers effectual as well as innocent. If *A* disinherits *B*, those authorities will, when *A* or his executor brings an action, enforce the provisions of *A*'s will against *B* (and against all other parties). *A*'s having the power puts *B* under a liability, makes him liable to have his jural situation and relations altered by *A*'s use of that power. And when *A* uses his power, his doing so imposes obligations on *B* which are enforceable under law. Indeed the use of powers is a major source of rights s.s. and the obligations that correlate with them. To have a power is to be, legally (and sometimes morally) speaking, in a position to alter effectively the jural situation and relations of oneself and of others.[10]

In many societies something like the liberal principle is operative at least in the minimal sense that there is a liberty to act wherever and whenever the legal code does not prohibit or require action. (This would not be the case in a society in which there was a rule such as "Everything is prohibited that is not explicitly permitted." In the theory of the American Constitution, for example, such a rule applies to the national government in its relations with the state governments. A literal interpretation of the notion of totalitarian government would suggest that such a rule would apply to the subjects of a thoroughly totalitarian regime.) Powers, and the rights s.s. and obligations they create, by contrast, exist only insofar as they have been explicitly created by the legal or moral system or code. But if powers and rights s.s. apply to fewer aspects of life than the liberal principle as such, their application marks a more substantial jural and moral capacity and relationship. The individual's liberty of action is ordinarily more extensive than his powers or his rights s.s., but his powers and rights s.s. permit him a greater degree of control over other persons and hence over those aspects of his life to which they apply.[11]

For this reason rights in the sense of powers are particularly valuable to A. They are the type of right, and perhaps the feature of legal and moral practice more generally, that most directly and substantially accepts the notion that it is a good thing for A to be able effectively to pursue his interests and objectives as he understands them. But this very fact about them creates serious difficulties for influential descriptive and normative theories of rights. As we see in the next chapter, it is ordinarily the case that X can be said to be a right of A's only if A regards his having or doing X as, in general, advantageous to him. Assigning rights is a means of advantaging A, not a means of imposing something upon him that he does not like and does not want. But notice that Smith's use of his power to bequeath something to Jones serves to give Jones a right to that something. Powers are not only themselves a species of rights, they are a method of creating other species of rights. The liability on Jones' part correlating with Smith's power includes the liability to acquire rights. At least in the case of the power under discussion, Smith can create Jones' right without Jones' consent. If the something to which Smith gives Jones a right is, in Jones' view, disadvantageous to him – say, a piece of property that is burdened with heavy taxes and impossible to sell except at heavy loss – it seems that we have to say that Jones has a right to something that he most emphatically does not want.

There are of course ways of interpreting the foregoing example that reduce the imposition on Jones that it apparently involves. For example, it might be said that the right in question is the right of inheritance and this right *is,* in general,

advantageous. Or one might argue that it is the exercise of
rights that must be advantageous, and in the example Jones
only has, he does not exercise, his right to the property. What
he does is discharge the duties that go with ownership of
property. Or it could be emphasized that although it might be
costly, Jones can in fact alienate his right to the property –
perhaps by declaring bankruptcy.

But the particular kind of imposition that this example represents hardly exhausts the difficulties that rights in the sense of
powers create for the theory of rights. Recall Hart's argument
summarized earlier. The concept of rights is said to presuppose
commitment to the principle of the equal right to freedom.
General rights invoke that principle directly and special rights
invoke it indirectly in that A's having a right X requires that
he acquire it through a procedure involving consent, agreement, or some other exercise of freedom on the part of all Bs.
There are obvious difficulties in justifying rights in the sense
of powers in terms of this line of reasoning. A's powers give
him the right to alter B's jural or moral situation without such
an exercise of freedom on the latter's part. A is authorized to
act in ways that might have far-reaching and seriously adverse
consequences for B without B's agreement or assent. And if B
attempts to prevent or hamper A's use of his powers, the state
will come to A's assistance against B.

If we shift from the language of equal freedom to that of the
liberal principle, a system of powers may indeed be evidence of
a commitment to the idea that objectives and desires, and the
individual's pursuit of their achievement and satisfaction, is a
primary good. There is no doubt that the availability of powers
contributes to the possibility that A can act, and act effectively,
on his interests and desires, objectives and purposes. But we
immediately encounter the same difficulties we noted in respect
to rights s.s. Aside from the possible softening effects of informal consultations and exchanges between As and Bs, a system
of powers provides the As (including, of course, collective "persons" such as corporations and labor unions) with a powerful
means of imposing their will on the Bs. Everyone's objectives

and desires may be conceded to be of value, but the objectives and desires of the *A*s are much more likely to be achieved and satisfied than those of the *B*s. Moreover, in this case the interferences, advantages, and successes of the *A*s cannot always be justified in terms of the acceptance thereof on the part of the *B*s.

There is, however, an argument according to which the contention of our last sentence, at least, is false. Consideration of this argument will also move us ahead to example 3(b); that is, to the case of powers in the sense we would ordinarily call authority or public authority. The argument is that the interferences warranted by the powers of the *A*s and the liabilities of the *B*s can be accepted because they obtain under a *legal or moral code or system* that the *B*s regard as contributing to the satisfaction of their interests, the achievement of their objectives, and so on. *A*'s powers are valid despite their ill effects in this or that case because the system under which they exist is consistent with and in fact serves the liberal principle. Similarly, *B* may thoroughly disapprove the president's (*C*'s) use of (or decision not to use) funds appropriated by Congress for child care centers, but the political society and the authority structure under which the president has the right (authority) in question is consistent with, in fact serves, that principle.[12] By moving from the particular level of the action of *A* or *C* to the general level of the system under which *A* or *C* has authority to take that action, we can find a basis for reconciling *A*'s or *C*'s interference with the principles of individualistic liberalism.

For very good reasons this line of argument has always been prominent in discussions of the general question of political obligation. It is rare indeed for the substance of laws and other authoritative actions to meet with the approval of all of those to whom they apply. But it has often been much easier to win approval of and support for a system of government and law of some sort and even for the particular system or regime established here and now.[13] Hence arguments for obedience based on the importance or value of the system have often been more effective than appeals based on the substantive characteristics of particular laws and commands.

For reasons that we have detailed elsewhere, even in the best-accepted and supported regime this line of argument only reduces, it does not altogether eliminate, either the fact of or the theoretical and moral problems about imposition and unfreedom in political societies. But there are special problems in using this argument to reconcile rights in the sense of powers held by private persons (as opposed to persons holding public authority) with the liberal principle. The nub of the matter concerns the extent to which the administration of powers, as with all types of rights, is left in the hands of A himself. The cogency of the argument for political obligation is greatly abetted where there are mechanisms by which those who are in authority (the Cs) can effectively be held responsible to those who are not (the Bs and Ds) for the substantive character of the use they make of it. It is indeed important that the president of the United States holds his authority in a regime which, qua regime, has the approval of large numbers of its members. But there is little doubt that the regime has and is able to retain such approval in part because it includes provision for voting the incumbent out of authority (without challenging or changing the structure of authority) if the authoritative actions he takes persistently arouse disapproval.

In the case of powers held by private persons, such lines of responsibility as exist are, to say the least, attenuated. Because A holds his powers under law, if B does not like the power or the use a particular A makes of it, he can urge those Cs who passed the law to alter it. If the Cs fail to do so, B might attempt to get them voted out at the next election. But A himself is not in a position of public authority and cannot be reached by the devices available to hold the Cs responsible for their decisions and actions. If A's actions do not accord with the law under which he has powers, then they simply fail as attempts at the exercise of the power in question. Such failure is simply that; that is, simply a failure and not in itself a legally punishable act. Nor is A's persistent use of his powers in ways that harm or disadvantage others a ground for punishing him or for depriving him of those powers. So long as the powers remain established by law, *A* has use of them "as a matter of right" – that is, according to his discretion. He may choose to use them in a manner that respects the desires, objectives, and so on, of *B*, but it is part of the definition of a power that he is not required to do so.

Example 3(b) certainly represents a common use of *right* and *rights*. There are, however, good reasons for treating such statements as involving more than one of several senses or types of right. To begin with, there is a more specialized concept that is well established as appropriate for use in cases such as 3(b). That concept, of course, is *authority*. As we will emphasize later, the other major senses of *right* (i.e., rights s.s., liberty, power, and immunity) can usually be explained as meaning that *A* is authorized to do or have *X;* but it would be odd to say in those cases that *A* has authority to do *X*. In 3(b) such an explanation would be entirely natural. To explain 3(b) by saying that the president has authority to withhold expenditure of the funds would be a further specification or delimitation of the meaning of the statement. By contrast, if the president had used *authority* at the outset, to replace it with *right* would produce a less exact statement. To mention only one point, use of *authority* brings out the fact that the president is accountable for the decisions he makes in ways that private persons exercising rights are not.

Finally, the very salience of authority in political life is reason for treating it separately from rights in the other senses. A part of the point here is that all legal rights in the other senses of *rights* depend upon the existence of public authority. Rights are established, defined, and interpreted by legally authoritative decisions, and respect for them is enforced through legal processes.[14] Further, authority is used in many ways that do not involve creation of rights in the other senses. The criminal law provides many examples. Laws against, say, reckless driving create obligations without necessarily creating rights.[15] Thus the existence and exercise of public authority raises theoretical and normative questions distinct from those raised by rights in the other senses.

For these several reasons, although we must recognize that *right to* is commonly used in the sense of *has (public) authority to,* rather than subsume this use under the general category of uses of *right* we treat it as a distinct category. In Chapter 6 we explore the similarities and differences between rights and authority.

V.   Rights in the sense of immunities

Immunities are like liberties in that they leave A at liberty to do the X the immunity grants and they deprive B of any ground on which to claim that A's doing X is other than innocent. But they differ from liberties in that an immunity is always a qualification of or exception to a specific and established obligation, duty, or liability. The law establishes an obligation, a liability, and so on, and then it creates exceptions to it in the form of immunities. In our example 4 the law creates a liability to be called before congressional committees under certain circumstances, a liability to be asked questions by such committees, and obligations to appear and to answer such questions when a committee chooses to exercise its authority to ask them. But the law also specifies classes of cases in which persons do not have to appear or do not have to answer certain kinds of questions. These exceptions to the general rule are called immunities. They leave A at liberty not to appear or not to answer. Correlatively, they put B or C (in this case the members of the committee) under a disability to require A to appear or to answer questions covered by the immunity and a disability to initiate processes leading to punishment of A for refusal to appear or to answer. Thus when B is in fact a C – that is, someone in public authority – the immunity is in effect a limitation upon authority. In other cases the immunity is a limitation on the rights s.s. or the power of B.[16]

The logic of immunities might be sketched as follows: General rules are laid down that require persons to testify in trials, empower persons to make wills that the state will enforce, forbid the private use of physical force, allow owners of real property to forbid others from entering upon it, and so forth. These general rules are then qualified to allow agents, in part at their discretion, to exempt themselves from the application of the rules or some aspect of them under certain conditions. Thus *A* can refuse to testify against himself in criminal cases or can choose to so testify; under some circumstances a person can render himself immune to the obligation that he would incur if he inherited chattels or real property; private persons can sometimes use moderate physical force for purposes of self-defense or self-redress; persons can sometimes enter upon private property adjoining a public road, without permission from the owner, if the road is blocked or otherwise unusable. Of course society itself establishes the possibility of immunities, it sets the limits of each of them, and it reserves authority to judge whether any particular claim to immunity is in fact within the limits that have been set.

There are a number of possible rationales for immunities. The following general points are close enough to their logic to be made with some assurance: Immunities reflect social recognition of both the value and the limitations of authoritative general rules as a means of regulating social life. General rules are possible because, descriptively speaking, there are recurrent patterns of action and recurrent problems in social life that can be subsumed and treated under general rules of conduct. Such rules are desirable because it is both efficient and just to treat similar cases similarly. But the scope of the regularities is rarely sharply defined, they are seldom free of significant exceptions, and they are not immune to substantial change. Some exceptions recur and can be predicted, and hence provisions for handling them can be worked into the rules themselves. It can be predicted, for example, that some members of the society will from time to time find themselves in situations in which it is dangerously impractical to rely upon assistance from those public officials who are ordinarily the only persons warranted in using physical force in the society. Hence the immunity that permits use of moderate force for self-defense can be viewed as itself based upon a general rule, albeit one that takes the form

of an exception to another more comprehensive rule. But discretion is left to the *A*s to decide how to interpret the scope of
the immunity and to decide whether and how to make use of
it. Hence immunities must be understood as involving more
than general rules and established exceptions to them; they
involve leaving the regulation of social life to the discretion of
private individuals. (Of course one can say something like,
"The rule is that the individual decides for himself." This is a
useful thing to say in that it brings out the point that the
individual's use of his discretion is authorized by legal rules.
Beyond this point, however, the formula is no more than a
somewhat inflated way of saying that there is no rule covering
the case.) The individual's decisions and judgments, it should
be reiterated, are subject to review by public authorities. But
the very fact that private persons are explicitly authorized to
use their discretion in the first instance would seem to betoken
either the belief that they are in some respects the best judges
of how the situation should be handled or perhaps the belief
that though their judgments are often mistaken, they should
be permitted to make them.

Thus the existence of immunities can be viewed as an attempt
to combine regulation of social life by authoritative general
rules with decentralized social regulation through decision by
the private persons involved in this or that circumstance.

This perspective on immunities, however, although appropriate enough to much practice, neglects some of the most
salient aspects of their use both historically speaking and in our
own time. The perspective we delineated rationalizes immunities in terms of their contribution to universalistic values and
modes of procedure. As the term *privilege* reminds us, however,
immunities and privileges have often served, and indeed continue to serve, highly particularistic purposes. As Roscoe Pound
emphasizes in the discussion cited earlier, historically persons
of wealth and rank were granted comprehensive privileges and
immunities that relieved them of burdens and protected them
against the demands and interferences of government and of
social life more generally. Since the immunities typically went

to those who were well supplied with wealth, status, and power, they had the effect of providing a legal basis and legal support for existing inequalities. Some of these, for example, immunities of the church and the immunity of the state to suit, had a justification going beyond the mere fact that they advantaged the agents or agencies that held them. This may also be true of some of the particularistic immunities that survived, or have been accorded after, the widespread attack on such arrangements in the seventeenth and eighteenth centuries. Perhaps the entire society benefits from the fact that in the United States, labor unions and labor leaders qua union officials are virtually immune from torts.[17] The least we can say, however, is that it is difficult to square such immunities with theories that place substantial emphasis on equality, whether the equality implicit in the liberal principle, equal freedom a la Hart, or some other kind.

The last point calls attention to ideas that were not a part of the rationale for immunities sketched earlier. If that sketch is correct it is evident that there is nothing in the concept of an immunity or in the historical use of immunities requiring all immunities to be granted in a manner that accords with ideas of individualism, of equality, or of equal freedom. As with the powers they sometimes qualify, the device of immunities has been used to buttress a variety of inequalities and to limit the freedom of action of some in favor of the autonomy and power of others. So far as the logic of the concept and practice is concerned, the device remains available for such purposes. If immunities are a species of rights, in respect to them the relation between right and notions such as the value of individual interests and desires, objectives and purposes, is purely empirical and has in fact often been one of disjunction and conflict.

VI. Concluding remarks

The discussion of immunities completes the examination of our original list of examples of uses of *rights*. It is important to emphasize that all the examples involve uses of *right* and *rights* and that our entire discussion has been concerned with relatively well-established uses of those terms. Technical terms such as *liberties, powers,* and *immunities* are ways of making a first sorting of the diversity of uses that occur in discourse employing *rights.*

Certain features have recurred as we moved through the list of examples. Talk of rights s.s., liberties, powers, and immunities all involve advancing warrants for having or doing something, warrants advanced against and carrying implications for other persons. All the uses of *rights* we have examined involve some kind of rules that are to govern the conduct of those involved in the interactions in question. These rules and the warrants based upon them are typically thought to have peculiarly strong standing or stringency; actions properly based on them are widely thought to be justified in a strong sense and the obligations, no-rights, and so on, that correlate with them are widely thought to carry a particular force. Finally, all the uses of *rights* we have discussed seem to involve a large element of what we have called self-administration on the part of the holder of the right; that is, it is for *A* to decide whether, when, and how to exercise the right, whether to waive it, to release *B* from obligations in respect to it. These features require more detailed examination in later chapters.

Even if the impression that there are features common to all the uses of *rights* is sustained or deepened by further analysis, it will nevertheless *not* be the case that description of these commonalities would constitute a single exhaustive analysis of *rights* as the concept is now used. The differences among the several senses of *rights* discussed thus far are both important and irreducible. Without denying or minimizing the significance of the commonalities, there are vital differences between having a rights s.s. and having a liberty, between having a liberty and having a power or immunity. The analyst may indeed want to assess and make recommendations concerning the merits of the various uses and the practices of which they are a part. His first task, however, is to display the similarities and differences among them.

We should also note that our discussion thus far by no means presents a complete analysis of the uses we have considered and that there are almost certainly distinct uses of *rights* that we have not taken up at all. Hohfeld's scheme of correlates and opposites, as useful as it is for making a first sorting of common uses of *rights*, does not begin to identify the full logic of the several uses it distinguishes. Such questions as who can hold rights s.s., powers, and so on; what can count as an X, a Y, and so on; and what moves and countermoves a valid claim to an X allows and rules out are barely touched in his analysis or the foregoing attempt to summarize and build upon his work. And his analysis is concerned almost entirely with established legal rights. It remains to determine whether his analysis applies to moral rights, to rights accruing to membership in nonlegal institutions, and so on. Also, it is unlikely that use of his categories will take us far in dealing with what Joel Feinberg has called the "manifesto" sense of *rights* – that is, cases in which the concept is used to urge the establishment of rights that have as yet no standing in the law or any other system or rules.[18]

The more explicitly normative or justificatory aspects of the foregoing discussion not only are incomplete but do little more than identify some problems that need to be resolved and some of the directions in which an argument might be developed in order to resolve them. The liberal principle emerges as a possible foundation for rights, but its formulation needs to be elaborated and clarified and the relationships between it and apparently competing principles (e.g., Hart's natural right to equal freedom) worked out. Again, the liberal principle seems to suggest that liberties held against the authority of the state are an especially important and defensible type of right. Testing and developing this suggestion is a major concern in what follows.

3

Aspects of
the logic of *rights* (I)

After some preliminaries that return to questions discussed in Chapter 1, this and the following chapter attempt to enter into particulars of the practice of rights that the essentially taxonomic enterprise of the previous chapter induced us to ignore. In the terms we employed in Chapter 1, we will be examining rules and understandings that form part of the theory intrinsic to the practice itself. We will find, however, that the attempt to give a systematic account of these rules and understandings will bring us into confrontation with questions at the third level of theorizing we discussed in Chapter 1, questions central to the descriptive-normative enterprise of political philosophy. Following the preliminaries just referred to, our discussion will be organized in terms of those features or elements of the practice of rights we identified in Chapter 2, namely, holders of rights (A); the rights As hold (X); persons with obligations, no-rights, and so forth, that correlate with A's X (B); the obligations, and so forth, that adhere to the Bs (Y); persons in positions of authority (C) and their obligations (Z); and persons $(D$s$)$ who are part of the practice but who are not As, Bs, or Cs in respect to a particular X or the exercise thereof. The categories A through D can be viewed as referring to social roles and the categories X through Z can be viewed as referring to aspects of the content of those roles. The reasons for the absence of a category referring to the content of the role of D will emerge in the course of the discussion. In the perspective just delineated, the preliminary discussion in this chapter (subsections I and II immediately following) can be viewed as identifying features of the setting within which the roles just referred to are played.

I. The social character of
the practice of rights

The practice of rights is a social phenomenon. What does this mean? First and most obviously, the practice is social in the sense that it involves interactions among people. The notion of a purely individual or private practice of rights, whether by a Robinson Crusoe living apart from other men or by an individual living in a society but asserting to himself that he has rights against himself (e.g., against his better or worse self), is metaphorical. If taken literally it would have the same well-rehearsed difficulties as the notion of duties to oneself.

To say that the practice is social in the first sense is also to say that its existence and operation presuppose social arrangements and patterns apart from the practice itself – arrangements and patterns that can be identified independently of the practice of rights. There is no sense to the notion of a society or set of social relationships consisting exclusively of the practice of rights.

We must distinguish between what we will call a weak and a strong sense of *presupposes* as we have just used that word. As Hobbes persuades us (although he deliberately [mis]uses *rights* as regards the state of nature in order to discredit the notion), the practice of rights would be impossible among men who could not, for example, meet minimum biological needs, communicate with one another, and maintain a degree of regularity and predictability in their relationships. In this sense the practice of rights presupposes some set of arrangements and processes by which the members of a society attempt, not entirely without success, to meet these objectives.

The character of the practice of rights, moreover, is affected in various ways by the particulars of the language, the economic and political institutions, and the traditions of the society or social milieu in which it operates. Consider, for example, the immense differences between the practice of rights within nations (say, France, Canada, Great Britain, and the United States) as compared with the same practice in relations among nations (including the nations just listed). Although the concept of rights that is used in relations among states has many of the same historical roots and logical features as the concepts employed within them, the practice differs so markedly that it has been suggested that it should be reserved to the municipal context.[1] Without attempting to specify these differences, many of them result from the enormous differences between the settings in which the practices operate.

It is, however, *logically* possible that arrangements for communication, for a degree of security, for economic activity, and so on, could change significantly without producing changes in the practice of rights. The practice presupposes that certain fundamental objectives be attained, that certain kinds of arrangements and patterns of action obtain, but the relationships between the practice and any particular set of such arrangements and activities is contingent. It is for this reason that *presupposition,* as we have used it thus far, is weak (which is not to say unimportant).

There must, however, be some social institutions and arrangements that, though identifiable independently of the practice, are logically necessary to it in the form in which it exists at any moment in time. To have a right is always to have a right to have or to do something. The practice of rights is logically impossible without some number of types of objects, some number of forms of action, that individuals have a right to have or to do. The list of such objects and actions has of course changed over time. Hence we cannot say that any particular object or form of action is necessary to the practice of rights in any and all conceivable versions. But at any moment in the history of a practice some such set of objects and actions will stand in a logically necessary, not merely a contingent, relationship to it. (We bear in mind, however, that there may be disagreements concerning the content of the practice. Strictly, we must say there is a logically necessary relationship between the practice and the objects and forms of action to which, in the views of the participants, the practice accords a right.)

There are cases in which, under some descriptions, there is a symmetry in the logical relationship between the objects to which there is a right and the practice. The availability of the objects is a necessary condition of the practice and the practice is a necessary condition of the availability of the objects. The concept *property* provides an example. To say that *A* owns property means that he has a certain set of rights concerning some object or objects. The concept *property* would not have the meaning it has in the absence of the concept *rights*. Equally, the notion of a *right* to property is logically dependent on the availability of the notion of property. *Right* is not synonymous with *property*, but neither can be understood apart from the other. (The type of relationship exemplified by *right–property* is sometimes called an internal relationship.)

In cases where there is such a symmetry what becomes of our assertion that the content of rights must be partly supplied by social arrangements identifiable independently of the practice of rights? There are several ways of handling this problem. First, one can say that property rights are always rights to some particular piece of property and that the latter can be identified independently of the fact that they are also subjects of property rights. One can have property rights in land, houses, cars, and so on, and the latter objects can be identified – as can such actions as speech, assembly, and petition – without reference to rights. And, evidently, the notion of a right to property as we know it would have no application without the social arrangements by which and in which we identify, create, construct, and use land, houses, cars, and the innumerable other objects in which we have property rights.

Second, we can describe property not as a part of the practice of rights but as a species of the genus of arrangements by which we assign value to, use, share, divide up, and possess the things of the world. Such descriptions do not give us the features distinctive of property in the sense of something in which one has property rights, but they call attention to the variety of social arrangements and patterns of action presupposed by the practice of according property rights. The distinctive species of possession known as having property in something would make no sense in the absence of more general notions, such as that certain kinds of objects are useful or valuable and that their utility is sometimes increased if they are in the control of individuals or groups.

Finally, one can follow the example of such writers as Locke and especially Hume and hypothesize away the present internal relationship between property and rights.[2] One can say, "Let us imagine (or find historical examples of) a practice of rights that does not include property and/or a notion of property that does not involve the notion of a right." Of course such intellectual experiments do not themselves alter the fact that there is a logical connection between the two concepts in present practice. As with the first two approaches, however, they afford a kind of intellectual purchase on existing practices that at first sight seems to be excluded by the logical connection between them. If every use of *property* necessarily implies *right*, it might seem that attempts at social criticism would be caught in a kind of logical bind. Critics could not call the notion of property rights into question without using the concept *property*, but their every use of that concept presupposes and in that sense affirms that there is a right to property. In fact, however, *knowing* that there is now a logical connection between the two, critics can compare the existing practice to an imaginary one (or to one from another time and place) and say, "Look at the advantages of the latter as against the former." This is what critics of property rights have done and it is also what was done, in reverse, by early defenders of those rights, such as Locke. Locke argued in favor of a practice in which rights and property would be logically tied; he did so by comparing such a practice with a situation in which no rights of this type were established. Later critics of the practices for which Locke had argued – for example, Engels[3] – attacked not only the practice but Locke's rationale for it.[4]

The larger topic we have been considering – that is, the social character of the practice of rights – is of polemical importance primarily vis-à-vis the contractarian tradition in social and political thought. From Hobbes to John Rawls contractarians have written as though, in fact, in logic, or ideally, the web of relationships of which the practice of rights consists provides not only moral and juridical foundations without which other arrangements are illegitimate, but the very source from which all social and political arrangements spring.[5] Thus Hobbes spoke of moving directly from an asocial to a social state via a contract creating rights and duties. Rawls finds it useful to think of an agreement made by men who know little more of one another and their circumstances than that all of the parties to the contract are self-interested and might try to do one another in.

The reader will recall Hume's objection that it is logically impossible for the obligation to keep promises and agreements to rest on a promise or agreement.[6] The practice of creating obligations, and rights as well, by making promises and agreements logically presupposes the concept of an obligation (to say nothing of the concepts that identify those actions that we promise to take, those objects that we agree to buy, etc.). It is not our objective to try to show, as Hume tried to do, that social institutions necessarily evolve in one sequence such that the development of promising, allegiance, notions of rights and duties follows, *temporally,* the emergence of commitments and patterns of action more directly tied to the expression and pursuit of individual interests. The considerations we have presented in this section, however, are in support of the more general point that practices such as rights are neither sui generis nor self-subsistent, that they presuppose and cannot be understood apart from a larger social milieu in which they operate. There may indeed be analytic advantages to constructing a hypothetical model in which a practice of rights is made to stand largely independent of any such milieu. Such a model might allow illuminating comparisons and might foster critical assessment of actual forms of the practice. But such comparisons presume knowledge of both or all the items compared, and hence presume knowledge of the relationships between actual forms of the practice and the larger social settings in which they operate.[7]

II.   The subject or holder of a right (*A*)

The considerations discussed in Section I apply to all practices. To identify the elements or features specific to the practice of rights we have to analyze the concepts peculiar to it, the rules that define rights, that determine who can have them, under what conditions and with what consequences they can be exercised, and the rationales for those rules and for the practice they constitute. Such an analysis makes up the agenda for much of this study. In the remainder of this chapter and the following chapter we begin the task by considering the several roles identified earlier.

What are the qualities or characteristics necessary to be a subject or holder of a right? The rules governing particular rights establish conditions that must be satisfied in order for a person to have them. For example, in most countries the right to travel abroad under the passport of that nation can be held only by its citizens. But this kind of rules does not interest us. Rather, we are concerned with the question of whether the rules governing the use of the concept *rights* lay down requirements that must be met in order to be eligible for any rights whatever, in order to be eligible for the role of subject or holder of rights.

Writers in the natural rights tradition of thought have stressed the universalism of at least certain fundamental rights. They have argued that certain rights accrue to persons not by virtue of any characteristic or quality distinctive of them or their society but simply by virtue of their nature or their humanity. Even in its most unqualified form this view excludes creatures and things other than human beings and hence does imply a list of preconditions. This exclusion has itself become controversial. Moreover, there are problems as to what criteria a being must satisfy in order to count as human for purposes of the attribution of rights. What does one say about the fetus, young children, mental defectives, habitual criminals, and so on? We try to shed some light on these questions by looking at some of the language prominent in discourse about rights.

A striking feature of such discourse has been the often un-abashedly self-assertive and insistent character of the speech and other actions of those who claim to hold rights. It is not only common but generally thought unexceptionable for *A*s to claim, maintain, assert, demand, and insist upon their rights. It is rarely taken amiss, indeed often applauded, if they do so forcefully, staunchly, resolutely, boldly, and even zealously. A right is something to which one is *entitled,* which one can un-ashamedly assert to the world and zealously guard against all in-fringements and encroachments. These features of the practice persist despite the fact that *A*'s exercise of his rights restricts the liberty and may otherwise disadvantage other persons.

Moreover, its insistent, self-assertive character is not a merely rhetorical feature of discourse concerning rights. Although in-dividuals cannot unilaterally determine what rights they have, the practice of rights leaves the individuals who have them a large measure of discretion in deciding whether to exercise them in a particular situation, whether to waive them tempo-rarily or even permanently, whether and how to defend them against attacks and encroachments. Whereas it is often clearly wrong to fail to do what is right or just, wrong to fail to dis-charge one's obligations, the notion that it is wrong not to exer-cise one's rights is not well established. If a *B,* a *D,* or especially a *C* tells *A* that it was wrong for him not to exercise his right *X, A* might justifiably respond that whether he exercises his rights or not is his affair and that *B* ct al. should mind their own busi-ness. Although not unqualified, this large element of individual discretion is perhaps the single most distinctive feature of the concept *rights.*

The operation of a practice with the foregoing features pre-supposes individuals not only who are capable of such self-directed, assertive conduct but who engage in it from time to time. Such a practice would fall into desuetude or change in the absence of some number of people able not only to understand what their rights are but to make the judgments and decisions, and to act upon them, that the exercise of rights permits them. It was a society well supplied with such individuals that seventeenth- and eighteenth-century theorists of rights seem to have had in mind. We might say that individuals with such capacities and the inclination to act on them are the paradigm case of subjects or holders of rights.

It does not follow that these capacities and inclinations are logical preconditions of eligibility for the role of A or even that all As in fact display them. In a society in which the practice of rights is well established, many individuals simply inherit certain rights and "exercise" them without even being aware that they are doing so. Notice that in addition to the verbs mentioned, we often use more passive terminology in talking about rights. One can *hold, possess,* or simply *have* a right. One can also *enjoy, benefit from,* and *profit from* the rights that one has. These locutions imply less by way of choice and self-assertion on the part of holders of rights. They are much used, often without the company of the verbs we mentioned earlier, in talking about the rights of so-called third-party beneficiaries[8] – children, collectivities, and, in general, As who have themselves taken no action to acquire, exercise, or defend their rights, who may not even know they have them, and who are dependent on others to assert and protect their rights on their behalf.

Even in the case of the most passive of As, however, the statement that a person holds rights usually implies that he has, at least latently or potentially, the capacity to evaluate them and to decide whether he wishes them to continue and to have them respected by others. Smith might acquire his right to live in Peters' house without the least effort. He might even live there unaware that he has a right to do so. But to have a right to live there is to be free to waive that right if he decides he detests the house and would rather sleep in the park. If Smith has learned that he has a right, he has learned of these options and could, under some circumstances, exercise them. Similarly, if we speak of the rights of children we imply that as they reach maturity they become able to make the choices that having a right warrants them in making. We should add that to speak in an unqualified manner of *human rights* is to imply that all creatures who can properly be called human beings have the capacities to make such choices.

We cannot claim that all common, well-established uses of *rights* accord with the conventions just discussed. We leave aside the special case of certain legal rights that cannot be waived and that generally involve a lesser measure of self-administration on the part of the holder of the right. In addition to these, however, one encounters with increasing frequency uses of *rights* with respect to classes of creatures and things that we would not ordinarily think of as having the capacities we have been discussing. The recently intensified concern with ecology and environment has been especially productive of such tendencies. One hears of the rights of animals, of trees, and even of inanimate objects, such as mountain peaks and seashores.[9] Often this kind of talk is no more than inflated rhetoric, and those who engage in it might concede that, rhetorical considerations aside, it would be more appropriate to speak of good and bad or right and wrong treatment of animals, good and bad policies vis-à-vis the environment. The fact is, however, that such uses of *rights* are increasingly common.

We must be clear concerning the differences in the logic of *rights* when they are attributed to subjects who cannot make judgments and choices concerning them. The emphasis on (and the encouragement of) a kind of independent individualism, of assertive action, obviously disappears. At most the subject of the right must be capable of benefiting from it, although even this requirement disappears if one speaks of the rights of trees or of objects in inanimate nature. If the attribution of rights to animals and elements of inanimate nature has the effect of weakening the assumption (and hence the encouragement) of independence of action in applications of the concept to human beings, a high (and unnecessary) price would be paid for those improvements that might be achieved as regards attitudes and policies toward the former. Also, it is clear that the roles of the *B*s, *C*s, and *D*s must undergo significant change when rights are attributed to creatures and things unable to form preferences, to make and act upon choices, to interpret and defend rights.

In particular, the respect for the interests and desires, objectives and purposes of A as A understands them, which is central to the concept and practice of rights, simply falls out of both.

It appears, to sum up, that we must distinguish among at least three levels or types of uses of *rights*. The first presupposes what we have called the paradigmatic subject of rights – that is, persons who know what it is to have a right, have well-formed convictions about what those rights are, and are capable of and inclined to assert, exercise, defend, and protect those rights. Such persons have the capacity not only for understanding, evaluation, and choice, but for assertive, insistent, and perhaps even aggressive conduct in the area of their rights. The latter capacities, we have suggested, although not necessary to the role of subject of rights, must be present in the society if there is to be a practice of rights such as has in fact developed in several countries of the Western world since the seventeenth century. The second type of use requires that the holder of the right be in principle capable, under some circumstances, of understanding and assessing the value of his right and making a decision as to whether he wishes to have it maintained and respected. He may have little capacity or inclination to act on such assessments and decisions, but he could give guidance to those who might act on his behalf. The third type requires no more than that it be possible to say that the subject of rights enjoys, profits from, or benefits from having rights. When rights are attributed to creatures and things incapable of forming or expressing such a judgment, the latter requirement can be satisfied if someone other than the alleged holder of the right thinks that the latter does or would benefit. Although more and more common, in such cases the distinction between being the holder of a right and being the subject or object of a good or bad policy or good or bad treatment disappears.

III.   The content of rights (X)

The rights that people have in any time and place depend on the rules that establish them. But, as with the question of the criteria of eligibility for the role of *A* as such, we can ask the more general question whether there are limits to what can be made a right. Are there some *X*s that there must be, or cannot be, a right to do or to have?

We will begin with two fairly obvious, albeit difficult to apply, rules concerning the use of *rights,* rules that are of interest primarily in connection with arguments about natural or human rights. First, there can be a right to do or to have only such *X*s as are in fact identifiable in the language in which the practice of rights in question takes place. It is possible to speak of one's rights without actually identifying them. But if questioning fails to elicit an identification of the actions or possessions to which one has a right, the original statement is shown to have been empty.

A second point, already suggested by our discussion of the characteristics necessary to being a holder of rights, is that *rights* is governed by a rule similar to that which states that *ought* implies *can* and *obligation* implies *ability.* An action or possession can be a right only if there is some *A* capable of serving as the holder of that right and only if there is some *B* capable of discharging the obligation(s), respecting the no-rights, disabilities, and so on, that *A*'s right to *X* imposes. Men and things being what they are, the notion of a right to jump fifty feet straight up is nonsensical. Equally nonsensical is the notion of a right to have someone else jump fifty feet straight up. (In both cases, of course, we mean nonsensical apart from jokes, metaphors, and other uses in which the rules governing the concept are deliberately violated.)

Arguments that some rights are common to all human beings, then, assume that certain concepts occur in all languages and that certain capacities and the possibility of exercising them are common to all human beings. Consider, for example, the following provision of The Universal Declaration of Human Rights: "Everyone has the right to a standard of living adequate for the health and well-being of himself and of his family, including food, clothing, housing and medical care and necessary social services, and the right to security in the event of unemployment, sickness, disability, widowhood, old age or other lack of livelihood in circumstances beyond his control" (Article 25.1).[10] Our first response to this statement is perhaps that the rights of a very large number of people are not being respected. We may also wonder whether such concepts as *medical care, social services, unemployment,* and *widowhood* form a part of everyone's language. If this is not the case, what is meant when it is said that members of societies without such concepts have the rights mentioned? *What* is it that they have rights to do or have? How would they go about demanding, exercising, or defending these rights? We must also ask who has what obligations, no-rights, and so on, corresponding to these rights. If this latter question could be answered one would have to ask whether it is within the capacity of those persons or agencies to discharge those obligations. If the answer is no, we must say not that the rights are being violated but that the concept of rights is being misused in the sentences we quoted from The Universal Declaration.[11]

At first glance the third limitation on what can be a right involves a paradox. We have argued that all Xs must be such that some A is able to do or have them, and that all obligations, no-rights, and so on, vis-à-vis X must be such that some B is able to discharge and respect them. It is also true that all Xs must be such that the As who have them are able to choose not to do or have them, and that any obligations corresponding to X must be such that all Bs are able to choose not to discharge them.

We have already discussed a part of this point with regard to A. We noted that ordinarily A is free to forego exercising his rights; we also observed that he cannot be blamed, and certainly cannot be punished, for his decision not to do so. We add only what is already implied, namely, that there is therefore no sense to the idea of a right to do something that one cannot choose not to do. There could be a right to cut or not to cut one's hair, one's fingernails, and so on, but there is no sense to the notion of a right to have one's hair or one's fingernails grow (although one might imagine a right to treatments that would influence such bodily processes). Most important, there is no sense to saying that A exercised a right when his behavior was literally beyond his control (for example one does not *exercise* [though he may *have*] a right to free speech if he speaks when hypnotized, drugged, or even under such coercion that he could not reasonably be expected to remain silent).

The situation with regard to B is more complex. At bottom the issue concerns the conditions under which B can be said to have, and can be said to have acted to discharge, his obligations vis-à-vis A's right to X.[12]

B is not at liberty to ignore or waive his obligations in the sense in which A is at liberty to ignore or waive his rights. If B decides not to discharge his obligation he is legitimately subject to crticism by others and must defend himself. If he fails to do so or if his defense is unsatisfactory, others will be justified in criticizing him and perhaps warranted in applying sanctions against him. There are, nevertheless, satisfactory justifications for refusal to discharge obligations. Noticing why this is the case is one way to see that having an obligation to do X is not the same as being under compulsion to do it, and that acting to discharge an obligation is not the same as being compelled. If compulsion has the force of necessity the question of justification simply has no place. One does not do X, he suffers or experiences it. On these matters Rousseau said the last word 200 years ago: "If I took into account only force, and the effects derived from it, I should say: 'As long as a people is compelled to obey, and obeys, it does well; as soon as it can shake off the yoke, and shakes it off, it does still better; for, regaining its liberty by the same right as took it away, either it is justified in resuming it, or there was no justification for those who took it away'."[13] By contrast, obligations are defined by rules that rest on reasoning intended to show *why* there is and should be an obligation, from which it follows that one might show that the reasoning is not good, that the obligation does not hold, and that one need not or even ought not discharge it. Insofar, then, as doing an action involves discharging an obligation, there is logical room for a well-grounded decision on $B's$ part to do the action or not. (Of course other considerations may affect whether any particular *B* will in fact make such a decision and will in fact be successful in acting on it.)

To say that *A* has a right s.s. vis-à-vis *B* is to say that *B* has an obligation to respect *A*'s right. To see the significance of this point in the present context assume that *A* knows that *B* is ill or is under some form of compulsion and therefore *A* makes plans to do or to take something, *X*, that he knows *B* does not want him to do or to have. Assume also that *A*'s calculations prove correct and he succeeds in obtaining *X*. Evidently the fact that *B* did not prevent him from having *X* does not, and by itself could not, show that *A* had a right to have it. If his calculations had misfired and *B* had successfully stood in his way, the considerations on which his calculations were based would not show that *B* had failed to respect a right of *A*'s. *A* could regret that *B* had escaped the effects of the forces on which he had counted, but he would have no grounds for criticizing *B*. By the same token, the fact that the forces in question prevented *B* from interfering with *A* would not show that *A* had a right to *X*.

For *A* to have a right s.s. to *X* vis-à-vis *B*, then, it must be the case that *B* has an obligation *Y* to respect *A*'s right. And for *B* to have an obligation it must be the case that he may, in the sense just discussed, choose not to discharge that obligation. It follows that *X* can be a right of *A*'s vis-à-vis *B* only if *B* is able to choose not to do those actions that would fulfill his obligation vis-à-vis *A*'s right. If the *Y* *A*'s right to *X* would require of *B* is something it would be impossible for *B* to choose not to do, *X* cannot be a right of *A*'s. If *B* could choose not to do *Y* but if in fact he does it only because he is threatened or out of some other cause or reason having nothing to do with obligation, and if *A* does *X* solely on the calculation that *B* will feel compelled to do *Y*, then, although *B* may have an obligation to do *Y* and although *A* may have a right to *X*, *B* cannot be described as discharging an obligation and *A* cannot be described as exercising a right. On the other hand, if *B* could choose not to do *Y* but in fact does *Y* because he feels compelled, and if *A* knows that *B* has an obligation to do *Y* and does *X* in the belief that he is justified in so doing, then *A* not only has a right to *X* but can be said to be exercising a right when he does *X*. The paradigm case of the operation of the practice of rights, however, is when *A* chooses to exercise his right *X*, knowing that *B* has an obligation that he could choose not to discharge, and when *B* chooses to do *Y*, despite the possibility of disadvantage to himself, because he believes that he has a well-grounded obligation to do so out of respect for *A*'s right.

The fourth limitation on *X* was also anticipated by our discussion of *A*. There cannot be a right to an *X* unless having or doing *X* is in general, and in *A*'s judgment, advantageous for *A*. If *A* did not anticipate good consequences from doing *X*, he would presumably decide not to exercise his right to do it. If he so decided on each occasion that the question of doing *X* arose, the right would fall into desuetude. For others to continue to insist that *A* had the right to do *X* would be pointless if not perverse. The point of saying that *A* has a right to *X* is to warrant *A* in doing *X*. If *A* no longer wants to do *X* he no longer has occasion to warrant doing it.

There are at least three qualifications to this last rule. First, since *A* cannot know for certain that it will prove to be advantageous to do *X*, we must say that he must *expect* that it will be advantageous. Presumably this expectation will be based on the results of doing *X* or similar actions on previous occasions. This expectation might well survive occasional disappointments. Second, in the case of rights of children and third parties, it may be that others will have to assist *A* or make the judgment on *A*'s behalf for a period of time. In this case the logical requirement is that they must think it advantageous for *A*. Their judgment ceases to be relevant when it becomes possible for *A* to judge for himself. In the absence of this principle the concept of rights could well change from an instrument for protecting a sphere of action on *A*'s part into an engine of imposition and repression.

Evidently this fourth rule does not place substantive limitations on what can count as an *X*. But it does call into question the notion that there are certain *X*s that must be rights regardless of time, place, and circumstance. If the *A*s who make up a practice of rights do not think that a certain *X* is to their advantage, then that *Y* cannot be a right in the practice. A critic of the practice might say that its members are foolish – that they do not understand what is advantageous and what is not – and he might try to persuade them to change their views. But until he has so persuaded them, the critic cannot say that they have a right to *X*.

Fifth, an *X* can be a right only if, in general, *A*'s doing *X* has consequences for persons other than *A*. To claim a right to do *X* is to claim to have a warrant for doing it. If no one else is affected by *X* there is no need for a warrant for doing it and to claim a right would be an empty gesture. Indeed we must go further and say that an *X* can be a right only if doing *X* is thought to inconvenience, injure, or in some way disserve the interests of some person or persons other than *A*. If *A*'s doing *X* always or even ordinarily benefited *B* (or was indifferent to the latter), the question of justifying *X* would not arise. We can make the same point from a slightly different perspective if we recall that to claim that *A* has a right to *X* is also to claim that *B* has an obligation, a no-right, and so on, vis-à-vis *A*'s right. We do not say that *B* has an obligation to do *Y* if, in general, he has no reason to avoid doing *Y*, shows no disinclination to do *Y*. We say that *B* has an obligation to do *Y* because we think at once that he ought to do it and that he would not be likely to do it in the absence of an obligation. In short, to say that *X* is a right is to say that some *A* is warranted in doing *X* *despite* the fact that doing it will be thought to have adverse effects on the interests of some *B*.

There are two important complications concerning this fifth point. First, it is not the case that each and every instance of the exercise of an *X* must be judged to have an adverse affect on the interests of some *B*. If no *B* expresses his dislike or objection to *A*'s doing *X*, it is perhaps unlikely that *A* will use the word *right* of what he does and unlikely that anyone will use *obligation* with regard to *B*'s doing *Y*. The members of a well-established practice of rights become accustomed to the exercise of certain rights and discharge their obligations concerning them without objection and perhaps in a nearly habitual manner. Moreover, we cannot specify in general terms how often the *B*'s must give expression to their dislike of *A*'s doing *X*. We can say only that if *A*'s sense of the need to warrant his doing *X* and *B*'s sense of having an obligation to do *Y* disappear, the concept of rights ceases to apply to *X*.

The complication concerning *disserves* B's *interests* is more important and more difficult. *X* can be a right only if some *B* thinks that *A*'s doing *X* disadvantages him. It is also the case that *X* can be a right only if the participants in the practice, which of course includes those who will be *B*s vis-à-vis *X,* have made the judgment that it is proper that *A* have a right to *X*. The members of the practice, although recognizing that *A*'s doing *X* is thought to disadvantage those among them who will be *B*'s vis-à-vis *A*'s *X,* judge it desirable to establish a right to *X*. Put another way, it is not enough that *A* qua holder of right *X* judge himself to be justified in doing *X*. This judgment must be established as part of the practice. In the case of legal rights such judgments are usually arrived at through formal processes and promulgated in authoritative rules. In the case of moral rights the judgments typically evolve over time and come to be embodied in conventions more or less widely known and accepted among the participants in the practice.

Numerous schemes have been advanced to explain and to justify the fact that the *B*s of a practice support such apparently curious judgments – that is, judgments that *A*'s having *X* is justified despite disadvantaging them (the *B*s). The simplest of these schemes stresses the reciprocal character of the arrangement: Jones is a *B* vis-à-vis Peters' *X*, but he is an *A* and Peters is a *B* in other circumstances or vis-à-vis some other *X*. Both are willing to accept the disadvantages accruing to the role of *B* in order to obtain the advantages attendant upon the role of *A*. Another such theme is Rousseau's notion that there is a difference between the private interests of each member of an association and the public interest or general will in which each person participates as a member of the collectivity.[14] On this

understanding, B's decision to support the establishment of
A's right to X represents a judgment that A's having that right
is in the interest of both A and B in their capacities as members
of the collectivity, interests that are most important and hence
must take precedence over the purely personal interests that are
disserved when they are in the role of B. A third argument,
closely related to Rousseau's, is John Rawls' view that the right
accords with the principles of justice that are arrived at and
agreed to in the original position.[15] Persons in the original
position agree to these principles because they see that, in general, social arrangements that accord with them will benefit all
members of the social order equally. In practice there will be
instances in which the arrangements disserve the immediate
interests of those who are, in the circumstances at hand, the
B's. But the latter will know that, in general, the arrangements
are based on principles that are fair to everyone. Moreover, if
they have agreed to the arrangements and themselves benefited
from them in other circumstances (or will do so), justice requires that they discharge their obligations under them.

Later we will argue for a modified version of the position we
ascribed to Rousseau. But the question of what constitutes an
acceptable rationale for rights will have to wait until we have
achieved further clarity concerning what a right is and hence
concerning what such rationales aim to explain and to justify.
For the moment the important point is that an X can be a right
only if doing X is warranted by the rules of the practice despite
the fact that, in his own judgment, B is disadvantaged by it.
This aspect of the logic of *rights* is important to understanding
a number of prominent features of the practice, particularly its
lively and disputatious character.

To summarize, in order to qualify as a right (1) an X must be
identifiable in the language of the practice of rights in question,
(2) there must be an A who is able to exercise the right and a B
able to discharge the obligation(s), (3) it must be possible for B
to avoid discharging the obligation(s), (4) the exercise of X
must be judged advantageous to A and disadvantageous to B,

and (5) the right X must be established in the rules or conventions governing the practice.

We must stress the differences between this list of requirements and substantive lists of actions and possessions that purport to state what are and are not, should and should not be, rights. The fact that an X meets the foregoing requirements establishes that, logically, it can be a right, not that it is in fact a right and not that it should or should not be a right. The fact than an X does not meet the requirements establishes only that, as the concept of rights is now used and as the practice is constituted at the moment of the discourse in question, it cannot be a right. Such facts do not show that an X should not be a right and do not show that it could not become one if the practice of rights changed.

We have also noted discrepancies (as distinct from the differences in purpose just listed) between our list of requirements and general declarations and theories of rights – that is, between our analysis and a form of discourse about rights that has been recurrent in political philosophy and sometimes prominent in political and social life. One response to these discrepancies is that the statements of which the general declarations consist are, despite impeccable grammatical form, nonsensical. Another is that the discrepancies demonstrate that the analysis is mistaken.

The first response is appropriate with regard to discrepancies between a declaration or theory and our requirements 2 and 3. It is indeed difficult to make sense out of the notion that there is a right to an action that in principle no one could perform or avoid performing. But it is unsatisfying to cast whole bodies of discourse, discourse that has been important in human interaction, into the nonsense can. This tactic is especially unsatisfying when the declarations have point precisely because they are at variance with the usual requirements of the use of concept. It is something less than a great achievement to point out that such statements as "Everyone has a right to paid vacations" conflict with the rule that an X cannot be a right unless it is established in the practice in which the discourse takes place. It is exactly the fact that the X in question is not so established that prompts the authors of the declaration to make the statement.

Perhaps, then, we should conclude that the prominence of such statements invalidates the analysis. There is one sense in which this conclusion is appropriate, namely, that we would not be justified in treating as nonsensical all discourse that is in conflict with the analysis. But it does not follow that the analysis is mistaken. Rather, the discrepancy between the analysis and certain recurrent forms of argumentation calls attention to important features of the practice of rights. We noted, for example, that uses of *rights* that do not accord with the rules we have discussed lack the stringency of the more ordinary uses on which the analysis is based. The statement in the Universal Declaration that everyone has a right to paid vacations does not identify, explicitly or implicitly, either a B who has an obligation or a Y that is the obligation of some B. Hence it does not say that any particular B has failed to discharge his obligation because the As, or rather the potential As in various societies, do not in fact enjoy paid vacations. Insisting upon this capital difference among uses of *rights* may even help in a small way to combat erosion of the stringency in those uses of *rights* on which our analysis is based.

At the same time, the person who enunciates a universal right to paid vacations is not merely saying that paid vacations are or would be a good thing. He is saying, rather, that a *right* to paid vacations would be a good thing. Presumably he wishes to bring about a situation in which it would be possible to say, "Everyone has a right to a paid vacation," and to have the statement possess all the stringency of statements that accord completely with the logic of *rights* that we have described. He departs from that logic in order to urge changes in the content of the practice of rights but he wishes to retain the logic in order that the new content benefit from the established rules of the practice. Although this kind of discourse is by no means the only impetus to change in the practice, it is valuable as one such impetus. It is also valuable as a mode of questioning and criticism that keeps alive awareness of the rationale for established rights and for the practice of rights itself.

We hasten to add that the foregoing understanding of declarations of and theories about universal or human or natural rights in no way supports the view that there are certain rights that are somehow natural or immutable in character. We make sense out of such declarations as adjuncts to the system of belief, rules, and conventions that makes up a practice of rights, not as discourse based on foundations that are "natural" or in some other way independent of that system of conventions.

4

Aspects of
the logic of *rights* (II)

IV.   The obligees and their obligations (*B* and *Y*)

Most of the basic rules concerning *B* and *Y* have begun to emerge in the course of our examination of *A* and *X*. If *A* has a right to *X*, *B* has obligations, no-rights, and so on (*Y*), that correspond to *X*. Sometimes the content of *Y* is explicitly stated in the rules establishing *X;* sometimes it must be understood on the basis of the characteristics of *X* and what is necessary or contributive to *A*'s doing or having *X*. But an action or nonaction can be a *Y* only if some *B* can in principle perform it, can choose not to perform it, and sometimes finds it disadvantageous to perform it. Finally, an action or nonaction can be a *Y* only if it is established in the practice in which *X* is established and of which *B* is a member. It follows that an agent can be a *B* only if there is some *Y* that he can perform, can choose not to perform, and sometimes finds contrary to his interests to perform; and he can be a *B* only if he is a member of a practice in which rights and corresponding obligations are established.

Despite the parallels between the requirements for *B* and those for *A,* there has not been a willingness to relax the former, to extend the role of *B* to categories of beings and things not evidently capable of satisfying those requirements. Apparently it is one thing to assign rights to creatures that lack the capacity for reflection and choice, another thing to assign obligations, no-rights, and so on, to them. Whatever the explanation for this situation, it serves to call attention to further features of the relationship between *A* and *B*.

The first of these might be called the reciprocity of that relationship. It is ordinarily the case that an agent who is an *A* with right *X* in context 1 may be a *B* with regard to the same *X* in context 2. The same is true of B. In context 1 Smith is an A with a right to religious worship, Jones is a B with a no-right to object to A's worship. In context 2 Jones is the A exercising the same right, Smith is the B with the no-right. And of course Smith can be a B vis-à-vis Jones' right to some other X. As the parallels between the requirements for the roles of A and B would suggest, participants in the practice readily and regularly switch from one role to the other in the course of interactions in the practice.

From Locke on, this element of reciprocity has been important in justifications for the practice of rights. If Jones has a right against Smith, Jones can oblige Smith to act in a manner contrary to Smith's interests. Such an arrangement is likely to be more palatable to Smith if he knows that, in his turn, he can put Jones under a comparable obligation. It is evident, however, that this particular justification ceases to be available insofar as it becomes established that a subclass of participants in the practice can be As but never Bs.

Arguments concerning the rights of animals and things also call attention to another dimension of the relationship between A and B and another requirement that must be satisfied in order to be eligible for either status. However much they may deserve them, trees, animals, fetuses, and so on, cannot assert, demand, or insist that they have rights. Rights must be accorded to them, asserted on their behalf, and protected against violation by persons with the capacity for such actions. Unlike children and third-party beneficiaries who may temporarily be unable to exercise their own rights, this dependency is permanent. In at least this respect the relationship between the Bs who have an obligation and the As who have but cannot exercise rights is (permanently) a relationship of superiors to inferiors. Whether out of a sense of guilt, duty, benevolence, generosity, or some other motive, the Bs accord and respect the rights of the As. It is an important point about the ordinary logic of rights that such concepts as benevolence, generosity, and especially charity ordinarily have no place in the relationship between A and B as such. B respects A's X because A has a right to it; A expects, insists upon, respect for X because he has a right to it. Aside from conditions involving special sacrifice on his part, it is inappropriate for B to feel that he has been generous or charitable in respecting A's rights. Similarly, it is, special conditions aside, inappropriate for A to be grateful to B for respecting his (A's) rights. There is an impersonality (even a coldness or hardness) that is characteristic of interactions that take place under the rubric of rights.

These features of the practice are not, however, *logically* tied to the reciprocity characteristic of the relationship among the members thereof. It is not logically impossible for superiors to accord rights to inferiors. They not only could do so but could do so out of a cold and narrow calculation of their own interests. Rights could be accorded to a great variety of creatures and things out of such a calculation. But the relationship between A and B undergoes a significant change if the As are in principle incapable of demanding that rights be established, of asserting their rights, of objecting to encroachments upon them. No longer subject to the restraints imposed by the actions of the As themselves, and conscious of the fact that, after all, the As have their rights at their behest, it is highly unlikely that the attitudes of the Bs will continue to be those attitudes characteristic of the participants in the practice of rights we know. The history of rights in societies in which it has been assumed that some members of the human population are intrinsically or irredeemably inferior to others is painfully instructive in this regard.

V. Other members of the practice (C and D)

The distinction between C and D, on the one hand, and A and B, on the other, is most easily drawn in the case of rights that arise out of transactions such as contracts and promises. If Jones contracts with Smith to sell Smith his car, Smith acquires certain rights against Jones and Jones certain obligations to Smith. (The converse is true as well, but we will ignore this complication.) But the transaction presupposes an established practice in which contracts can be made. This practice includes other members who are not parties to the contract between Jones and Smith. These other members do not have the same rights and obligations vis-à-vis the contract as do Jones and Smith, but they stand in a variety of relationships to that contract. The distinction between A and B and C and D, then, is prompted by these two facts: (1) persons other than A and B are members of the practice that is a necessary condition of A and B acquiring the X and Y in question; (2) these other persons (Cs and Ds) do not have the same X and Y that A and B have.

A number of questions arise concerning this distinction, including the following: How should the distinction be drawn with regard to the various types of X, and indeed can it be drawn with regard to all Xs? What distinctions, if any, should be made within the categories C and D? What, if any, are the qualities necessary to having the role of a C and a D? What are the probable consequences of including within C and D this or that selection of those agents who, on logical grounds, are eligible for that role?

In the case of rights that arise out of contracts and related transactions, Cs and Ds are distinct from A in that they do not have the right A has and most obviously distinct from B in that they do not have the same obligations as B. They could have B's obligations only if they too were parties to the contract that B had made with A. Whether Cs and Ds have any obligations vis-à-vis A's X is a question to which we will return shortly.

It is not as easy to distinguish between B, on the one hand, and C and D, on the other, in the case of Hohfeldian liberties. If A has a constitutional right to free speech, assembly, and so on, it is incumbent upon all members of the practice of rights to which he belongs to respect those rights. Hence it might seem that in the case of such rights there is no room for the distinction between B, on the one hand, and C and D, on the other. It would seem that the only problem is to determine the scope of the membership of the practice.

If less clear-cut than in the case of contractual rights, the distinction is nevertheless a useful one. It is true that all mem-

bers of the practice must respect A's liberties. But in a practice
of any complexity it would be surprising if every exercise of
such rights provided all Bs with occasions to show their respect
for them. A's attempt to speak against fluoridation of the water
supply in Billings, in Arles, or in Bremen is not likely to provide an occasion for the citizens of Tampa, of Bordeaux, or of
Munich to demonstrate that they respect A's right to free
speech. Indeed there is an important sense in which A's speech
may not provide members of his immediate audience with
such an occasion. Insofar as the members of that audience welcome A's speech, agree with its contents, hope for its practical
success, it is inappropriate to say that they are allowing him to
speak out of a sense of respect for his right to do so. They ought
to let him speak, but the fact that they do not interfere with his
speech is not properly described as acting upon that ought (any
more than it is properly described as a failure to act upon it –
those in the audience let A speak because they respect his
opinion, not because they respect his right).

In the case of liberties, then, Cs and Ds are distinguished
from the Bs by the fact that, in practice, A's exercise of his
liberties does not always occasion a demonstration of their
respect for those liberties. But if we left our account of C and D
at this conclusion it might appear that the distinction between
A and B and C and D was in fact a distinction between those
who have a role to play with regard to A's X and those who do
not. In fact, the distinction is among those with such a role.
What, then, are the positive characteristics of the role of C
and D?

Assume that Peterson, a citizen of Billings with no very strong
convictions about the subject of fluoridation, happens along the
street where A is addressing a crowd. Peterson observes a group
of antifluoridationists at the back of the crowd and hears them
complaining bitterly of the shocking and scandalous character
of A's remarks. "We cannot tolerate that sort of thing in Billings," says one. "You are right," says another, "let's run him
out of here."

Or assume that Peters, an ordinary citizen of Tampa, is sitting in a cafe talking with friends. The local newspaper is at hand and it carries an article concerning campaigns for fluoridation, recounting the number of communities that have fluoridated their water supplies, the tactics that profluoridationists have employed, and so on. "Why can't we do that here?" says one. "The advantages are obvious." "I wish we could," says another, "but we won't be able to as long as those A.F.'s [a local antifluoridation group] are allowed to disseminate their lies to everybody in the city."

Finally, assume that Jones is talking to Roberts about a contract he has with Smith. "I no more than agreed to sell the car to Smith," says Jones, "when Williams called and offered me half again as much money for it. I'm going to do whatever is necessary to get out of that deal with Smith."

This is the point to begin distinguishing between the Cs and the Ds; that is, between persons in positions of authority (Cs) and persons not occupying such positions (Ds). If Mr. Peterson of Billings is a policeman, he has a duty to remind the antifluoridationists that A has a constitutional right to give the speech and that they have no-right to interfere with it; in fact, he has a duty to arrest them if they do interfere. In the case of the contract, if it is established that Jones has a legal obligation to Smith, it might become the duty of the sheriff or other legal officer, after the appropriate legal processes, to see to it that Jones discharged that obligation. On the other hand, in the Tampa example, as policeman or other representative of legal authority, Peters has no proper concern with the cafe conversation until there is evidence that those participating in it are going to do more than object to the views of the A.F.'s

The person in authority is not simply another B. His obligation is not simply to A, nor is the content of his obligation the same as that of other Bs. On the first point, we might say that his obligation is *to* his superiors in the authority structure in which he holds his position. This formulation has the advantage of emphasizing that it is they who are immediately responsible to call him to account if he does not fulfill his duties. One can also say that he has duties or obligations *under* the rules that establish and govern the authority structure and according to which his conduct is to be judged. As to the content of his duty, it is not simply to respect A's right; it is to enforce respect of that right on the part of all the members of the practice.

In thinking about C, however, we must remember that a large number of the rights that have been established since the seventeenth and eighteenth centuries have been conceived of as, first and foremost, rights against legal authority. They were created for the explicit purpose of limiting authority and protecting the citizen against its misuse. From this perspective the policeman, as part of the authority structure, has obligations to each and every A. As we will see, this point is of great importance in regard to the role of those who are not in authority – that is, the role of the Ds. But it also calls attention to peculiarities in the role of the Cs. At one and the same time they have a special role in enforcing the obligations of the Bs vis-à-vis A's X, and particularly stringent obligations to respect A's X. Although they are like the Bs in that they have obligations to the As, they are to oversee the relationship between the As and the Bs. Although they are like the Ds in that they are distinct from the As and Bs, they are ultimately to be controlled by the Ds.

It is often possible to speak with assurance about the situation of the Cs because their duties are spelled out in the rules governing the positions they hold.[1] Sometimes there are legal and moral rules that impose well-specified obligations on the Ds as well. In France, for example, what are sometimes called Good Samaritan laws impose an obligation to give assistance to persons in various sorts of distress.[2] If those in distress have a right to this aid they are As with a right to assistance; those with an obligation to aid them are simply Bs with an obligation to give assistance. But it is not the case that the members of a society have a *right* to all the protections and forms of assistance that the laws and conventions of the society grant them. There are obligations corresponding to all rights s.s. but there are not rights corresponding to all obligations. For example, I have an obligation to obey the law. But although some laws clearly create individual rights to the obedience of other members, it does not follow that every citizen in my society has a right to my obedience to all laws. If my city passes an antilitter ordinance, I have an obligation under that law not to litter. But if I litter, even if my doing so harms or inconveniences Smith, I do not violate a right belonging to Smith. (I may violate one of Smith's rights if I litter on his private property. But then I would be violating not only an antilitter ordinance but the laws that determine the particulars of the right to property.) What I do, simply, is fail to discharge my obligation. Smith may have a right, or perhaps an obligation, to report my violation to the authorities; but he misdescribes the situation if he reports that I have violated a right of his. The view that each citizen has an individual right to the obedience of all other citizens to all laws inflates the concept of rights out of all recognition and deprives it of its distinctive utility.

It is possible, then, that a *D* could have an obligation to assist *A*s in the exercise of their rights without thereby becoming a *B* vis-à-vis those rights. It would be possible for our man Peterson in Billings, now neither a *C* nor a *B,* to have a legal or a moral obligation to act to prevent the antifluoridationists from interfering with *A*'s speech. Perhaps he has an obligation to try to dissuade them from their plan, to call a policeman if they begin to act on it, or even physically to try to prevent them from interfering with *A* if no policeman is at hand. And although *A* would be an immediate beneficiary of *D*'s efforts, *D*'s obligation would be not to *A* personally but to all members of the practice *under* the rules and conventions thereof. Again, Peters in Tampa could have an obligation to take issue with the suggestion that the "lies" of the A.F.'s be suppressed; Roberts could have an obligation to remind Jones of his obligations to Smith.

We say there *could be* such obligations because there is nothing in the logic of the concepts involved that would impeach such an arrangement. There is no question that there are individuals and groups who, in a manner going well beyond the obligations they may have as *B*s, think of themselves as under an obligation to support and defend the exercise of rights in their society. Outstanding examples would be the American Civil Liberties Union, comparable organizations in other countries, and members of international organizations, such as Amnesty International.

As a generalization, however, it seems to us that the notion that the Ds in a practice have obligations vis-à-vis the rights of the As does not have wide currency and that few such obligations are clearly established. This judgment is supported by the very fact that it is often thought praiseworthy for a D to act to support the rights of an A. If D had an obligation so to act, his doing so would be praiseworthy only when he did so under particularly hazardous or demanding circumstances. Put another way, if such obligations were well established the activities of such organizations as the American Civil Liberties Union and Amnesty International would involve *no more than,* would be *merely,* the discharge of obligations shared with the other members of the society. Anyone familiar with such organizations knows that this is not the way their members ordinarily view their own activities. Nor is it difficult to find individuals who view the members of such organizations as busybodies who meddle in affairs of no concern to them. The judgment is also supported by the fact that one frequently encounters appeals to the members of a practice to take a more lively interest in the protection of rights, to greater vigilance and an increased willingness to give time, effort, and money to the safeguard thereof. The recurrent appeals of such groups as the NAACP and the League for the Defense of the Rights of Man are good examples. Those who launch such appeals may or may not favor establishing legal and/or moral obligations on the part of all Ds. The important point here is that appeals and requests would be inappropriate if it were accepted that there is an obligation to perform the actions in question. Appeals and requests would be replaced by reminders and warnings.

What, then, is the relationship of D to A and B and what should that relationship be. To begin with, the person who is a D vis-à-vis X in circumstance 1 may well be an A vis-à-vis the same X in circumstance 2. Peterson is not interested in the fluoridation issue and will neither give nor listen to speeches about it. But he may very much want to give, hear, or at least have presented speeches about the proposed bond issue to raise salaries of teachers in the local schools. Or he may believe that it is of value to his society, and hence to himself as a member of that society, for there to be public discussion of the issues that come before the community. Of course there is no *necessary* connection between silencing the speakers on fluoridation and silencing speakers taking up the question of the salaries of teachers. But a variety of kinds of connection can develop between them such that the one increases the probability of the other. These include legal precedents that authoritatively restrict the right to free speech. They also include the strengthening of social and psychological characteristics that prompt encroachment on the rights of others or discourage resistance to such encroachments. Thus for a number of reasons the Ds may have an interest in defending the exercise of the rights of persons other than themselves.

We can make a similar point from a slightly different perspective. We have identified four roles in the practice of rights. B and C have definite obligations that correlate with A's rights s.s. Leaving aside A's own efforts in this regard, if the Ds are inactive the burden of guaranteeing A's rights falls on the Bs and the Cs. Now by stipulation B often has an interest in encroaching upon A's rights: by stipulation the exercise of A's rights disadvantage B qua B. C's position is analogous to B's at least to the extent that A's rights and liberties limit authority. Here again it is well to remember the importance of suspicion of authority in the development of the practice of rights.

The foregoing considerations provide general grounds on which to think that it would be dangerous to leave the active protection and support of rights to the Bs and Cs. A good deal of historical experience points to the same conclusion. We have already noted that the practice of rights presupposes some number of As who understand and are able to assert and defend their own rights. But we hardly need to document the fact that the unaided individual, whatever his personal qualities and capabilities, has often been unable to protect his rights against the encroachments of Bs and Cs hostile to their exercise.[3] If the Ds remain passive or indifferent in the face of such hostility, the rights of the As are likely to suffer. The most dramatic and appalling cases of this sort have been those involving minorities, such as the blacks in the United States. Receiving little or no support from the Ds in their society, for long periods of time the rights of this segment of the population were in the less than tender care of the Bs and Cs. The often dreadful consequences of this arrangement are of course in part explained by the generalized prejudice against the hostility toward the minority in question. The Ds (as well as the Bs and Cs) failed to come to the defense of the rights of blacks, native Americans, and so on, not out of an understanding of their role as Ds in the practice of rights but out of indifference or hostility toward the As in question. But it is not much of a practice of rights that succeeds in protecting only the rights of the popular members of the society or the actions most widely approved in the society. It would be an exaggeration, but not more than that, to say that the raison d'être of the practice of rights is the protection of unpopular individuals and unpopular forms of action. If the Ds of a society will not act to protect such individuals and such actions, their role would be reduced to intervening in conflicts of narrowly personal interest between this A and that B – perhaps exactly the kind of case best left to the care of the As, Bs, and Cs.

Our last remark brings us to the considerations against the Ds having an *obligation* to support A's rights and that counsel restraint in playing the less than obligatory role that the practice seems in fact to accord to them. To begin with, there is the danger of inhibiting the actions of the A's. It is ordinarily for A to decide whether to exercise his rights and how to assess and respond to threats to them. If D intervenes without having been asked to do so by A, this feature of having a right is altered. If it happens regularly A's capacity to exercise and defend his rights may actually deteriorate.

Second, regular and uninvited interference on the part of the

*D*s carries the dangers of what might be called busybodyism with regard to moral rights and vigilantism with regard to legally established rights. The practice of rights represents one of the many respects in which societies employ a division of labor. In according rights to *A*s and corresponding obligations to *B*s and *C*s, a society in effect turns over to those who occupy these roles primary care of the interactions that take place in respect to them. At their best such role allocations facilitate the development of reliable expectations, understandings, and competencies and permit the efficient use of time, energy, and other resources. They also contribute to clarity concerning responsibility for successes and failures. The vigilante and the busybody, outside of the realm of the established division of labor and the interaction pattern based on it, will not have the as it were institutionalized opportunities to develop sensitivities and competencies presented to day-to-day participants. However good his intentions, our man Peterson is not likely to have developed the skills in crowd control that the police officer acquires through training and repeated experience. If his attempts to calm the antifluoridationists incite them to violence, it is impossible to change his assignment, to give him further training, or to discipline him for misuse of his authority. A well-developed division of labor provides mechanisms for dealing with failures and breakdowns; it is in the nature of ad hoc interventions that dealing with them is difficult if not impossible. Although perhaps efficacious in this or that instance, the ad hoc intervention may disrupt the relationships and expectations on which the day-to-day operation of the practice depends.

At the general level at which we have been discussing the question, then, there are conflicting considerations concerning the proper role of the *D*s. It is certain that the practice of rights could not be sustained if the exercise of rights never received active support from the *D*s. (If support from the *D*s was never necessary, the rights in question would no longer be controversial and the *A*s would be able to take the actions guaranteed by the rights even if they were not so guaranteed. In such a circumstance the practice could be sustained but there would be

little point in sustaining it. One would expect that the practice
would wither away.) On the other hand, persistent, uninvited
interventions by the Ds may interfere with the independence
and freedom of action that are among the values that the practice serves and it may disrupt the network of role relationships
of which the practice largely consists. The presence of these conflicting considerations may explain, and in any case seems to
justify, the comparatively indeterminate state of the role of D
in actual practice. Each D is left to decide whether and how to
intervene in cases that present themselves. The Ds can be called
upon to justify these decisions and they are subject to criticism
if others find the justifications inadequate. By comparison with
the situations of A, B, and C, there are few well-defined rules
on the basis of which Ds can reach and justify their decisions.
An appeal for assistance is certainly a potent consideration, but
it is not conclusive in all cases. Owing to the heavy dependency
of the practice on the support of the Cs as well as the special
danger that the Cs pose for it, evidence of the failure of a C to
discharge his special obligations properly carries heavy weight.
Judgments are required as to the significance of the right and
the encroachment in question, both for A and for the larger
practice of rights in which A has a right to X. If B's infraction
consists of walking across A's lawn to save a few steps on his way
home, D may properly decide, even in the face of A's request
for assistance, to allow A to fend for himself. If B treats A abu-
sively or disrespectfully there will be a better case for intervention on D's part. If a C violates A's rights under cover of the
exercise of his authority, the case for giving some kind of assistance will be very strong. But these and other precepts that
one might list are no more than general guidelines for decisions
that are, and in our judgment should remain, highly contextual
in character.[4]

Two questions concerning C and D remain on our agenda for
this chapter. The first concerns the qualities or characteristics,
if any, that an agent must possess in order to be eligible for the
role of C and/or D. The second concerns the implications or
consequences of according the role of C and/or D to this as op-

posed to that selection of those agents who, criteriologically, are eligible for them.

Insofar as we are explicating an operative practice as opposed to setting up an ideal, the answer to the first of these questions will turn on the role of C and D in that practice. To be eligible for these roles an agent must be capable of the actions they require. In the case of C the requirements of the role – or office, as we would ordinarily say – are spelled out in the rules and conventions that specify the authority that the office carries. The requirements of the role of D are not closely specified. Hence it might appear that the qualities necessary for eligibility for this role must be equally indeterminate. Indeed our argument that the Ds as a class have few, if any, established obligations might suggest that there are *no* characteristics or qualities necessary to eligibility for the role of D.

Put another way – by comparison with A, B, and $C - D$ is more an analytic than an existential category. People have rights; have obligations, no-rights, and so on; and have authority. The role of those who do is worked out in the practice of rights and related practices. The task of the analyst is to trace systematically and explicitly the contours of categories that figure prominently in social life. But it has been one of the burdens of our argument to this point that no equally well-defined phenomenon corresponds to our category D. It is for this reason that we have tended to identify D negatively, as comprising agents who are neither As, Bs, or Cs. Perhaps we should view D as no more than a residual category in which we can include any and all agents or agencies that are not As, Bs, or Cs. If we set requirements for eligibility for this category we would do so purely for terminological convenience, not because they correspond to requirements that figure in the practice.

There is, however, a distinction between those non-As, non-Bs, and non-Cs, that are capable of reflection and choice and those that are not. If the practice of rights seldom assigns obligations to the members of the first of these categories, it does distinguish between good and bad and right and wrong actions on their part and it does hold them responsible for the actions they take that affect the practice. If there were no non-*A*s, non-*B*s, and non-*C*s capable of choice, this latter distinction and our entire discussion of the proper role of *D* would be without point. The *A*s, *B*s, and *C*s could discuss the question of how they themselves should act so as to control the consequences that, as a causal matter, the existence of non-*A*s, non-*B*s, and non-*C*s have on the practice. But if the non-*A*s, non-*B*s, and non-*C*s are incapable of choice there would obviously be no sense to the enterprise of identifying criteria of proper and improper action on their part.

Our category *D*, then, is intended to correspond to a role that is part of practice; it comprises those persons who, in respect to this *X* in these circumstances, are not *A*s, *B*s, or *C*s but who are capable of reason and choice with regard to their conduct vis-à-vis the *A*s, *B*s, and *C*s and who are in some sense part of the practice with the latter. Because the practice has specified few, if any, obligations or firm rules of conduct for this role, we cannot say that an agent is eligible for it only if he is capable of performing this or that particular type of action. We can say that an agent is eligible for the role only if he is capable of reflection and choice concerning those of his actions that affect the practice. Taking this requirement to mean that *D* must understand that the practice consists of relationships involving rights and obligations, liberties and no-rights, and so on, and hence must understand such concepts as *rights* and *obligations,* we assume that it means that the status of *D* is available only to agents with the capacities we found necessary for the roles of *A* and *B*. The practice of rights affects and is affected by agents and things who lack those capacities, but participation in it is possible only for those who have them.

Who, then, are the *C*s and *D*s vis-à-vis any given *X*? How is this question decided? What are the implications or likely consequences of deciding it this way rather than another?[5]

In order for an agent to be a *C* vis-à-vis a particular *X* there must be some rule, convention, or understanding that is established among the members of the society and according to which that agent has authority to take some range of actions.

Hence the question of who is a C is to be settled by examining the rules, conventions, and so on, that grant authority. The issue of how the latter question is settled is to be answered by examining the rules and procedures by which and through which allocations of authority are made.

Sometimes these rules and conventions are well worked out and clearly established. For example, it is clear that certain agents of the federal government in the United States are now Cs vis-à-vis threats, emanating from state governments, to the exercise of the right of freedom of speech established by the First Amendment to the U.S. Constitution. In other cases there is ambiguity and controversy concerning the rules. An example would be the extent to which agents of the federal government are Cs vis-à-vis threats, whether from state governments or private citizens or groups, to the right to various kinds of equal treatment. Many more examples of ambiguity and controversy could be drawn from international law and relations – for example, the extent to which the United Nations and its various agents are Cs vis-à-vis threats to rights listed in the Charter or the Universal Declaration. In the latter case, moreover, the procedures by which ambiguities are clarified and controversies settled are not clearly established.

Even when the authority given by such rules and conventions is clearly established, acting on it is often a sensitive matter requiring prudential and partisan political calculations as well as knowledge of the basis and extent of the authority that the rules grant. This is perhaps particularly true when it is a question of interventions across the lines of what in some respects are distinct practices – for example, across the boundary lines of nation-states or the boundaries of the units of federal systems.[6] Together with the complex, often ambiguous, and sometimes rapidly changing character of systems of rules, this fact means that it is often difficult to specify with exactitude who the Cs are vis-à-vis any X and just what their authority includes. For present purposes, however, the important point remains that questions about C (and hence about this aspect of the question of the boundaries of the practice) can arise only if there are some established rules and conventions. Either there are such conventions or it is simply a question of an initiative by some person or groups and a response to it by others. In our nomenclature it is a question of a D, not a C. Thus the Cs vis-à-vis an X are those who have authority to intervene under some established rule or convention, the normative question of who should be and will be a C and what his authority will be is decided through the processes by which the rules are passed and the conventions evolve, and the descriptive question of who is a C (of the boundaries of the practice in this respect) is to be decided by examining the rules and conventions and the manner in which they are interpreted and applied in the practice.

There are also some established conventions concerning who are the Ds. For example, it is reasonably well established that those who are members of a practice in the sense that they are As and Bs in it are also Ds. Whatever might be the status in this respect of the nonstudents who live in the immediate vicinity of certain major universities, there is little doubt in this enlightened age that faculty and registered students have standing to protest and otherwise to attempt to remedy violations of the rights that are established under the rules of the university community. Whatever might be said about Minnesotans or Oregonians, Georgians are ordinarily accorded such standing with regard to rights established under Georgia law, Nevadans under Nevada law, and so on. Southerners are more apt to accept the interventions of other southerners, New Englanders of other New Englanders, and so on. In short, where something like boundary lines – whether territorial, functional, or some other species – have evolved with some clarity, those who are "located" within them are usually thought to have a legitimate concern with and perhaps some responsibility for protecting the rights that are established within the practice. However they answer it, the question of whether to act to support the rights of other members of the practice properly arises for them.

In addition to such conventions, there are what might be called doctrines or ideologies intended to specify who the Ds are vis-à-vis certain rights. The most prominent and most sweeping of these has figured in some versions of the theory of natural rights. According to this doctrine there is, at least with regard to the most fundamental rights, one and only one practice of rights that comprehends all the human race. This doctrine insists that all human beings possess and should enjoy the exercise of fundamental rights. It also implies that all men have a responsibility not only to respect these rights in their own actions but to sustain and support them whenever and wherever they are threatened. Violations of the fundamental rights of Puerto Ricans in New York and dissident novelists in the Soviet Union ought to be as much a concern of Peterson in Billings as are the consequences of the actions of antifluoridationists in his home town.

The reception accorded to "northern agitators" in Albany, Georgia, to "nonstudents" demanding free speech in the University of California, and the affection with which virtually all governments embrace such notions as "self-determination" and "internal" or "domestic" questions is perhaps sufficient indication that this doctrine is less than universally accepted. But it is accepted by substantial numbers of people and it takes practical importance from the fact that it provides the underlying rationale for activities of respected organizations such as Amnesty International and the League for the Defense of the Rights of Man. Thus it figures in conflicts that arise when those who accept it attempt to support rights in what those who follow a more particularistic understanding of the role of D regard as *their* practice.

The existence of a rule or convention that accords authority is a necessary condition of being in the role of C. It is not a sufficient condition of playing that role, and certainly not of playing it successfully. In the case of D, conventions and doctrines such as we have been discussing are neither a necessary nor a sufficient condition of having the role of D. They may facilitate playing the role and playing it effectively but they do not guarantee either.[7] If Peterson is distressed by violations of the rights of migrant workers in California or of novelists in the Soviet Union he may, in regard to right and wrong, attempt to

intervene without showing that there is an established convention or doctrine that justifies his doing so. Because his action
will affect others he must justify it. The availability of a well-
developed convention or doctrine may make it easier to do so
in the sense that at least some of the materials out of which to
form a justification will be there at his disposal. To the extent
that the convention or doctrine is accepted by those to whom he
must justify his actions, his justification and his action are likely
to meet with a more cordial reception. But it is characteristic of
questions about the status and role of D that there are few
conventions or doctrines sufficiently well established that one
can justify an intervention merely by showing that it falls under
one of them. By comparison with the arguments often available
to an A or a C, Ds are more likely to be successful if they sup-
plement or bolster general principles and arguments with considerations tied more closely to the particulars of the case at
hand. These points also hold about attempts by the As, Bs, and
Cs to limit the number of Ds and to prevent or criticize attempted interventions.

For these reasons it is difficult to give a general or a conclusive answer to the question of who is a D vis-à-vis any X,
and hence also difficult to identify the outer limits or boundaries of the practice in which X is established. Neither the universalistic theory according to which there is one practice that
includes all persons capable of reflection and choice nor the
particularist understandings that exclude all participation across
sharply drawn territorial, functional, or other boundary lines
capture the complexity of day-to-day events and interactions.
Certain conventions are reasonably well established, but the
boundary lines are redrawn and the role defined and redefined
through a complex process involving initiatives and responses
to them, justifications and criticisms of them. Similar processes
occur with regard to the As, Bs, Cs, and indeed X itself, but
they are most pronounced with respect to D. The role of D is
the most changeable feature of a fluid and changeable dimension of human affairs.

The practice of rights consists in part of rules and conventions that provide socially established warrants for types of actions that affect, often adversely, persons other than the agents to whom it accords the right to take them. The same rules establish obligations and responsibilities to respect and support those actions when, at their discretion, the holders of the rights choose to exercise them. The rules have such standing as human beings choose to accord them. The scope of the practice depends upon the number and the distribution of persons who accept the rules; its degree of integration depends upon the clarity of the rules, the extent to which they are interconnected, and the firmness with which they are accepted. In some well-established social and political entities, the practice forms a bounded, integrated pattern of human interaction that can be resistant both to outside intervention and to change. Because the standing of the rules depends upon their continued acceptance by human beings, they are susceptible, both as a logical and as a practical matter, to change. We have noted respects in which features of the practice, particularly the role of D but also the very fact that the rules and conventions cannot be applied without interpretation, leave an element of what might be called open texture in the practice. Because the practice consists in part of established, more or less integrated rules, we can say that certain understandings of and certain proposals concerning the practice are invalid, inappropriate, or unacceptable at given times and places. The open-textured, permeable character of the practice prevents us from saying that those understandings and proposals could never be valid, appropriate, or acceptable and prevents us from saying that understandings and proposals that are now valid and appropriate must always be so.

5

Rights and rules

The prominence of the terms *rule* and *convention* in the previous chapters is in part a consequence of the larger premises and methods on which those discussions are based.[1] It is also due to characteristics specific to the practice of rights itself, characteristics that could hardly be ignored in any account of the practice.

As we noted earlier, *rights* is a legalistic concept and the tradition of thought and action concerning rights can readily be interpreted as part of the tradition of legalism that is salient in modern Western history. This aspect of the practice of rights is most clearly evidenced by the fact that many established rights are created and defined by rules that have standing in law. But legal rights are not the only variety that involve conduct directed and guided by rules and conventions. When we say that *A* has a moral, familial, professional, or other nonlegal right to *X,* we ordinarily presuppose that the *X* has been specified by established rules. To claim a right to *X* is to appeal to such a rule. If *B* challenges the claim, the challenge is met at least initially by reminding him of the rule.[2] Thus even when not legal in a strict sense, rights are legallike phenomena and the interactions that involve them are legalistic in character.

These propositions about rights and rules, however, are significant more because of the questions they raise and the problems to which they direct attention than because of the answers and resolutions they provide. We all know what rules are; we encounter, follow, break, ignore, interpret, enforce, regret the existence of numerous rules in the course of our everyday activities. In this sense we know what it means to say that rights are defined by rules and that *rights* is a rule-dependent concept. But our very familiarity with rules, their very ubiquity in our affairs, signals a need for systematic analysis. A concept that figures as widely in our lives as *rule* is not likely to be univocal or to yield easily to efforts at systematic analysis. For the latter purpose we must treat such propositions as "All specifically human behavior is . . . rule governed" and "Rights are established and defined by rules" as points in need of further analysis, not as a satisfactory conclusion to the analytic enterprise.

Some headway can be made by identifying generic characteristics of rules and rule-guided conduct. We have attempted such an identification elsewhere,[3] and we have summarized a part of that discussion in Chapter 1. Rules in all senses save mere regularities are conduct-guilding devices (1) that presuppose forms of action susceptible of choice and guidance; (2) that are thought to be important; (3) about which criteria of right and wrong, good and bad, wise or unwise have developed and been widely accepted. (4) These criteria have been accepted for reasons that can be stated and that can and do serve as guides to the interpretation and application of the rules to particular cases. Rule-guided conduct, accordingly, involves choices among alternatives. Such choices are made on the basis of the directive provided by a rule the agent accepts. He applies the rule in the light of the reasons that, in his view, support acceptance of the rule. Thus rules in all relevant senses are to be distinguished from mere descriptive generalizations and rule-guided conduct is to be distinguished from instinctive, habitual, compelled, and other forms of behavior that are explainable without use of such concepts as *choice, right and wrong, reasons for and against.*

These points about the generic features of rules and rule-governed conduct are important because they place the whole vast array of rule-governed practices and activities, and hence the practice of rights, in the realm of human action.[4] The implications of this fact for the study and interpretation of the practice of rights are substantial. It implies that the practice of rights cannot be treated as a mere collection of regularities detected by observers. We must search out the choices and deci-

sions made by the actors in the practice, the rules they accept
and follow, the rationales for those rules, and the warrants, justifications for, and criticisms of action that appeals to those rules
and rationales are thought to provide. Such an investigation can
indeed be expected to identify patterns of action among the participants in the practice. But these patterns will be best understood as a result of shared rules accepted and followed by the
participants, not as consequences of the workings of causal
forces of which the participants are unaware and/or over which
they have no control.

I.   Types of rules

The kind of investigation implied by the rule-governed character of rights will yield limited results if the investigator operates with a univocal, undifferentiated concept of *rule, rules,* and
rule-governed conduct. There are characteristics common to
most uses of these concepts and calling attention to them is a
useful means of avoiding certain misunderstandings and mistaken research strategies that are all too common in social science. But we will not progress toward an understanding of the
practice of rights unless we notice the considerable variety of
types of rules (and the ways they figure in the practice) that share
those characteristics.

A.   Regulations and authorizations

We can make a beginning on this enterprise by returning to
the point that many established rights are created and defined
by legal rules. Although this generalization is not likely to be
disputed, when unpacked it turns out to be complex. This is
because the concept *rules* stands for a considerable variety of
devices that vary from one another in significant ways.

The term *legal rules* most readily brings to mind *regulations*
of the sort exemplified by "Come to a full stop at red lights,"
"It is unlawful to burn leaves from 8:00 A.M. to 6:00 P.M.," "It
is a felony to be in possession of heroin," and a host of others.
Sometimes prohibitions and requirements such as these specify

obligations that correlate with legal rights. Examples would be regulations prohibiting owners of hotels, restaurants, and other public accommodations from discriminating against certain classes of potential customers. Such laws are clearly intended to protect the constitutional rights of clients by putting hotel keepers under specific legal obligations to respect those rights.

We should notice at once, however, that the rules that create the legal rights themselves (the X as opposed to the Y) rarely take the form of regulations that prohibit or require particular forms of conduct. It is for A to decide whether to exercise his rights. The legal rules authorize A to act in certain ways and they may prohibit others from interfering with his taking those actions. But they impose no requirements or prohibitions on A. This is most obvious in the case of rights in the sense of powers, but it is true of most examples of all the types of rights we have identified. For this reason we cannot fully explicate the statement "Rights are defined by legal rules" in terms of rules of the type we have called regulations. We need an additional type or sense of *rule* if we are to give an account of this (obviously central) aspect of the practice of rights. We will call such rules *authorizations.*

B. *Precepts*

The foregoing feature of rights is not the only one that defies analysis in terms of rules in the sense of regulations. We must ask why it is that legal rules, of whatever type, are thought to have binding force for those to whom they are addressed; we must ask why it is that the addressees are thought to have an obligation to obey them, respect them as valid authorizations, or adopt whatever other attitudes and courses of action may be deemed appropriate. Legal rules themselves rarely, if ever, state that those to whom they apply have obligations to obey or respect them. The widely held view that there is an obligation to obey the law is grounded not in particular legal rules as such but in some more general premise or premises thought to hold for all rules that have legal standing. Some such premise has been widely enough accepted in numerous times and places to have achieved the standing of a rule. But it is not, to repeat, a legal rule. Political societies do not punish their members for disobeying the rule "Obey the law," they punish them for disobeying particular legal rules. Such societies *do* encourage their members to accept and act upon the rule "Obey the law." If they do not achieve substantial success in this endeavor, obedience to particular legal rules is not likely to be widespread and the notion that legal rules impose obligations is likely to lose standing. Thus an account of the role regulation-type legal rules play requires an understanding of their relationships to the nonlegal rule "Obey the law." We will call rules of this type *precepts,* and we will be concerned not only with "Obey the law" but with such analogous precept-type rules as "Rights should be respected."

C. *Instructions*

Regulations, authorizations, and precepts such as "Obey the law" are interwoven with a variety of prudential or *instruction-type* rules that provide guidance as to how the former types should be regarded and responded to. Examples in the practice of rights are rules that advise vigor and insistence in defending rights, that condemn "standing on one's rights" when doing so has bad consequences for persons in comparatively disadvantaged situations, and that instruct concerning the ways in which rights can be most effectively exercised. Such rules never have legal standing and seldom have moral standing. Yet they may be widely accepted and acted upon, may be taught by one generation to the next, and in general may have great prominence in the workings of the practice of rights.

D. *Constitutive rules*

Finally, there is a type of rule that is intimately connected with those we earlier called authorizations. Rules of this type specify what must be done for an action to count as an instance of the exercise of certain rights. Take as an example the right to vote in elections. This right is accorded and protected by constitutional and statutory authorizations and regulations, undergirded by precepts, and surrounded by a variety of instruction-type lore that counsels the *A*s on how to use the right so as to serve their purposes most effectively. The right would be empty in the absence of further rules that specify what counts as voting. As with authorizations, these rules do not require *A*s to vote and do not prohibit them from doing so. They tell them what procedures they must follow if they are to accomplish the objective of exercising their right to vote. Of course these rules are closely akin to, indeed presuppose, the semantic rules that govern use of the concept *vote*. But many actions that would satisfy the generic semantic rules governing *vote* will not count as exercising the right to vote in this or that legal or institutional context. Detailed provisions concerning registration, form of ballot, manner and procedure of casting a ballot, and many others typically govern this action in the sense of specifying what must be done in order to succeed in voting. We will call such provisions *constitutive* rules.[5]

II. Rationales for the several types of rules

These distinctions among several types of rules will permit us to take further our earlier remarks concerning the implications of the rule-dependent character of the practice of rights. We said that rules and rule-governed conduct necessarily involve reasons and reasoning. To the extent that the practice of rights is rule dependent it must involve reasons and reasoning. Our next task is to try to determine whether the modes of reasoning appropriate to the several types of rules resemble and/or differ from one another.

We will begin with authorizations. Reasoning concerning this type of rule varies with the substance of the right that the particular authorization establishes. Arguments for or against the right to free speech will hardly be sufficient to justify or disjustify a right to vacations with pay or a right to hold and dispose of real property. We may be able to generalize somewhat over classes or types of rights – for example, civil-liberties-type rights such as freedom of speech versus civil-rights-type rights such as access to public accommodations, or either of first two versus welfare-type rights such as to medical care or unemployment compensation. Such generalizations have been the basis of arguments that some classes of rights are categorically preferable to others.[6] Clearly, however, important differences remain within these categories. Arguments for the right to freedom of speech may be more akin to arguments for freedom of assembly than to arguments for a right to unemployment compensation, but free speech and free assembly are not the same and the arguments for them cannot be identical.

Further complications result from the differences among the types of rights that we surveyed in Chapter 2. Rights s.s. are not the same as liberties, privileges, or powers, and the argumentation that supports them and their interpretation must reflect the differences. The bulk of the following remarks concerns rights s.s. and liberties.

Whatever the content of this or that right, all authorizations of rights are, trivially, authorizations of rights and not something else. Now to be an authorization of a *right,* a rule must define a moral or jural entity that counts as a right. It must, in short, accord with the semantic rules governing the concept *right.* We explored aspects of these rules in Chapters 3 and 4. The requirements and limitations we noted establish boundaries within which reasoning in support of rights authorizations must remain. For example, they establish that such reasoning must justify the policy of according to the As a sphere of action that is, comparatively speaking, autonomous; in this sphere the As can do X without obtaining the assent, agreement, or permission of particular Bs, Cs, or Ds. To have a right to do X is (among other things) to have an authorization to do X that is conclusive against some range of objections on the part of Bs, Cs, and Ds.

There is a good deal of controversy concerning the scope of the autonomy that must be established in order for it to be said that there is a right. Disputes concerning the First Amendment to the U.S. Constitution, for example, have sometimes taken the form of whether claims validly based on the right to freedom of speech are absolute (i.e., hold against all objections) or whether claims based on freedom of speech must be balanced against claims based on other considerations, such as order and security.[7] Disputes between natural rights theorists and utilitarians sometimes reenact this disagreement at a higher level of abstraction. They also concern the pattern of reasoning that best justifies whatever degree of autonomy their proponents have decided a right should establish.

Despite these important differences all reasoning in support of rights authorizations must justify some degree of autonomy on the part of A. If reasoning does not do this job it does not support rights. (See Chapter 8 for an examination of some prominent attempts to support such autonomy.) This feature of reasoning about rights authorizations entails another, namely, that all reasoning about rights must also justify the restrictions that A's autonomy implies for B, C, and D. The character of these restrictions differs among rights s.s., liberties, powers, and immunities as well as varying with the substance of the particular right in question. In all cases, however, rights authorizations must be accompanied by precepts and/or regulations that apply to B and perhaps others. It is indeed appropriate to think of granting rights as a way of establishing or enlarging the autonomy and freedom of the As. But we must also recognize that granting rights to As restricts the freedom of Bs. Reasoning in support of rights authorizations is always, at least implicitly, reasoning in support of regulations and precepts. If no rules of these types can be justified, no rights can be justified. (Thus if an ideological position – say, anarchism or antilegalism – opposes all regulations, it also opposes all legal rights; and if it opposes all rules that restrict conduct, it opposes all rights.) Because regulations and precepts also play a role in numerous contexts outside of the practice of rights, this feature of reasoning in support of rights authorizations is not unique to it. But it is necessary to it; it is a categorial feature of such reasoning.

The relationship between authorizations and constitutive rules is more complex, and its implications for reasoning in support of the former are less tightly drawn. Defense of a rights authorization always presupposes some delineation of what will count as an exercise of the right defended, and hence implies that some defensible set of constitutive rules can be worked out. But there may be several possible and acceptable sets of constitutive rules. Consider again the right to vote. A defender of this right might be indifferent as to whether the voting is done by secret or open ballot, whether preregistration should be required, and so on. Once a particular set of constitutive rules has been adopted, the X being defended will include those rules. But defenders of the right might think this feature of the right insignificant and hence neither defend nor attack it.

Most of the unqualified generalizations that can be made about reasoning in support of rights authorizations, in sum, hold by virtue of the relationships between authorizations and the other types of rules that are part of the practice of rights. Because the semantic rules governing *rights* summarize, indeed embody, many of these relationships, many of the generalizations can be stated in terms of the semantic rules (which is, I suppose, one way of saying that, and why, we are doing conceptual analysis). Thus it would appear that the generalizations hold only insofar as the semantic rules are (at least tacitly) accepted and followed by participants.

This inference, however, is too strong, too unqualified. If the semantic rules define what a right is, it would seem to be a necessary truth that arguments for rights must accord with those rules. Arguments that do not satisfy the requirements of those rules might be cogent arguments for something else, but they simply would not be arguments for rights. To begin with, however, the semantic rules do not form a strict calculus that imprisons discourse about rights in precisely delineated categories, nor can the rules be mechanically applied to particular cases. To have a right to do X is indeed to have a degree of autonomy in deciding whether to do X. But what will count as having autonomy is a matter of great controversy, which can rarely be settled merely by reciting a semantic rule.

It is also possible to question established semantic rules without departing from rights discourse. If someone categorically rejects all the rules governing rights, his arguments will not be arguments for a right. But someone who knows the rules might urge changes in them and yet succeed in making arguments for rights that are not only intelligible but cogent. Those who argue for the rights of the fetus are implicitly rejecting the rule according to which only beings capable of choice can hold rights. Someone might object that their arguments are therefore irrelevant to discourse about rights. Such an objection might convince proponents of the rights of the fetus to alter their position and to argue, rather, that it is wrong to treat the fetus in certain ways. But the proponents might also argue that the semantic rule ought to be changed, that we ought to alter our conception of rights so as to make it applicable to the fetus and perhaps to other creatures now excluded by the rule. It is a truism that most discourse about rights accords with the rules governing the use of the concept. But it is not a truism, nor is it a true, that all discourse that violates those rules in any way whatever is unintelligible or is discourse about something else. Rather, discourse that violates rules is often of particular interest. Because the semantic rules define the formal characteristics of the practice of rights, to accept and conform to them is to accept (and even to reinforce) the practice as it is. If doing so cannot be questioned, defended, and attacked, the practice as such cannot be defended or attacked and cannot be deliberately changed. Knowing that defending and attacking these rules is defending and attacking the practice, we can hardly say that doing so is unimportant.

III.   Rhetorical uses of *rights*

These remarks bring us back to a topic we postponed earlier, namely, discourse that uses the concept of rights in arguing for rights that are not as yet established. It is a distinctive but at first sight puzzling feature of rights discourse that proponents of new rights very often cast their arguments in the form of assertions that the rights they are proposing already exist, are al-

ready established. Declarations of rights are only the most prominent example of this phenomenon. "I have a right to X,"
uttered in the absence of any established rule creating such a
right, is commonplace in circumstances much more mundane
than national independence movements or the sessions of con-
stituent assemblies.

Locutions of this type first attracted our attention as exceptions to the generalization that right claims presuppose established rules creating and defining the rights claimed. Our distinctions among different types of rules and the kinds of reasoning
that can support them permit a more differentiated analysis of
such locutions. We must distinguish between (1) arguments for
adding new rights to an established practice of rights and (2)
arguments (a) for establishment of such a practice for the first
time or (b) for structural changes in an existing practice. In
case 1 the argument presupposes and builds upon semantic rules
that determine the generic features of the entity that one is arguing for a right. If it is an argument for a new legal right it
also presupposes the concept of regulation-type rules that define
the obligations, no-rights, and so on, that correlate with rights.
It also presupposes precept-type rules such as "Laws should be
obeyed" and "Rights should be respected" as well as the possibility of defining constitutive rules that determine what counts
as an exercise of the proposed right. Here the person who says,
"I have a right to X," is counting on the fact that his audience
will be familiar with rules of these types and will understand
what his contention implies, namely, the addition of an au-
thorization-type rule and the necessary regulations and constitutive rules. The sort of utterance we are considering is also used
when a speaker believes that an authorization for X is established but in another realm or at another level of discourse. A
speaker urging a legal right to X may believe that a comparable
moral right is already established. Similar tactics can be used
within systems that distinguish between levels of law – for example, in federal systems where a right established at one level
of government might be proposed at another. In such cases the
statement "I have a right to X" is true, but it is not yet true in

the desired context or at the desired level. Proponents use the rhetorical device we are discussing in the hope of extending acceptance of a rights authorization to a new setting.

More generally still, when the precept "Rights should be respected" is well established in a society or group, the concept *a right* becomes available for uses that do not satisfy the strictest criteria of its established uses. "I have a right to X" becomes a particularly strong locution for defending a position or action, a locution that renders irrelevant a wide range of objections. If a speaker succeeds, however prematurely, in attaching this concept to his claim, he has made important headway in getting de facto acceptance of the claim in the situation at hand. If he wins de facto acceptance often enough, the claim may become accepted in the stronger sense that a rule becomes established and a new right is added to the practice. This process is perhaps the most common means of extending the list both of nonlegal rights resting on judicial interpretation and other methods not involving formal legislative enactment. It also contributes to legislative enactment in that it prepares acceptance of the opinion that there should be a legal right to X and hence the idea that the legislature should pass the necessary rules.

In regard to 2(a), establishing a *practice* of rights where none exists, we must first make a further distinction between establishing such a practice ab initio and adopting (adapting) one already established in another society or group (diffuse versus borrowed, as anthropologists say). Communication patterns in the contemporary world guarantee that most, if not all, cases now fall into the latter category. Indeed it may be that, in general, the former category is of value only as a kind of ideal construct with which to compare actual cases. Detailed historical studies might permit us to reconstruct the process by which our present concept of a right developed in the Western tradition or spread to societies in other traditions. But such a reconstruction, which we will not attempt here, would certainly portray an evolutionary process through which concepts such as *right* (versus *wrong*) and *justice* were gradually modified to produce the notion of having a right to X. Certain writers – for example,

Hobbes and Locke – might be especially prominent in the story, but it is unlikely that the concept we now have sprang full-blown from the mind of any person.

The important point in this context is that if the concept is not established in a society or group, the rhetorical tactic of arguing for a right by asserting its existence is not available or works differently from the way it does when used as discussed previously. In a society without such a concept, the statement "I have a right to X" would either be without meaning or (if the *word* was available but not the concept) would have a meaning different from the one we know. A society might have a concept with only some of the features of *rights* as we know it – say, the feature of providing a conclusive warrant against a definite range of objections but not the feature of being "possessed by" persons free to exercise it or not. (*Rights* may have had these features in feudal societies.) In such a case a person could say, "I have a right to X," when he did not in fact have one, but he would be speaking for a class or caste of people. If the assertion were successful its implications would be different from those of analogous assertions in the practice we know.

A possible generalization from the foregoing discussion is that the uses of *rights* we have just been considering are parasitic on those more usual uses that presuppose established authorizations and regulations. The aim of the person who claims a right that he does not yet have is to bring about a situation in which the ordinary use will be fully available concerning the X in question. It is possible to have such an aim, and to succeed or fail in attaining it, only because the concept has a definite rule structure. But these uses are not *merely* parasitic; they may influence the ordinary use and may effect important changes in the rules governing the concepts. If such uses become common, the notion that right-claims not supported by established authorizations are merely rhetorical devices might be undercut. If this happened the concept would have changed. New semantic rules would have developed and there would be a possibility of new kinds of parasitic uses – uses parasitic on the new semantic rules.

From a somewhat wider perspective, the use of the claim to have a right in order to win that right is not so much parasitic on the ordinary uses of the concept as simply one of the ordinary uses. Such uses typically accord with all the rules governing the concept save the one requiring that an authorization specific to the X in question be antecedently established. Second, it is not an uncommon use of the concept. Indeed much of the most celebrated discourse involving rights includes uses of this type. These uses may pose problems for the analyst who is trying to generalize about the practice, but there is no evidence that they have been particularly puzzling to the actors involved. Either they are simply accepted as valid right-claims (the optimum outcome from the standpoint of the speaker) or they are understood as contentions that a particular right should be established.

Yet more generally, uses of *rights* apparently in the indicative mood but in fact hortatory focus our attention on an extremely important feature of rule-governed practices and the concepts that are part of them. When we talk about established practices we imply regularity and settled form, a certain fixity and predictability. A concept, a practice, is something, not anything whatever. It has a shape or character that permits us to distinguish it from other concepts, practices, and institutions and that allows us to make judgments such as whether a particular action is or has been correctly or incorrectly, felicitously or infelicitously done. The rules that govern the practice provide, indeed constitute, its form, its identity as a distinct and discernible aspect of human affairs.

Such practices and their rules are not fixed in the sense that they cannot or do not change; they are not distinct in the sense that they are hermetically sealed off from all other practices and arrangements; they are not structured in the sense of possessing a form that permits no alterations and additions. Sometimes, as in numerous constitutions, a definite procedure for making changes is incorporated in the rule structure itself. Insofar as the practice of rights is a legal practice, such procedures are commonly available for changing the content of the rights that the practice includes at any point in time. Such procedures, however, are neither self-actuating nor self-implementing. Human beings must decide to make use of them and must arrive at decisons concerning the changes that should be initiated and effected. They can do so, and they can initiate the much larger number of changes that are effected in less formalized ways, because there is a wider set of rules, procedures, and shared understandings within which they can interact. From one perspective this wider set permits efforts to bring about change because *it* is stable enough to allow communication and other forms of meaningful interaction. From another perspective it allows efforts for change because it is sufficiently open and incomplete (and perhaps because it is highly complex) to allow the kinds of tactics exemplified by my saying, "I have a right to X," when in fact I do not. Such tactics can be employed both because the concepts involved and the kinds of contexts in which they are employed are familiar and understood and because they are open to exceptional, deviant modes of action. If *all* aspects of language and all patterns of human interaction generally were in flux, they would be unavailable to those caught up in that flux. But it is a fact that exceptional modes of speech and conduct – in short, change – are a part of language and human interaction. The rhetorical device we have been considering has been one of the deviant and exceptional elements through the use of which the practice of rights has changed. In this sense it is at once deviant and parasitic and an integral part of the practice.

6

Rights and authority

In this and the following chapter we will take up more explicitly than heretofore a kind of question that has always been a part of moral and political philosophy but that has become increasingly prominent in recent years. The question arises in the following manner. There are a substantial number of concepts that frequently appear when agents in moral and political domains direct, guide, assess, and justify conduct. These concepts are commonly used to warrant and praise, criticize and blame conduct and proposed forms of conduct. They include *rights, authority, good, right, ought, just* and *justice, public interest, common good* and *general welfare, obligation* and *duty, free, freedom* and *liberty, equality,* and *responsibility.* Such statements as, *"A* has a right to do *X,"* *"A* has authority to do *X,"* *"A* is at liberty to do *X,"* "It would be good (right, in the public interest) for *A* to do *X,"* *"A* has a duty (obligation, responsibility) to do *X,"* "It would promote freedom (equality) if *A* did *X,"* all commonly serve, among other things, to advance a warrant for *A*'s doing *X.* Actors who use these words advance that warrant and implicitly claim that they can substantiate it if asked to do so; auditors who leave such statements unchallenged thereby concede that *A* is warranted in doing *X.*

Of the several types of questions that arise from and about this situation, the one that will interest us concerns the distinctions that are nevertheless to be drawn among these concepts and the uses to which they are properly put. Are there important differences in the conditions under which they can properly be used and the implications of their proper use? Are there differences at some levels of analysis – for example concerning the realms of moral and political life in which they are properly employed, and similarities at others – for example at the level of general ethical theories, such as utilitarianism and contractarianism? Our analysis of *rights* to this point provides reference points from which we can commence an examination of relationships between *rights* and the other concepts just mentioned. We will concentrate on the similarities and differences between *rights* and *authority* and, in the following chapter, *rights* and *liberty* and *freedom*. Taking up these relationships will also permit us to note a few of the similarities and differences between *rights* and *good* and *public interest*.

We have noted some of the several senses in which *rights* is commonly used. There is also a large number of established uses of *authority* and we cannot attempt to identify them with any precision. Our primary concern is with the sort of legal authority possessed by officers of governments, particularly that species of legal authority that Max Weber called rational-legal. It will be illuminating, however, to make an occasional comparison with what Weber called charismatic authority, with some analogues to rational-legal public authority in nongovernmental organizations, and with *authority* in the sense in which we say that a scholar is *an* authority on a certain subject.[1]

I.   Similarities between *rights* and *authority*

The chief similarities between *rights* and *authority* concern the fact that both involve the existence of a rule or convention that itself serves to authorize the holder of the right or the authority to act in a certain manner. That is, once established the rule or convention specifies a form of action and provides a warrant for taking it that, at least in particular cases taken one by one, does not depend upon the substantive merits of the action itself. This similarity between the two concepts is reflected in a degree of interchangeability between them. To have authority to do X is to be in a position to do X as *a matter of right* or even *to have the right to do it*. To have a right to do X is to be *authorized to do it*.

A further similarity is that, by their decisions to exercise their right or their authority, both As and Cs can, as a matter of right, place other persons under an obligation, a no-right, and so on. Or more precisely, owing to the rule on which their right or their authority depends, their decision to exercise the latter instantiates obligations, no-rights, and so on, to which others are liable as members of the practice in question. The rules that lie behind rights and authority are similar not only in authorizing the actions of A and C but in imposing obligations on those who are Bs vis-à-vis the exercise of the right or the authority. If you are a B vis-à-vis my established right to do X, my decision to exercise that right is sufficient to impose an obligation on you not to interfere with my doing so. If I have authority to do X or to promulgate a rule or command requiring you to do X, my decision to exercise that authority is sufficient to impose an obligation on you not to interfere with my doing X and/or to obey the rules and commands that I set forth.

It is true that rights differ from authority in that they do not authorize their holders to promulgate general rules requiring others to act in a certain manner. A does not lay down a rule requiring B to act in a manner that respects A's right. All potential Bs have an obligation under the rule that establishes A's right, and A's decision to exercise the right instantiates that obligation for actual Bs. If B refuses to discharge his obligation, A qua A has no authority to command or order him to do anything. (A may have the privilege of self-help or self-redress for limited purposes.) Rather, A must appeal to a C who does have such authority. Despite this difference it is important to emphasize that A's having a right does justify him, and him in particular, in criticizing B for failure to respect that right. A has his right under an established rule, but it is *his* right; it is first and foremost for him to defend the exercise of his right. Although he lacks authority to promulgate rules and commands, he is justified in criticizing B and in various other ways pressuring him to discharge his obligations. In the case of rights held under civil (as opposed to criminal) law, his having a right to X authorizes him and only him (gives him standing) to initiate legal processes intended to yield authoritative commands against *B*. Thus in several ways the possession of a right, although not giving *A* the authority to issue rules and commands, does authorize him to intervene in and interfere with the conduct of other persons in various ways.

II. *Rights* and *authority* versus *public interest*

In the foregoing respects, possessing a right and possessing authority, though not the same thing, resemble one another closely. The points of resemblance between them distinguish the two of them from *good, public interest,* and *common good.* If *X* is a right of *A*'s or is within *A*'s authority, *A*'s doing *X* is sufficient to occasion an obligation for those who are *B*s vis-à-vis *A*'s *X*. Questions can still arise about whether it would be good, right, or in the public interest for *A* to do *X* and for *B* to discharge his obligation *Y*. But to show that *A*'s doing *X* would not be good or in the public interest is not sufficient to show that it is not his right or within his authority and not sufficient to show that *B* has no obligation. (Though if this could regularly be shown in respect to *A*'s doing *X*, the rationale for the rule establishing the authority or the right would be undermined and one would hope that the rule would cease to be accepted or would be changed.) By contrast, to show that *X* would be good or in the public interest is not sufficient to justify use of the strong language of obligation in respect to *B*. To show that *X* would be good or in the public interest may provide a justification for *A*'s doing *X* but it does not itself create obligations and does not authorize the sorts of interference with *B* that are authorized by proper uses of *rights* and *authority*. *B* might say, "I concede that *X* is in the public interest and that it would be good for me to avoid interfering with your doing *X* if I can. But I am in the course of doing *X'*, which is also in the public interest. Unfortunately my doing *X'* necessarily interferes with your doing *X*. Your justification places me under no obligation and my justification for X' is as strong as your justification for X. Hence I see no reason why I should alter my course of conduct." In short, unlike *rights* and *authority, good* and *public interest* do not generate obligations and hence do not themselves warrant the same kinds of interference with the conduct of others that *obligation* entails.

There is a further point here that will take us into additional differences between *rights* and *authority* as well as between *rights* and *good* and *public interest*. As noted earlier, the exercise of rights must, in general, be advantageous to those who hold them and disadvantageous to those who are *B*s in regard to them. This feature of rights may be a reason for according *A* special standing to criticize and to initiate legal actions against *B*s who fail to respect *A*'s rights. It is ordinarily *A* who must judge whether X is advantageous to him and, at least in the first instance, whether *B*'s actions interfere with X. (Of course this judgment is not final if legal proceedings are initiated.) These features of rights place heavy burdens on any *B* who wishes to show that he need not or ought not discharge his obligation vis-à-vis *A*'s right. Unless he can show that the right ought to be disestablished or suspended so that he would no longer *have* an obligation, he must convince *A* either that *A*'s interests would not be disserved by *B*'s proposed actions or that he should waive his right and release *B* from his obligations. If *A* is not convinced by the considerations that *B* advances, and if *B* goes ahead with his contemplated course of action, *A*'s position as holder of the right warrants him in criticizing *B* for failing to discharge his obligations and perhaps in initiating processes that will bring other sanctions to bear. Other persons may criticize *A* in various ways for not accepting *B*'s arguments, but until such time as *A* does so he continues to enjoy the warrants that his right to X give him.[2] *Rational-legal authority* differs from *rights* in that (1) authority is lodged in offices that carry specified duties and responsibilities as well as authority and (2) the justification for *C*'s doing X gives no special weight to X being advantageous to *C* himself. As a holder of authority, *C* qua individual person does not have the sort of control over the scheme of authority and obligations that A has over the corresponding scheme surrounding his right to do X. Even when the interpretation of the rules of which this scheme consists is accorded to a particular office (and hence to the person who holds that office at any moment of time), it rarely has the highly personal dimension that rights take from the role that A himself plays in deciding whether his rights serve his interests and whether actions of B threaten them.

But *authority* is similar to *rights,* and the two differ from *good* and *public interest* in that the question of whether C has authority to do or command X turns not on the substantive merits of X but on a preestablished rule. Just as with his arguments about A's rights, B cannot show that his obligation vis-à-vis C's authoritative command does not hold merely by showing that discharging it would have bad consequences for B, for C, or even for all those affected by his exercise of his right or authority. If C's actions comport with the rules under which he has authority, he is thereby authorized to take those actions. If C chooses to do so B will have obligations regardless of the consequences of discharging them. To show that the consequences would be bad might be to show that the rules should be changed. Or it might show that the authority and the obligation are overridden by superior considerations in the case at hand. But in neither case is this the same as showing that C does not have authority and that B does not have a valid obligation. We may indeed hope that the formation and the interpretation of rules will be influenced by the expected consequences of acting on them. But entertaining such hopes does not alter the fact that the rules by which rights and authority are established stand between judgments about consequences, on the one hand, and decisions as to whether there is authority or a right and whether there are obligations, on the other.[3] This is not the case with regard to *good* and *public interest*. There are precept-type rules that do and that should guide decisions about whether doing X would be good or in the public interest. But from the fact that X accords with those precepts it does not follow logically that X is good.

The precept-type rules are useful because they encapsulate or abbreviate the results of previous experience with recurrent types of actions and their consequences.

III. Differences between *rights* and *authority*

The personal character of rights is the basis of additional similarities and differences between *rights* and *authority*. First of all, there is the question of the degree of discretion allowed to *A*s and *C*s. Earlier we stressed that *A*'s discretion is very great and we argued that its scope is in fact the single most distinctive feature of the practice of rights. It is not unlimited. United States courts have held, for example, that under some circumstances defendants cannot waive the right to counsel. They have also held that the failure of an accused person to assert or insist upon his rights does not justify law enforcement officers in not respecting them.[4] The first example, although complicated by the fact that many of the rules that establish the rights of the accused serve the effective administration of justice as well as the interest of the defendants, comes very close to establishing the notion, always anomalous with regard to moral rights and ordinarily so in legal contexts as well, of an obligation to exercise a right. The second example, although speaking primarily to *B* and *C* rather than *A*, requires that *A* be treated in a manner that accords with his rights even if he does not attempt to exercise them or to insist that they be respected. As with the first example, it tends to make persons other than *A* the guardian of *A*'s rights. What in practice is more important, especially with regard to legal rights, is the process by which the rules establishing rights are interpreted; that is, the process through which authoritative decisions are reached as to exactly which actions are included in the right to do *X*. *A* has a right to freedom of speech and of association. But the process of deciding what is included in and excluded from *speech* and *association* permits others to exercise a substantial influence on *A*'s exercise of these rights. *A* may be advised against, criticized, and even punished for actions that *he* is confident fall under the warrant that those rights give him. Indeed he may be punished for types of actions that courts and other authoritative agencies had previously held to fall under those warrants.

In addition, a variety of what might be called external criticisms, that is criticisms drawn from aspects of morality and law other than rights itself, are commonly encountered. An important example is criticism of people who insist on their rights despite the fact that their doing so causes substantial hardship or suffering to others. Another example is criticism of an A for exercising rights despite the fact that doing so threatens the integrity of the practice of rights. Criticisms for failure to exercise rights are less common but not unknown. Persons who submit without protest to violations of such rights as the freedom from unwarranted search and seizure or the freedom of speech may be criticized for failure to defend rights that are important not only to them personally but to social and political arrangements on which the well-being of all members of the society depend. Although rights are personal, they are not purely personal. The fact that they are socially established and supported and the fact that whether they are exercised or not has important consequences for others provide bases for criticisms of the manner in which they are exercised.

Nevertheless there are few, if any, obligations to exercise rights, and the individualistic traditions and assumptions that surround the practice have discouraged what we just labeled as external criticisms of their use. A's discretion in exercising his rights is substantial. This feature of rights constitutes one of the most important sources of differences between *authority* and *rights*. The most significant of these differences is that, in principle, C is always formally accountable to other persons for the manner in which he exercises what everyone admits to be his authority. One manifestation of this fact is that persons in authority are typically required to swear an oath to discharge their authority in a faithful and responsible manner. No such performance is required of those who possess rights. More important, rational-legal authority structures specify to whom C is accountable for the exercise of his authority, and democratic societies add to this the principle that those in elected office are accountable to the electorate. This feature of the practice of authority formally establishes the notion that non-*C*s are not only justified in but even responsible for evaluating *C*'s exercise of his authority. *C* can be punished for acts not within his authority but taken under color thereof. By contrast, if *A* does *X* under the false claim that he has a right to do it, he can be punished for doing *X* (if *X* is prohibited by law) but not for doing *X* under the claim that he had a right to do so. The notion of an ultra vires exercise of rights, of actions taken under color of rights, has no standing. Again, if non-*C*s judge that *C* has exercised his authority thoughtlessly or with bad consequences, they may appropriately decide that he should be removed from his position in the authority structure. Such actions are not punishable under law, but he is subject to political sanctions for them. The practice of rights has no comparable feature. *A* can be criticized for exercising his rights thoughtlessly or so as to produce bad consequences, and widespread misuse of a right could lead to its being eliminated from the practice. But *A*'s rights cannot be taken away from him on such grounds.[5]

This is an appropriate point to glance at *authority* in the sense of that characterizing someone who is *an* authority on a particular subject matter or activity. Harold Cherniss is an authority on Plato, Ted Williams is an authority on batting, and Buckminster Fuller is an authority on building geodesic domes. By contrast with the authority of the president of the United States, their authority derives not from a position or office that carries authority with it but from the superior knowledge and/or skill that they have demonstrated concerning the subject matter and/or activities of concern to them. Their authority does not carry with it the right to issue commands or promulgate rules that others have an obligation to obey. But we do say that authorities in this sense *command respect* and the respect they command is manifested by willingness on the part of others to accept and/or act upon the opinions, judgments, and counsels they advance. Questions about discretion and accountability, as those terms are used in political and legal contexts, are difficult to apply to authorities in this sense, but such persons lose their status as authorities if they do not continue to satisfy the canons of excellence peculiar to the activities in which they engage.

Although we cannot fully explore the logic of *an authority,* the concept is nevertheless of interest here. From Plato forward a number of thinkers have rejected, and considerable political practice has implicitly avoided, a sharp distinction between *authority* in this sense and *authority* in the sense of the right of command vested in a particular office. Plato's concept of the philosopher-king merges these types of authority by making possession of the characteristics of an authority on morals and politics a necessary (perhaps a sufficient) condition of properly occupying (at any rate the highest) offices that carry the right of command. If his views in this respect have seldom been fully accepted or applied, ideas similar to his have been commonplace in most discussions, both theoretical and practical, of political authority since he wrote. Even in epochs (such as our own) in which the notion of an authority on moral and political matters is in disrepute among (if not unintelligible to) many, we continue to hope (if not to insist or even expect) that those who hold positions of public authority will be, if not authorities a la Cherniss or Fuller, at least knowledgeable about and competent concerning the activities in which they must make authoritative decisions.[6] Civil servants are required to demonstrate such knowledge and competence through formal testing of various sorts, the biographies of would-be judges are sometimes examined for evidence of the qualities thought requisite to the role they must perform, and candidates for elective office must present their qualifications for public scrutiny.

It is true that demonstration of genuinely superior qualities often prompts talk of leaders and statesmen as opposed to mere officeholders and politicians. Perhaps this fact indicates that being *an authority* is neither necessary nor even particularly relevant to holding authority in the *in authority* sense. Even if we accepted the latter view, however, doing so would not alter the point of interest here. Persons in authority who are also regarded as authorities *on* the matters that fall within the authority of their office are accorded a degree of respect and a range of discretionary action beyond that allowed to persons who are no more than *in* authority. Churchill, de Gaulle, Masaryk, and perhaps Roosevelt were viewed by many as having an exceptional understanding of the issues and problems faced by the societies in which they held public authority. For this reason their judgments and decisions were widely regarded as authoritative in both the *in* and the *an authority* senses. Although other factors (such as the crisis conditions that obtained during much of their tenure in high public office) must also be considered, the exceptionally wide discretion they enjoyed was due in part to this fact.

If we try to deal with this matter in the conceptualization we have been using, the following remarks suggest themselves. Having a right to do X ordinarily carries with it broad discretion in deciding whether and how to exercise that right. A possible explanation for this fact lies in the point that rights are expected to advantage those who have them, together with the view that those who have them are thought to be the proper (and perhaps the best) judges of whether a particular exercise of their rights will in fact advantage them. There is a presumption that leaving the *A*s free to choose how to use their rights will maximize the good or benefit they derive from having them. The *A*s, as we might put it in the present context, are authorities in the *an authority* sense on whether a particular use of their rights will benefit them. They are not authorities on the question of whether their decisions will benefit the *B*s, *C*s, and *D*s. But rights are *expected* to disadvantage the *B*s. From this perspective rights are justified on the assumption that this disadvantage will not be excessive (or will be adequately compensated for by some other feature of rights) as long as the *A*s stay within the limits defined by the rules that establish the rights. Thus mechanisms of oversight and control are necessary but there are reasons for employing them so as to emphasize the discretion of the *A*s.

Authority in the *in authority* sense also gives a right to act to those who possess it. But such authority is established and accorded to particular *C*s not for the purpose of benefiting the *C*s but to benefit all the members of the society. If the *C*s are authorities in no more than the *in authority* sense, the only grounds on which to think that their decisions will benefit society are the general grounds on which the case for establishing authoritative positions is built (as opposed to the grounds on which to put a particular person in one of those positions or the grounds that support the substance of particular authoritative commands). Because authoritative offices and positions are defined by the rules that create them, it is not surprising that those not in authority are concerned to limit the discretion of the *C*s in interpreting and applying the rules. The very assumptions that argue for allowing discretion to *A*s urge restricting the discretion and assuring the accountability of *C*s.

If, however, the *C*s are thought to be authorities in the *an authority* as well as the *in authority* sense, the case of the *C*s would take on greater similarity to the case of the *A*s. There would then be general grounds on which to expect that the decisions the *C*s make in exercising their (in) authority would, substantively speaking, benefit all members of the society. Just as we want to keep *A*s within the rules that define their rights; just as we want to hold authorities on Plato, on architecture, and so on, to general canons of evidence, good design, and so on; and just as the British, French, and Czech people did not give up the idea of limits on authority when they were governed by Churchill, de Gaulle, and Masaryk, evidence that *any* particular *C* was *an* authority on the matters that came before him would not justify abandoning the idea of limited authority or accountability. But the context in which the rules limiting authority are interpreted and the mechanisms of accountability employed would be substantially altered. The practice of authority would look more like the practice of rights than our preceding discussion argues it now does.[7]

Rights and authority are among the devices by which societies warrant certain other-regarding actions on the part of their members. Both involve constraints and mechanisms of accountability. But in the case of rights these mechanisms have not been emphasized. In various informal ways societies have encouraged a large measure of individual discretion in the uses to which rights are put. In the case of authority, by contrast, formal mechanisms of constraint are typically well developed and the informal traditions, although varying according to time, place, and level of office, put substantial stress on accountability.

Both rights and authority give individuals advance authorizations to interfere in important ways with the lives of others. Given this fundamental fact about them, the suspicion with which authority has been viewed and the restraints with which it has been surrounded are understandable; the very considerable discretion left to holders of rights is perhaps surprising. The explanation for the difference between the two is in part historical. The tradition of individual rights began largely as a reaction to a history of abuses and misuses of power and authority. The warrants that rights provide were viewed primarily as warrants that would hold against authority. They were conceived as guaranteeing the possibility of actions that do not seriously harm other people but that had nevertheless been forbidden or interfered with out of a desire to enlarge and protect authority. However necessary it might be, governmental authority had proved to be dangerous and individuals needed protection against it. In this setting the possibility that rights would be misused was not emphasized and the purposes of establishing the rights suggested a large measure of discretion for the *A*s. Governments have continued to limit rights and have regularly violated them. Thus experience has reinforced the original conception of rights with its attendant tendency to leave it largely to the holders thereof to decide how to use them.[8] The same experience has maintained and strengthened the suspicion of authority and the desire to surround it with constraints and restrictions designed to ensure that it is exercised in a responsible manner.

As a practical matter, of course, we have overdrawn and oversimplified the contrast between rights and authority. In some societies the picture we have presented would have to be nearly reversed. In the Soviet Union such exercise of rights as one can find is closely controlled and it is well established that rights must be exercised in a manner consistent with the regime's conception of the socialist order. The fact that X is a right does not itself exempt A from criticism and even punishment for doing X. Solzhenitzin had a "right" to publish his novels only if Soviet authorities judged that his doing so accorded with the interests and welfare of the Soviet workers.[9] At the same time, although great efforts are apparently expended to ensure the accountability of lesser bureaucrats, one could hardly say that the authority of the top leader is closely defined or that their exercise of that authority is narrowly controlled.

Nor are these points peculiar to totalitarian or authoritarian regimes. We have already mentioned some of the problems that arise in interpreting and applying rules – whether rules that grant authority, that establish rights, or whatever. Because persons in authority provide the authoritative interpretations of rules that grant authority, these problems are often resolved to the advantage of the authority of the Cs. But it is hardly necessary to go into the logic of rule following and interpretation to support the observation that presidents, prime ministers, and indeed petty bureaucrats often enjoy great discretion in the exercise of their authority. Although voices are from time to time raised against this fact, it is perhaps fair to say that there is general recognition that a considerable degree of discretion, at least at higher levels of authority, is not only inevitable but desirable.

The fundamental facts of formal and political accountability for the use of authority remain, however, and constitute a difference between rights and authority that is important in both theory and practice. However great the authority of, say, the American president or the German chancellor and however great their discretion in exercising that authority, neither can claim to be exempt from formal and political accountabilty for the use they make of it. A showing that action X was indisputably within their authority does not still the question of whether they should have done X and whether they should be deprived of their position of authority because they did X. By contrast, if the lowliest citizen in the land can show that he had a right to do X, there is an important sense – namely the meaning of the concepts in question (!) – in which the question of the propriety of his having done X is properly closed. If X is a legal right the question of punishing him for doing X is closed. Whereas the traditions surrounding authority encourage assessment and criticism, praise and blame, of actions admittedly within the authority of the agent, they discourage such assessment and criticism of actions that one has a right to take. Both authority and rights establish a range of authorized actions, but the latter concept serves to insulate the actor from assessment to a greater degree than the former.

The foregoing differences between rights and authority call attention to a tension between the practice of authority and the practice of rights. Authority is often defended on the ground that it is needed to regulate conflicts that arise in the course of interactions among the members of a society. Yet through the practice of rights societies that establish authority also insulate certain of the other-regarding actions of their members against control by the authorities they have established. Even if A's doing X produces serious problems, his having a right to X prohibits C from interfering with his doing it. It is hoped that the decision to establish and maintain rights is premised in part on a judgment that the exercise of rights, despite its adverse effects on B, will not create unacceptable social consequences. In other words, one hopes that it is premised on the belief that the advantages gained by according and maintaining rights will outweigh any costs or disadvantages that the exercise of those rights may produce. As with any such judgment, this one might prove to be mistaken concerning a particular right or even concerning the practice of rights as such. Of course particular rights or, in principle, the practice of rights itself can be suspended or abolished if the consequences of exercising them are too serious. Moreover, such suspensions and abolitions could not be described as uncommon if one considers the full range of societies that claim to grant rights to their members. In societies in which rights are well established and supported by a firm tradition of respect, however, suspending them is controversial and difficult to sustain, and abolishing them is exceedingly un-popular. If the exercise of rights creates problems that it is the responsibility of those in authority to control or resolve, the fact of their exercise can complicate the task of the Cs. If A's speech threatens to incite a riot and if he has and insists on exercising a right to give that speech, C cannot properly quell the riot by preventing the speech. If a strike threatens to block the nation's transportation network and bring about extensive economic and other losses and if there is a right to strike, the Cs cannot pre-vent the losses by forbidding the strike. The discretion the As have in deciding whether to exercise their rights serves to limit the discretion available to the Cs in deciding how to discharge their responsibilities. There may be conflicts between serving the purposes for which rights are apparently established and serving some of the purposes for which authority is established. This conflict is sharpened and rendered more difficult to resolve by the discretion typically accorded to the As and by the stringency attached to the obligations of the Bs and Cs.

IV.   *Rights* and *authority:*
attribution and distribution

The final comparison we will make between rights and author-ity concerns the similarities and differences, and their implica-tions, in the manner in which they are attributed to and distributed among those who hold and exercise them.

There are significant similarities in respect to the kinds of criteria that are used to determine eligibility for rational-legal authority and for possession of prominent legal and moral rights. Consider the rules that establish the office of president of the United States. Anyone who is over thirty-five years of age and a native-born citizen of the United States is eligible for the office. We can best contrast these requirements not with less restrictive definitions of eligibility but with, for example, the rules of succession according to which the only person who could have legitimately become the king of England at the death of Henry VII was the particular member of Henry VII's family later to be known as Henry VIII. On the side of rights, a comparable rule would be the constitutional doctrine that all citizens of the United States have the right to freedom of speech guaranteed by the First Amendment to the Constitution. Both rules are impersonal in that they do not name or otherwise identify particular persons and in that they establish a rule that will be the basis on which all judgments concerning eligibility will properly be made. The rules are not universalistic; they do exclude substantial numbers of persons from eligibility. However, they are comprehensive in the sense that they leave very large classes of people eligible for the office and the right. They are also open-ended in that they set no limit to the number of persons who might become eligible without change in the rules.

In respect to the actual distribution of authority and rights (as opposed to eligibility for possessing them), however, there are important differences. The number of persons who can hold a particular office or position at any one time is specified by authoritative rules. Many persons are eligible to become president of the United States, but only one person can actually hold that office at any moment in time. Hence there is competition for office and the criteria of eligibility are supplemented by processes of selection among those eligible for and desirous of the office.

By contrast, any number of persons can simultaneously possess most rights. With regard to most rights in the sense of liberties, eligibility for and possession of the right are coextensive. In respect to most rights s.s. and most powers, eligibility for the right must be supplemented by participation in one of the types of transactions that creates rights of these kinds, but formally speaking, eligibility for the right is coextensive with eligibility to enter into such transactions. Moreover, in a number of societies from the seventeenth century on there has been a secular trend to broaden the rules of eligibility so as to exclude ever fewer and ever smaller categories of people. In this (somewhat formalistic) sense, development of practices of rights has contributed to equality in these societies.

Related movements have also limited the number of social and economic inequalities considered relevant for purposes of determining eligibility for positions of authority. But owing, among other things, to limitations upon the number of positions of authority, the practice of authority continues to create hierarchy and inequality. Jones has and exercises rights *against* other persons and those persons have obligations to Jones in respect to those rights. But those persons may have and exercise the same rights against Jones. The relationship between them in respect to rights is, as we might say, horizontal in character. By contrast, we speak of Jones having authority *over* Smith and of Smith being *under* Jones' authority. Again, the fact that Jones has authority over Smith in respect to X excludes Smith from having authority over Jones in respect to X. (Smith may have authority over Jones in respect to X at another time.) The hierarchical character of authority relationships is not qualified by reciprocity of the sort that marks rights and it remains a superior-subordinate relationship as long as Jones retains his authority over Smith. The hierarchy and inequality are emphasized and given additional dimensions insofar as in-authority-type qualities are prominent.

There are at least two qualifications to the foregoing remarks, two respects in which the points just discussed do not distinguish authority from rights. The first concerns rights created by contracting and related devices. All or nearly all persons in a society may be, formally speaking, eligible to use these devices and hence to acquire the rights that can be created by them. But in fact these devices are used more often by some persons than others and the availability of the devices – that is, the fact that a society sustains the practice of using them to create rights – systematically benefits some members more than others.

Whereas many rights (especially liberties) are acquired simply by becoming a member of a society, contractual and related kinds of rights in the strict sense are created only if some agent takes an initiative on his own or some other agent's behalf.

Those who, for whatever reason, take no initiatives will have such rights only insofar as someone else intiates a right-creating action that is directed toward or otherwise involves them. We might say that procedures for creating such rights are of special advantage to those persons who we earlier called the paradigmatic holders of rights.

Whatever initiatives Jones may take, others ordinarily enter into right-creating agreements with him because they believe that he has something that they want and can best get by doing so. For this reason the more power, goods, skills and so on, that Jones has to offer, the greater his potential for concluding right-creating arrangements. Hence we can expect that the distribution of such rights in a society will tend to resemble the distribution of property and valued skills and capacities. Because the latter are unequally distributed, the former will ordinarily be so as well. Insofar as contractual-type rights such as rights to property have legal standing, the existence of mechanisms for creating them will serve to give a legal basis to, legal reinforcement for, other inequalities. Given the elaborate legal protections for property rights in numerous contemporary societies, the availability of mechanisms for creating such rights fosters and maintains not merely inequality but stratification analogous to the hierarchy created by authority arrangements. In theory such a result could be avoided or at least minimized by policies that eliminate or reduce nonlegal inequalities. (High inheritance and capital gains taxes are examples, as are programs to distribute wealth, education, and other goods in a more equal manner.) Virtually all contemporary societies have enacted some programs of this sort, but it could scarcely be argued that any of them have set out to eliminate differential benefits from such rights. The tendency of rights of this type to reinforce and extend inequalities, especially rights concerning property, is one of the reasons that persons favoring a more egalitarian society should be critical of them.

As a practical matter, and this is the second qualification alluded to previously, the foregoing points about contractual-type rights also apply to the *exercise,* and especially the effective exercise, of rights that accrue to mere membership in a society. Having a right is only a necessary, not a sufficient, condition of exercising it or exercising it effectively. One cannot exercise (although one may act in a manner protected by) a right that one does not know he has. Knowledge of constitutional rights may be more widely distributed than knowledge of contractual rights and the possibilities of acquiring them, but it is not equally distributed in the societies we know. Nor is there anything like an equal distribution of the economic and other resources and capacities that are often necessary effectively to exercise rights that one knows one has. Persons at higher economic, educational, and social echelons are clearly better able to take advantage of such liberties as freedom of speech and press, of various rights of the accused, and so on, than those at the lower echelons. This can be true even in cases in which a large number of people can not only have but exercise the same right at the same time. Jones' decision to exercise his right not to testify against himself need not compete with Smith's decision to exercise the same right. But if Jones has reason to believe that exercise of his right will jeopardize his job, whereas Smith holds a tenured position in a university, there is an obvious respect in which Smith is better placed to take advantage of the right. Although any number of persons can have the same liberty at the same time, it is seldom possible for any number to exercise that liberty at the same time. Both Jones and Smith have a right to free speech, but they cannot both exercise their right at the same time and place. It would be unrealistic to think that decisions as to which of them will speak are uninfluenced by the fact that one is more wealthy, prestigious, powerful, or skillful than the other.

V.   Concluding remarks

1. Both rights and authority warrant certain actions on the part of those who possess them (i.e., make it possible to say that certain actions were done *by right* or *as a matter of right*).

2. In both cases actions taken *by right* occasion obligations to

which some *B* is liable by virtue of the rules establishing the right or the authority and warrant *A* and *C* in criticizing (in ways that vary from *right* to *authority* and according to circumstances) *B* for failure to discharge that obligation.

3. Both differ from *good* and *public interest* in that they are created and defined by rules and in that actions that conform to those rules thereby acquire a warrant (i.e., without consideration of whether the consequences of the action will be desirable).

4. Eligibility for possession of both is typically defined by rules that are impersonal, comprehensive, and open-ended in the previously discussed senses.

5. The two concepts differ in that having authority permits *C* not only to act in ways that affect others but to promulgate rules and commands *to* others; having a right permits *A* to act in ways that instantiate obligations to which *B* is already liable but not to promulgate new rules that create liabilities to additional obligations and not to command *B* (except in a weak sense that is really a reminder of a preexisting obligation) to discharge his obligations.

6. Several differences can be grouped under the general headings of discretion and accountability. *A*'s decisions to exercise, waive, or even renounce his rights are ordinarily not properly subject to assessment and criticism. With some exceptions, they are his rights to use or not as he sees fit. Persons holding authority also decide when and how to exercise it. But their decisions are definitely subject to review and, depending on the office, the policy, and numerous other variables, also to criticism and material sanctions. Moreover, the authority is lodged in, "belongs" to an office or position, not the individual who occupies that position at any particular time. The occupant may renounce the office and thereby his right and duty to exercise the authority it carries, but if he retains the office he cannot renounce its authority. Further, the notion of action "under color of authority (law)" has no application to rights. Persons who act on the false pretense that they have a right to do the action in question simply do not succeed in exercising a right;

the claim to a right not actually possessed is not itself punishable (though of course it might be subject to moral criticism as deceitful and might be actionable in law if it constitutes fraud). More generally, in a variety of formal and informal ways and to varying degrees the exercise of authority has been viewed with suspicion and has been restricted, checked, and subject to oversight and mechanisms of accountability. Practices of rights have, as a comparative generalization, allowed and encouraged discretion on the part of the *A*s.

7. Despite the formal similarities noted under item 4, authority tends to produce and reinforce hierarchy and inequality in a society, whereas, with the exceptions noted earlier, the practice of rights has tended to increase equality and reciprocity.

Rights and authority establish and protect areas in which those who hold them can act in ways that have substantial and often objectionable consequences for others. As authoritatively established practices both seem to presuppose a judgment that they have, as a generalization, socially desirable effects. But the assumptions on which this judgment rests, the understandings of how the desirable effects are produced, are substantially different between the two practices. Both presume widely accepted rules that define and establish the practices (and legal rights further presuppose authority itself). But rights, whether legal or otherwise, leave the initiation of conduct largely to the unregulated action of the individual members of society. So long as these decisions remain within the framework of rules that define the practice, social coordination is achieved by uncentralized social and political process. Participants in this process have no formalized or institutionalized responsibility to concern themselves with the broad social consequences of the use they make of their rights, the assumption apparently being either that the question of the social good is not raised by the exercise of rights or, more plausibly, that it will in fact be best served by uncentralized interaction so long as that interaction remains within the limits defined by the rules of the practice. (The individual freedom of action allowed by the practice should itself be regarded as a social good.) Authority, on the other hand, concentrates initiative and decision in a comparatively restricted number of persons. At a minimum the practice assumes that issues and disputes will arise that will not be resolvable, except at excessive social cost, by interaction among nonauthoritative agents. On this view the common good is served by the mere existence of authority, by the existence of agents whose decisions will be binding not because of their substantive merits but because of the fact that they emanate from an agent with established authority to settle or decide them. But the persons who hold positions of authority are typically charged with the definite responsibility of attending to the common good and exercising their authority in a manner that serves the latter. Their decisions are legally binding even when they do not serve the common good, but they are subject to criticism and the loss of their positions of authority if they consistently make decisions and follow policies thought to be contrary to the common good. The assumption seems to be that there are respects in which society requires persons who make explicit pursuit of the common good their direct and paramount concern and who are given the position and other resources thought requisite to doing so in an effective manner.

The practices of rights and authority coexist in numerous societies. In respect to legal rights the latter (i.e., authority) is necessary to the former because the rules that define rights are authoritative in character. Many have thought that a *proper* practice of authority presupposes a practice of rights that establishes limits on authority. More generally, the assumption seems to have been accepted that rights and authority are different but compatible practices that make complementary contributions to social and political life. In a few societies this assumption has been sustained by experience at least in the sense that both practices have continued to operate effectively over substantial periods of time. Nevertheless, the logics of the two practices, and the larger assumptions on which they depend, are not only different but in competition with one another in important respects. It is to be expected that there will be continuing tension between them.

7

Rights and freedom

Just as to have a right to do X is always to be authorized to do X, so it is always, in some sense of *free*, to be free to do X. Just as rights can be thought of as a species of authority, so they can be viewed as a species of freedom. Thinking of rights in the latter way is useful because it calls attention to some of their important characteristics and some of the reasons that they have been highly valued.

Clearly, however, *rights, having a right,* and so on, cannot be reduced to, are not mere synonyms of, *freedom, being free,* and so on. A can be free to do X and yet not have a right to do it, and A can have a right to do X and yet as a practical matter be unfree to do it. "A has a right to do X" always means that there is, or in the view of the speaker should be, an established rule according to which A has a warrant for doing X. "A is free to do X" is indefinite on this point and often means no more than that in fact no B will attempt to prevent A from doing X or that no material conditions will impede his doing X. The refinement concerning A's having a warrant for doing X could be made clear only by supplementing *free, freedom,* and so on, with additional concepts.

For these and other reasons that we consider as we proceed, we should not expect that analyzing the relationship between *rights* and *freedom* will yield an exhaustive analysis of *rights.* Rather, we are exploring separate concepts that are intertwined in complex ways in our practices. Our hope is not to reduce the one concept to the other but to achieve a clearer view of the complex interrelationships between them. It is hoped that doing so will also help us further to clarify and assess prominent arguments for the practice of rights.

I.   Rights, freedom, and human action

Despite the differences just noted, numerous writers have argued that there is an especially close relationship between *rights* and *freedom* and indeed that the closeness of that relationship is the most important feature of the concept of rights. In some formulations the connection between them is primarily normative or justificatory. On this view rights are important and valuable primarily because having them enlarges or enhances freedom. Other formulations, which may also emphasize the normative connection, argue that there is a conceptual or logical connection between them as well. On this view the concept of rights is intelligible only if its connections with the concept of freedom are understood. The first view can be abbreviated along the following lines: "*A* should have a right to do *X because* his having such a right means that he is free to do *X*." An abbreviation of the second view would be as follows: "*A* has a right to do *X* and *therefore* he is, in some sense of free, free to do *X*."[1]

We begin with the second view and see whether clarifying it helps us to assess the first as well. We argue that the second view is always true of rights, that it is always the case that having a right to do *X* is, in some sense of *free,* to be free to do *X*. But we suggest that this connection between *rights* and *freedom* is not unique to *rights* but rather obtains between freedom and a very large class of concepts. We also argue that the first view does not follow from the second and indeed that the truth of the latter never provides a sufficient reason for having or exercising a right or for having and participating in the practice of rights.

In what sense or senses of *free* is *A* always free to do *X* if he has a right to do *X?* In Chapter 2 we noted the sense in which rights are moral or jural possessions of *A*. *A* cannot, by himself, create rights for himself. But if he has a right it is ordinarily for him to choose or decide whether and how to exercise it. His use of his rights, in other words, is not properly at the leave of other persons. Certain forms of conduct on the part of other persons may indeed be necessary to his exercising his rights at all and certainly may be necessary to his exercising them effectively. The conduct of other persons is not and cannot be a sufficient condition of A's exercising his rights or not. A can exercise his rights only if he decides or chooses to do so, and no statement or set of statements about any other person or persons will state the sufficient conditions of (though they may state conditions necessary to) A's deciding or choosing to exercise them or not.

We also noted wider senses in which it must be possible for A both to choose to do and to choose not to do the things he has rights to do. It must, for example, be within A's physical capacity both to do and to choose not to do the X. This does not mean that his doing X or not must be independent of all conditions and influences other than his own choice or decision; many such conditions may be necessary to or otherwise affect his doing X. But if his "doing" X or not can be sufficiently explained without reference to his decision or choice, it cannot be said that he exercised a right. For example, if A "does" X under hypnosis, while in a psychotic state, under extreme duresss, because of force applied to his body, or in a mindless, unthinking, habitual manner, he does not exercise a right. Decision or choice (and hence some degree of reflection) must enter into his doing X.

Actions that satisfy the criteria just discussed can plausibly be called free actions or actions done freely; they satisfy rules governing some uses of *free, freely,* and so on. Hence it is a point about the concepts that exercising rights is always, in some sense, acting freely. There may be other senses of *free* or *freely* in which rights are free actions, but there is at least this sense. To this degree at least, those who argue that there is a conceptual connection between *rights* and *free* are on solid ground. If one values free action in this sense, one can therefore say that exercising rights (and hence having rights such that one of the conditions of exercising them is satisfied) is a good or valuable thing.

On this analysis of the sense in which exercising rights is always acting freely, however, exercising rights cannot be distinguished from a very much larger class or "family" of events that must also be described as free actions. Indeed the foregoing sketch of *exercising a right* has many of the features prominent in philosophical analyses of *human action* as such – that is, analyses of the category of things that people *do* as distinct from things that *happen* to them – that people undergo or suffer as a consequence of forces they are unable to control. Many theoretical and practical difficulties and complexities surround this distinction and there is much disagreement as to how (and indeed whether) it should be drawn. We will not take up these problems in detail here. The basic idea behind the distinction is deeply embedded in our conceptions of ourselves and in our social practices. To challenge it categorically would be to call those conceptions and practices into question in fundamental ways. Because at present we are explicating one of the conceptions and practices in which the distinction is embedded, we are justified in assuming that we can employ it without attending to all the problems concerning it.[2]

If we accept the distinction and put exercising rights in the category of human actions, we see that the sense in which exercising rights is acting freely does not distinguish that type of action from a very large class of events. If exercising rights is acting freely, so are discharging obligations, acting justly or unjustly, exercising authority, and indeed choosing roast beef rather than fried chicken for dinner. This is hardly the sort of distinctive and distinctively important connection between *rights* and *freedom* that proponents of rights have had in mind. The sense in which exercising rights always involves acting freely does not, contrary to Hart, establish that discourse about rights forms a distinct "dimension," "branch" or "segment" of morality in which we are concerned exclusively to maintain "a certain distribution of human freedom."[3]

One problem in the theory of action, however, cannot be overlooked in this context. There is an argument according to which the fact that exercising rights is an action (in the somewhat technical sense in which that term is used in contemporary philosophy) does *not* itself warrant us in saying that doing so is acting freely. Exercising rights, on this view, is an action and is not categorically distinct from any other member of the (huge) family of actions. But of none of the members of this family as such can it appropriately be said that they are freely done. The argument has to do with what have been called the significance conditions (as opposed to the truth conditions) for the use of *freedom, freely,* and *free* in ordinary (as opposed to philosophical) discourse. Analysts working in the highly ethereal regions of the theory of action may use *free, freely,* and *freedom* of the exercise of rights, of obeying or disobeying a law, of the decision to buy a pair of shoes or to order roast beef instead of fried chicken for dinner. But would persons making or affected by those decisions do so? If so, under what conditions? "I freely choose roast beef" is perhaps less than a staple item of dinner table conversation. In ordinary talk, J. L. Austin observed, " 'free' is only used to rule out suggestions of some or all of its recognized antitheses."[4] If nothing in the circumstances of the dinner suggests that *A* was compelled, required, deceived, or otherwise unfree, the claim to have "freely chosen" roast beef has no point or significance and is likely to be puzzling to auditors. *A* simply chooses roast beef. His choice is no more free than it is unfree. In ordinary talk, to quote Austin again, " 'freedom' is not a name for a characteristic of actions, but the name of a dimension in which actions can be assessed."[5] The philosopher or social scientist, using *freedom* in an extended, abstract sense, may say truly that *A* freely chose to order what he did. But that statement would be neither true nor false in the discourse at the dinner table. It would, rather, be pointless (or perhaps a philosophical joke). That there is some sense in which *A* chose roast beef may be a necessary condition of saying that *A* acted freely in ordering or eating that dish;[6] it is not a sufficient condition of making that statement with significance.

Austin's argument suggests that the generalization "all events properly characterized as human actions can also be characterized as freely done" is misleading as an account of ordinary discourse about such actions. Of course, many actions will indeed be "freely done." Moreover, the generalization may stand without qualification if *freely* is used in a special philosophical sense. But the generalization misleads us concerning the ways questions about freedom arise and are dealt with in day-to-day affairs. Hence to say that exercising a right is always a free action in the same sense that all human actions are free actions is (not so much false as) misleading concerning the practice of rights.

Austin's argument is no doubt a healthy corrective to inflated philosophical use of *free* and *freely*. But he himself seems to have overgeneralized the valid point that he was making. Joel Feinberg's remarks in respect to a related thesis are relevant here: "we do not ordinarily raise the question of responsibility for something unless that something has somehow excited our interest, and as a matter of fact the states of affairs that excite our interest are very often unhappy ones. But sometimes unexpected happy circumstances need accounting for too, and sometimes the interest aroused is the desire to give credit or blame."[7] Substituting *freedom* for *responsibility*, Austin is right that we do not raise the question of freedom about just every run-of-the-mill action that we take or experience. We do not do so because many actions, being perfectly familiar to us, "do not arouse our interest." But our interest in saying that an action was freely done might be aroused by considerations other than the suggestion of some specific constraint lurking in the circumstance. The philosopher who raises this question, for example, is doing so for just the reason Feinberg suggests, that is, out of a desire to understand human affairs in a philosophical way. The philosopher's remarks may indeed lack point in the context of the dinner table conversation. But they are hardly intended to be a contribution to that conversation, and hence this is perhaps less than a devastating objection to them. Moreover, the remark "*A* freely selected roast beef" might have point in (nonphilosophical) dinner table conversations – conversations that do not satisfy Austin's tests. For example, someone might say that *A* freely chose roast beef if *A* had always disliked the dish but suddenly, with no prompting, decided to give it a try; or it might be said of someone who chose the dish in the face of advice that it was usually badly prepared in the restaurant in question; or of a person who had been on a diet that excluded red meats. Similarly, someone might say that *A* freely exercised his right to join a political party not because there was a suggestion that he overcame pressure but simply because he had never before displayed any interest in partisan politics, because the party in question was in a politically moribund state, or because he previously had been convinced by the arguments of George Washington's First Inaugural. In such cases *freely* seems to function as a way of giving emphasis to the verb *to choose;* it serves as a kind of explanation for a surprising action that people are trying to understand. (Or perhaps as a way of indicating that there is no "explanation" for the action beyond the fact that *A* chose to do it.) True, the explanation *might* be intended to ward off the interpretation that *A* did the surprising act because of some pressure or influence at work upon him. But nothing beyond dogmatic insistence on Austin's analysis requires that this be the case.

For these reasons Austin's analysis requires us to qualify but not to abandon the suggestion that actions are freely done and hence that the most general connection between *rights* and *freedom* is not distinctive to *rights*. We should also recur to a feature of *rights* that emphasizes ways in which connections between *rights* and *freedom* very often satisfy Austin's analysis. For *A* to *claim* a right to do *X* ordinarily presupposes that there is some *B* who thinks that his interests will be disserved by *A*'s doing *X*. If this were not the case the act of claiming to have the right would lack significance. *B*'s belief that *A*'s doing *X* will disserve his interests provides *B* with a reason to prevent *A* from exercising that right, and perhaps to act so as to make *A* unfree to exercise that right. Thus a threat of unfreedom, which Austin makes a necessary condition of significant uses of *free,* will be present, and it will be not only true but significant to say that *A* has a right and that, in choosing to exercise that right, *A* acts freely.

In practice, of course, not every exercise of a right – not even every claim of a right – arouses the concern of some *B*. In settled practices many rights are taken for granted and the idea that they disserve *B*'s interests all but disappears. Or at least some rights may be so well established that *B* will not seriously consider taking action to prevent *A* from exercising his right. Insofar as this situation obtains, *A* is not likely to claim his rights and it will be significant to say that he exercised them freely only if doing so "excites our interest" in the sense in which Feinberg has used that phrase.

To sum up thus far: First, as with all human actions, claiming and exercising rights can be said to be freely done in the sense that they are done by choice or decision, done in a manner that cannot be sufficiently explained or accounted for without (positive) use of concepts such as choice and decision in describing the action. This may be a special, extended sense of *freely* that has little currency outside of philosophy. But it is a philosophical issue we are considering, and if this is the sense of *freely* in which philosophers have argued that there is a conceptual connection between *rights* and *freely, freedom,* and so on, then it is important but not distinctive to *rights*. Second, many actions, including the exercise of rights, can be said to be freely done when, in addition to involving choice or decision, they are done in a manner or under circumstances such that the doing of them "excites our interest." Here again the connection between *rights* and *freedom* is not distinctive to *rights*. Finally, claiming and exercising rights can be said to be freely done when, in addition to the first point, they are done under circumstances in which there is a suggestion of unfreedom of some sort to be rebutted. Such circumstances commonly obtain. Once again, however, these circumstances are by no means unique or even distinctively prevalent to the claiming or exercise of rights. They are common in respect to the vastly larger class of actions that are regarded by some *B* as immoral, illegal, or merely unconventional.

The thesis, then, that there is a conceptual connection between *rights* and *freedom* is true for several senses of *freedom*. In respect to the senses of *freedom* we have examined thus far, the thesis is also true of a vastly larger class of concepts. Therefore it is not enough to distinguish *rights,* to put it in a unique position in moral and political practice. It is instructive about *rights* and the practice thereof, but the instruction it offers is mainly in the direction of calling attention to parallels and analogues between the practice of rights and other aspects of human affairs. Most important, if this is the sense in which *rights* are tied to *freedom* and if rights are valuable because of their tie to freedom, then rights are not distinctively valuable; they are valuable in the same way – for the same reason – that the whole class of events called human actions is valuable. The value of human actions as a class is no trivial matter. Indeed one might argue that it is the value on the acceptance of which all moral and perhaps all social relations depend. The liberal principle, which is an expression of that value, is of fundamental importance for exactly this reason. But those who wish to defend the particular aspect of moral and social relations called the practice of rights must have reasons that go beyond this general principle in ways relevant to the specifics of that practice as such.

II.   Rights and the protection of action from interference

A further relationship between *rights* and *freedom* is suggested by the point that some B will commonly think that A's exercise of his right to X will disadvantage him (B) and will want to prevent A from exercising that right. To the extent that this is the case, having a right will be valuable to A only if it means that exercising that right will, in some way, be protected against B's interference. And this is, as we have already had occasion to note, one of the things that it means to have a right. Just what the warrant the right provides amounts to, and just how (if at all) it will be made effective as a practical matter, varies according to the Hohfeldian sense of *right* and according to whether the right is legal, moral, or of some other kind. In the case of legal rights in Hohfeld's strict sense, it means that B has a legal obligation not to interfere and that some C has both the authority and the duty to hold B to the discharge of that obligation. If we focus on this – the strongest – sense of a right, we can say that the connection between *rights* and *freedom* is that the freedom to exercise rights receives a kind of protection that other types of actions are not, or are not necessarily, accorded.[8]

There is no doubt that this is an important feature of rights and that it is this connection with *freedom* that many who have defended rights in the name of freedom have had in mind. Without detailing them again, it is essential that we bear in mind the differences among the several Hohfeldian senses of right, and the differences among legal and other kinds of rights. It is also important to remember that some legal rights s.s. are, as lawyers say, "imperfect"; that is, there is no remedy in the law if *B* fails to discharge his obligations vis-à-vis *A*'s right. (For example, American authors have a right to royalties for sales of their books in the Soviet Union, but no legal remedy is available if the Soviet government refuses to pay those royalties.) Most important, however, is the fact that this feature of rights does not distinguish the exercise of rights from many other forms of action. Legal and moral codes afford protection to forms of action that are not – except on highly inflated uses of the term – properly regarded as rights. Many of the prohibitions that such codes impose protect freedom in the sense that they place *B* under an obligation to refrain from actions that would impinge upon the freedom of other people to act in the ways they wish. But *B*s who violate the prohibitions are punished for that violation itself, not for violating the rights of some *A*. Once again, therefore, there is an important relationship between *rights* and *freedom,* but that relationship is neither distinctive to nor definitive of *rights.* Arguments cast in terms of the value of freedom in this sense cannot provide a distinctive or a sufficient defense of rights.

III.   Rights and the protection of freedom against interference by the state

Discussion of rights protected by law reminds us of a further, more specialized respect in which rights have been understood

and defended as a means of safeguarding freedom. Very prominent in the modern tradition of rights is the notion that rights
should protect not freedom in general but specifically freedom
from excessive interference on the part of the state. In the
natural rights version of this tradition it is argued that certain
rights are grounded in considerations that in some sense ante-
date or are independent of legal and perhaps all conventional
arrangements. They accrue to the *A*s by virtue of properties or
characteristics that do not depend upon legal or perhaps any
other conventional arrangement. Incursions upon or interferences with these rights are always morally wrong. Hence any
alleged authority to interfere with them must be bogus, and
they in effect constitute limitations on authority and especially
upon the authority of the agent thought to have proved itself
most given to such interferences, namely, the state.[9] These
rights protect individual freedom against the state by restricting
the authority of the state to act. (In doing so, of course, they
necessarily restrict the extent to which the state can act *to
protect* freedoms other than those encompassed within the
natural rights. If Peter's exercise of his natural right to hold
property impinges upon Paul's freedom to partake of the boun-
ties of nature, the state cannot act to protect Paul against Peter
in this regard.)

The notion of constitutional rights, sometimes influenced by
ideas about natural rights, sometimes not, is another version of
this line of thought. Here again rights protect certain freedoms
of action against intrusion by the state and here again they do
so primarily by placing limitations – this time legal limitations
– upon the authority of the state to act. As we argued in an
earlier chapter, these constitutional rights are best thought of
as liberties in the Hohfeldian sense. They deny to the state the
authority to make the actions in question other than legally
innocent, and hence they make any interference with those
actions an ultra vires action on the part of the state. In their
classical form such rights protect the actions in question only
in the sense that they eliminate one possible source of interference with the freedom to engage in them. As with natural

rights, in the case of constitutional rights there is a particularly close and important connection between rights and freedom. The idea that the state is especially prone to interference with individual freedom suggests that a threat to freedom is always present and hence use of *free, freely,* and so on, can be said to satisfy the Austinian significance conditions discussed earlier. Because there is no requirement that the individual take advantage of the rights, the point of establishing them is primarily, if not exclusively, to protect A's freedom to exercise them if he is inclined to do so.

These features of rights against the interference of the state, together with the prominence of such rights in the tradition of discourse concerning rights, are doubtless among the most important reasons that rights and freedom have been closely identified. The relationship between them, both conceptually and in terms of justification, *is* substantial and important. But rights against the interference of the state form a numerically small subclass of the rights that obtain in modern practices of rights, and even in respect to them the relationship with freedom is much less than the whole story concerning either their logic or the arguments for having and respecting them. On the conceptual question, we use the especially clear case of such rights as a vehicle for presenting senses of *freedom* in which neither these nor any other rights involve freedom. We then conclude the chapter with a few remarks concerning justification, remarks that bring us back to H. L. A. Hart's thesis mentioned earlier but that otherwise are preliminary to a more extended discussion in a later chapter.

Rights against interference by the state protect freedom in the sense of the autonomy of action of the individuals who have those rights. A moral and/or juristic barrier is erected around those individuals that shields them against intrusions into the "space" in which they act. The extent or degree of the autonomy they protect, however, immensely valuable as it is, should not be construed as isolating individual members of the practice from one another or from social and political arrangements and institutions. Such rights do create moral and juristic space in which individuals can act, but the very processes that create that space also enmesh those individuals in an elaborate web of social and political arrangements and relationships from which they could extract themselves only at the cost – among many others – of giving up the rights. Although viewed by many critics as fragmenting and isolating influences, there is an important sense in which establishing the practice of rights creates and strengthens the very interpersonal relationships that such critics desire.

The autonomy within society protected by rights against state interference is far from complete. Consider the constitutional right to free speech in the United States. Within the conceptual confines of the practice of rights, this right makes it juristically innocent to speak under certain circumstances. But the practice of rights is only one practice among many. It is not only possible but commonplace to judge actions that fall within it by criteria that come from surrounding practices. The fact that A has a right to make certain statements is no bar whatever to raising the question whether the statements are cogent, prudent, well-grounded, vulgar, inconsiderate, divisive, destructive, insulting, and many other good and bad things. Having a right to X protects A from a certain range of interferences on the part of other people; it is very far from isolating A from all influences and interferences.

IV.　Concluding remarks

Most of the foregoing discussion has been concerned with the conceptual connections between *rights* and *freedom* as opposed to the question of whether, or the extent to which, rights not only can but should be justified in terms of their contribution to freedom. But of course these questions are intimately connected and the points we have been considering are of the greatest importance to the issue of justification. In justifying rights we are justifying something, not anything whatsoever. *What* we are justifying is given, is constituted, in part by the conceptual facts we have been discussing. Depending upon the level at which the justificatory discourse is taking place – for example, whether one is justifying an exercise of a particular right, the inclusion of a particular right or type of right in the practice of rights, or the practice of rights as such – one can call these facts into question in various degrees. One cannot ignore them; one cannot ignore them simply because to do so would be to ignore constitutive features of the very phenomenon that one is trying to justify or disjustify.

We identified three generic senses of *freedom* in which there is a substantial connection between *rights* and *freedom*. The first of these is freedom in the sense in which all human actions can be said to be freely done; that is, done in a manner that cannot be accounted for without attributing decision and choice to the actor or actors in question. The fact that exercising a right is always acting freely in this sense is a reason for valuing that form of action, but it is equally a reason for valuing an indeterminate (and indeterminable) but very large number of other activities as well. For this reason this feature of rights cannot provide a sufficient justification for the distinctive features of exercising any particular right, of including any right or type of right in the practice, or of maintaining the practice of rights as a part of human arrangements.

The second sense in which *rights* is conceptually connected to *freedom* is that establishing a right to do X always involves establishing some form of protection, against the interferences of other parties, for the doing of X. This second sense goes beyond the first in that it means that the society will take steps to facilitate A's action by placing restrictions on the actions of parties who attempt (or who can be expected to attempt) to interfere with it. The character, scope, and efficacy of the steps society takes vary substantially from practice to practice, type of right to type of right, and indeed situation to situation. It is nevertheless a conceptual point that a right always involves the availability of some such protection. Because the protection is protection of acting on decision and choice, it is properly called protection of freedom in the first sense of that concept just discussed. Because in practice it is always protection of some particular, determinate form of action against some particular interference or anticipated interference, it is properly called protection of freedom in a more concrete, substantive sense of freedom than is entailed in the first sense. A denial that doing X should be protected constitutes a denial that there should be a right to do X. And to deny that there is or should be some such protection of *any* X is to deny that there is or should be a practice of rights. For these reasons there can be no such thing as a defense of rights that is not cast in part in terms of the value of freedom in this sense. By parity of reasoning there can be no such thing as an attack on rights that is not in part an attack upon the value of freedom in this sense.

Nevertheless the value or disvalue of freedom in this sense cannot be a sufficient defense of or attack upon rights. There are several reasons for this. First, as in the case of freedom in the sense of decision and choice, this feature of rights is not distinctive to rights. Numerous types of action that are not rights are also protected against interference by other persons. Thus the argument that it is desirable to provide such protection justifies arrangements other than rights and does not justify features of rights that go beyond this one. Second and more important, in protecting A's freedom to do X by establishing a right to do it, society necessarily restricts B's freedom to do those actions that interfere with A's doing X. Because the same policy both protects and limits freedom, that policy cannot be adequately defended in the name of protecting freedom. At the very least, the justification for the right must weigh the desirability of protecting the freedom to do X against the justifiability of interfering with B's freedom to do other actions. It may be true, as H. L. A. Hart argues, that the entire practice of according legal and moral rights presupposes a more basic "natural" right to freedom of action according to which all infringements on action – including those that result, for B, from according A a right to do X – must be justified. Even if so, arguments for freedom as such (whatever that might be) support *only* this "natural" right. All "conventional rights" require

8

Rights and
the liberal principle

I. Introduction

Here is a skeletal summary of the findings reported in the foregoing chapters: To have a right is to have a warrant, provided
by socially established rules, that holds against some at least
loosely specified range of objections and that authorizes A,
usually on his decision, to engage in a type of action that A
judges to be advantageous to himself and that is often judged,
or can be expected often to be judged, disadvantageous to some
B or Bs. For A to claim a right X is for him to assert that he has
such a warrant for X. To exercise a right is ordinarily to decide
to do X in the belief that the action will advantage A and will
be held to have been warranted despite the fact that it disadvantages B. In ways that vary according to the (Hohfeldian) type
of right in question, the rules that warrant As doing X also
impose restrictions on B and sometimes C and warrant Cs (and
sometimes Ds) in acting to protect As doing of X against interference. To say that a society has a practice of rights is to say
that these arrangements are available to its members.

The primary question we take up in these final chapters is
whether, and if so how, a practice with these features can best
be justified. In the terms we employed in Chapter 1, having
examined aspects of the theory and practice of the practice of
rights, we turn now to a search for an optimal pattern of justificatory reasoning in support of the practice. We should, however, pause at the outset of this search to note some of the
special characteristics of this enterprise and the questions it
involves. We discussed some of these peculiarities in abstract
terms in Chapter 1, but it is well to note the particular forms
they take in respect to the practice of rights.

The question of a justification of the practice itself, to begin with, is a question that is not much asked, at least in its own name, by participants. Participants regularly take up questions concerning the proper content, scope, and distribution of the particular rights of which the practice consists. But these questions arise within the practice of rights and presuppose that practice.

Second, the question is logically peculiar. In the view of some writers the question is not only peculiar, it is bogus or even nonsensical. Particular rights, their exercise, their waiver, their violation, and so on, are not somehow derivative of the practice itself or some comprehensive justification thereof or therefore, they are constitutive of that practice. If there were no particular rights such as free speech or property, if there were no instances of the exercise of such rights, there would be no practice of rights. The practice is not something over and above, something in addition to particular rights and their exercise; it *is* those rights and their exercise. The justification for those rights is not derivative of a general justification for the practice; it is, simply, the justification for each of those rights. The search for a justification for the practice as distinct from justifications for its particular elements is a pursuit of a will-o'-the-wisp.[1]

To begin with the logical objection, it is true that the practice of rights has no existence apart from particular rights and the interactions that take place in connection with them. But it does not follow that the practice is reducible to the "sum" of the characteristics of particular rights. A particular right is, trivially, not just that right but also a species of the generic phenomenon of rights. This generic phenomenon has no essential feature or features. But there are certain features that are common to, that are characteristic of, a great many rights. If we are called upon to decide whether a particular moral or jural attribute is properly called a right, we look to see whether it is marked by those features characteristic of rights. Many such decisions are so easily made that they scarcely merit the term. Others are in effect decisions to expand the use of the term *right* beyond the established limits of its application. But the matter can sometimes be settled because the concept of rights has a relatively well-settled application, an application over a range of more or less recurrent features. If each right were the particular right that it is and nothing more, there would, and could, be no way other than by entirely arbitrary fiat to settle the matter.

Particular rights, then, are species of a larger genus. It does not follow that sufficient justifications for particular rights can be derived from justifications for the genus. As with the species that form any genus, particular rights have characteristics that distinguish them from other members of their genus. Justifications must take their species-specific characteristics into account. Nor is the foregoing discussion meant to imply that participants in the practice of rights are necessarily self-conscious about the genus and its common characteristics. But if the generic phenomenon of rights is unjustifiable, no particular right qua right can be justifiable (though actions warranted by a right might be justifiable under some other description). Participants may or may not be self-conscious about whether the generic phenomenon is justifiable. If they are not, the justification they *have* or *give* for their actions (as opposed to the justifications that there are, that *could be given*) may be less complete, less fully articulated than could be the case.

It is worth noting, however, that at least a degree of self-consciousness concerning the practice as such is implicit in its operation as we know it. Leaving aside ways in which participants may be said to support the practice merely by participating in it, some aspects of participation approach an explicit defense of the practice. It is not uncommon for persons whose rights are threatened to issue reminders about the importance of respecting rights as such. Often this is done merely by employing a certain tone of voice, a certain facial mien, a certain demeanor and set of gestures, in objecting to threatened denials or interferences. In other cases the justifications are given more definite verbal form, if not so much in interactions concerning particular rights, then at least in the course of passing on knowledge and understanding of the practice to persons not fully integrated into it. Precepts such as "Respect the rights of others" have a prominent place in the education of young people, and in the lectures, sermons, and so on, that persons suspected of some form of deviant behavior receive from those who are responsible for counseling and correcting. To advance such precepts is to defend, in however unsystematic or unsophisticated a manner, the set of arrangements and beliefs of which the practice of rights consists and that makes particular rights possible.

Finally, numerous theorists and ideologues have addressed themselves systematically to the question of whether individual rights are an appropriate or defensible part of our moral, political, and jural arrangements. Discussions of this question were perhaps most prominent during the seventeenth and eighteenth centuries, when the practice of rights as we have analyzed it was taking shape and taking its place as a part of Western social and political life. The writings of the Levellers in England and the French and American revolutionaries among others gave substantial attention to individual rights and explicitly defended them on various grounds. And such writers as Edmund Burke, Joseph de Maistre, and Louis-Ambroise de Bonald, although vigorously defending older notions of pre-scriptive and corporate privileges, took direct issue with the individual rights that Paine and Condorcet, Jefferson and Price were advocating.

Nor did this debate end at the close of the eighteenth century. The revolutionaries won the debate in the sense that the notion of individual rights became firmly established in political discourse and also in the sense that numerous rights were authoritatively accorded in a number of countries. But the very fact that individual rights became established left them subject to the attacks of critics who objected to the dominant configuration of Western political ideas and practices. Hence an admittedly subordinate but nevertheless recurrent theme of nineteenth- and twentieth-century political thinking has been the argument that individual rights do not form an appropriate part of social and political arrangements. The recurrence of these challenges lends import to the task of assessing the practice

of rights at a tolerably elevated level of generality. Having
identified and analyzed major features of the practice, our task
now is to determine whether it can be defended and, if so, of
what considerations that defense should best consist. Our procedure will be to begin with a range of considerations relevant
to all the (Hohfeldian) types of rights we have encountered. The
discussion of these considerations will, if successful, lay a foundation for the assessment of the several types of rights. We will
then build on that foundation in respect to a particular type of
right, sometimes called civil liberties or the "Great Rights," that
is of especially great significance to politics and political
thought.[2]

II.   Individual and society

The rights that have been our primary concern belong to and
are exercised by individuals. If such rights are to be defensible –
indeed if they are to be comprehensible – the individual must
be an identifiable, comprehensible, and morally and juridically
appropriate "unit" of analysis and assessment. Major traditions
of justification for rights, the natural rights tradition, and the
sometimes associated contractarian tradition, begin with the
assumption that these conditions are satisfied. More specifically,
they begin with the assumption that the individual is not only
a distinguishable entity but one possessed of or characterized
by natural, inherent, or intrinsic value, which demands respect
and protection as such. On this mode of individualism the practice of rights is based on recognition of the intrinsic value of the
individual. Particular rights recognize and accord protection to
aspects or, better perhaps, manifestations of that intrinsic value.

  Given the degree of autonomy of action that rights accord
to the individual, some version of this assumption is probably
essential to justifying the practice. It is no accident that the most
radical and determined critics of rights – for example, de
Maistre, de Bonald, and (to a lesser extent) Burke – have been
critics of individualism; it is not less an accident that defenders
of rights, including the present writer, have viewed rights as

valuable largely because of their contribution (or hoped-for contribution) to individualistic values and a society marked by a significant degree of individualism.

It is evident from our explorations to this point, however, that understanding and justifying the practice of rights requires that we understand more than the individual and his intrinsic value as such. More exactly, it requires an understanding of the individual and individualism that departs significantly from the conceptions thereof that are characteristic of the natural rights and contractarian traditions. As Burke understood so well, rights are more than possessions and/or attributes of individuals.[3] They are warrants for actions that affect other persons. This is the element of truth in the view of writers such as Spinoza and T. H. Green that rights are essentially powers.[4] Even such apparently passive (alleged) rights as the right to life or the right to be treated with respect involve actions that constitute and manifest life and that constitute and manifest those attributes – whatever they may be – that demand respect. Moreover, it would be insignificant to say that there is a right to life or to respect if the statement did not entail restrictions and requirements on other persons. In many of the contexts in which it is significant to assert them, honoring rights to life and to respect entails acceptance by *B* of restrictions and requirements that are likely to be onerous and objectionable to him. (Current controversies concerning abortion illustrate this point very forcefully.) In this and other respects rights are a qualification of, a limitation upon, individualism and the individualist will have reason to be skeptical of them.

For these and other reasons that we have discussed, no set of statements about the individual (or about individuals as depicted in natural rights theory) can constitute a sufficient justification for the practice of rights. The practice has characteristics and consequences that involve more than individuals, and justifications for it must take those characteristics and consequences into account.[5] Nevertheless it is a fact that individuals possess and exercise rights, and this fact is one of the most salient characteristics of the practice. The problem of justifying the practice is above all to justify this feature without overlooking or rendering incomprehensible those aspects of the practice that cannot be accounted for simply in terms of characteristics of individuals. An adequate resolution of this problem would require a theory of action and a theory of society. What follows might be viewed as a sketch of those elements of such a theory that seem to us to link most directly to the topic of rights.

III. The liberal principle explained

We have seen that one of the most prominent features of rights is that it is for A to decide whether to exercise a particular right or not. In the generic terms we used in the previous chapter, rights involve action on A's part. Hence they presuppose agents capable of action. They postulate agents who have interests, desires, purposes, intentions, objectives, and other types of reasons for acting in certain ways. In exercising rights, individuals act on their interests or desires, pursue their objectives or purposes. For this reason to justify according rights is at least to justify the belief that it is, as a generalization to which there may be important exceptions (indeed to which the practice itself makes important exceptions), a good thing for individuals to have, to act upon, and to satisfy the interests and desires, the objectives and purposes that constitute the reasons for their acting to exercise the rights accorded to them. As a first step toward a justification for rights we take up the question whether the beliefs just mentioned can be supported and defended. This discussion should be viewed as an attempt to explicate and defend the liberal principle, that is, to explicate and defend assumptions that we view as fundamental to an individualistic society and polity.

The first of the beliefs in question – that individuals *have* interests, purposes, and so on that constitute reasons for action – is about a matter of fact and is subject not so much to justification as to the kind of proof required for alleged statements of fact. It is worth emphasizing, however, that the statement would not be susceptible of proof or disproof if we did not have con-

cepts that allow us to form and give expression to the belief and
if the logic of these concepts did not allow of proving and dis-
proving statements in which they figure. We have the concepts
action, reason for, desire, interest, purpose, and *objective* and
the rules governing their use specify what counts as having and
acting upon them. Hence we can meaningfully raise the question whether human beings have and are able to act upon these
attributes. When we state the matter this way it is obvious that
this question is settled in a very strong sense. It is part of our
very conception of human beings that they have these characteristics.

Because concepts are socially established, the possibility of
rasing questions about the interests people have depends upon
the social relationships of which those concepts form a part.
Moreover, *pace* contractarians from Hobbes to Rawls, the fact
that A has an interest in X is not a brute fact that can be
understood in terms of some natural or pre- or extrasocial
reality. Just as not all Xs that can be identified in a conceptual
scheme are possible rights in that scheme, so not all identifiable
Xs are possible interests, desires, or other reasons for action.
Apart from some special scenario (say a bingo game), there is
no sense to the notion of A's having an interest in the number
22. Also, the question of which of the available objects any A
will in fact develop an interest in cannot be answered apart
from patterns of social life in which A has participated or at
least with which he is familiar. It is unlikely that an American
will desire to attain proficiency as a bowler in cricket or that an
Englishman will seek to become a first-rate tight end in American football.

Talk about individuals having interests, desires, and so on, is
always embedded, at several levels, in a pattern of social life.
To take the justification of individual rights back to the idea
that individuals have and act upon interests and desires is not
to take it out of the realm of the social. It is a fact that individuals have desires and interests, purposes and objectives. This
fact gives substance to the notion of the individual as a bearer
of rights and as an agent who acts upon those rights. But this

fact about individuals is also, in more than one sense, a fact about individuals as participants in social life.

The second belief mentioned above is that it is a good thing that individuals have and are able to act upon interests, purposes, and other reasons for action. This is not a factual belief in the same sense as the one just discussed. There is, nevertheless, an important sense in which it involves a factual question. Having and acting upon interests, desires, and purposes is part of our concept of a human being, a concept that is moral as well as biological. This shows up in many ways but perhaps most vividly in respect to persons who, because of congenital defects, disease, accidents, and so on, possess the characteristics we are discussing to a very limited degree or even not at all. We regard such cases as tragic and we seek ways of restoring or stimulating the development of the capacities they lack. What is more, we have a very special conceptual apparatus in which to think about such persons and very particular norms of conduct, often part and parcel of the conceptualization, governing our interactions with them. To fail to use this conceptual set or to observe these norms is a species of insensitivity amounting to a serious moral fault.[6]

It is a conceptual fact that having and acting upon interests, purposes, and so on, is deeply embedded in our notion of a human being, and it is a fact that this is a normative notion. In this sense of *fact,* it is a fact that it is a good thing that individuals have and act upon interests and purposes. A justificatory theory might build upon this fact in constructing arguments for individualistic arrangements in general and for practices such as rights that warrant and protect action to pursue interests, satisfy desires, and achieve objectives.

The concepts in terms of which the second belief can be viewed as factual are of course subject to question. Much recent work in the social sciences, most dramatically the work of behaviorists such as B. F. Skinner, is in effect an attempt to question these concepts and to replace our notion of a human being with one that makes no reference to action and reasons for action such as interests, purposes, and objectives.[7] If such attempts were successful, the facts we have been discussing could not be used as building blocks in a theory of rights. If the concepts can be called into question it is presumably also possible to defend them in a sense of *defend* that goes beyond tracing the established conceptual patterns. But the concepts we are discussing are extremely basic to our understandings of ourselves. For this reason attacking or defending them is an enormously complicated and sensitive task. To mention only one tolerably obvious point, attacking or defending these concepts would require that we somehow suspend the belief that we the critics are interested, purposeful agents. The very notion of attacking or defending presupposes that the critic continue to understand himself (at least) as interested and purposive. Hence arguments for or against these concepts would be guilty of affirming, if only by taking for granted, the very concepts they purport to suspend and call into question.

We are not suggesting that these problems are insurmountable; that the concepts in question are unanalyzable primitive terms presupposed *in their present form* by all discourse about human affairs. For one thing, it would be quite beyond the scope of this essay to defend such a thesis. For another, it is hard to deny that the concept of a human being has in fact undergone significant changes because of argumentation concerning it. For example, there are important differences in the concept of a human being in religious as opposed to nonreligious thought. Religious thought offers an argument as to *why* it is good that human beings have the characteristics we are discussing – namely, that these characteristics are given by a divine agent or agency – that nonreligious thought will not so much as countenance. It is possible that secularization has altered the ordinary language concept of a human being. The same speculation might be entertained in respect to the influence of psychoanalytic theory.

As we suggested in our earlier discussion of the concept of action (Chapter 7), however, differences in the status and proper characterization of the notion that it is good that human beings have and act upon interests, desires, and purposes do not alter the fact that this *is* a part of our normative concept of a human being. Nor do such differences alter the fact that this notion enters into the practice of rights in an extremely important way. Without questioning the value of going yet deeper than this notion by trying to provide a grounding for it, doing so is for this reason not necessary to present purposes.

Two further points are important here. First, those who have argued against individual rights have done so in a purposive way: in the hope of achieving some objective, serving some interest, satisfying some desire. Hence if their arguments against rights involve a categorical attack on the notion that it is good that persons have interests and desires, pursue objectives and purposes, those arguments will undercut their own position as well as the one they are attacking. Thus they must attack the desirability of certain interests, desires, and other reasons for action and at least implicitly defend certain others. Second, defenders of the practice of rights must do the same thing. This second point is implicit in our discussion in the last several paragraphs. Because it is a part of our notion of a human being that such creatures have and act upon reasons for action and that this is a good thing, any categorical objection to these characteristics objects not just to the practice of rights but to all human practices. It is an argument for a different conception of a human being and a different set of human practices. Once again, then, defending this second belief is not a task that is imposed in any distinctive way upon those who attempt to justify the practice of rights. For these several reasons we will not take up this task in a systematic way.

Much of the foregoing discussion is also relevant to the third belief mentioned at the outset of this section, namely, that it is a good thing for individuals to satisfy their desires, to serve their interests, and to achieve their purposes and objectives. Although not a sufficient basis for an argument for rights, the relevance of the belief to such an argument is manifest. It is also manifest that this third proposition cannot be adequately

defended in the manner in which we have defended the first
two we have discussed, and indeed cannot be defended at all in
the unqualified form in which we have stated it thus far.

Some headway can be made, however, by pursuing further
the reasoning we have employed in respect to the first two beliefs. If human beings have reasons for action, if they are able
to act upon them, and if these are good things, there is a fairly
obvious sense in which, as a generalization, it should also be
accounted a good thing for the interests and desires to be satisfied and for the purposes and objectives to be achieved. One way
to make the point involved is to notice what can be called the
transitive character of these concepts. We do not intend to
restrict *transitive* to the narrow grammatical sense of a verb
taking a direct object. The Oxford English Dictionary also lists
what it calls the philosophical use of the term, namely, "Passing
out of itself; passing over to or affecting something else; operating beyond itself; opposed to immanent." Reasons for action
such as interests, desires, purposes, and objectives pass over to
something else, operate beyond themselves in that if one has an
interest in or a desire for some thing or state of affairs, one's
purposes and objectives are to achieve or accomplish, to bring
about or attain some thing or state affairs. To satisfy an interest
or desire, to attain or achieve one's objectives and purposes, is
to acquire, obtain, reach, and so on, the thing or state of affairs
in question. There is no such thing as an interest or desire apart
from the object thereof.

To begin with, therefore, to argue that it is good to have
interests and purposes but *categorically* to deny that it is a good
thing to satisfy or attain them would be to write a recipe for
unbearable frustration. The first contention would encourage
the development and pursuit of particular interests and purposes, and hence necessarily of interests in and the purpose of
acquiring or attaining certain objects or conditions. The second
would place an enormous obstacle in the path of attaining those
objects or conditions. Societies follow exactly this policy in
that they stimulate and encourage the development of particular
interests and desires but restrict the permitted modes of acting

upon and satisfying them. They also follow the policy in the more general sense that they encourage purposiveness and "interestedness" as such but all but categorically prohibit acting upon certain purposes and interests. Contrary to certain recurrent modes of romanticism (represented in recent times by Norman O. Brown and in some respects by Herbert Marcuse),[8] it is not easy to see how a society could avoid such policies altogether. Because according rights also involves assigning obligations, a society that includes the practice of rights manifestly could not avoid such policies. (Thus, once again, individualists in the sense of believers in the liberal principle are appropriately skeptical of rights.) But these considerations show no more than that the proposition "Satisfying interests and desires, achieving objectives and purposes, is a good thing" could not be defended *simpliciter*. The considerations do not support the conclusion that, as a generalization, the proposition is not widely accepted and they do not support the view that it is indefensible. Owing to the "transitive" character of interests, desires, and so on, categorical rejection of this proposition is conceptually incompatible with the continued meaningfulness of the concepts *interest, purpose, desire* and *objective* as we now use them. Our concept of intention would be different if no one were ever able to act on one's intentions (albeit it is common enough not to be able to act on one's intentions). Analogously, the concepts under discussion would be different than they are if no one was ever able to satisfy desires or achieve objectives. The view that it is never good to satisfy desires is incompatible with the second belief discussed earlier. For these reasons the notion that it is, as a generalization, a good thing to serve interests and satisfy desires, and so on, should be accounted a part of the concepts *desire, interest, objective,* and *purpose*.

IV.   The liberal principle defended

There is, in sum, a line of reasoning according to which the three beliefs we identified at the outset of this discussion are defensible. This reasoning is important to an individualist social and political theory because it gives substance to the notion of the individual human actor in a way that not only takes account of but is explicitly founded upon respects in which the individual is a part of a social order. In the terms we employed in the introduction, it preserves the emphasis on individual action that has been characteristic of liberalism from Hobbes forward and yet is responsive to the criticisms of theorists such as Burke and Bradley, Durkheim and Mead. The reasoning is particularly important to a justificatory theory of rights because rights presuppose such actors.

Manifestly, however, this reasoning is not itself *sufficient* to justify according a right in any of the senses of the term we have identified. To accord A a right to X is always to prefer the interest or desire, objective or purpose that constitutes A's reason for doing or having X to the interests, desires, and so on, that give B reasons for acting in ways that would violate A's right. Because the reasoning we have developed thus far provides no grounds on which to prefer one reason for action over another, that reasoning cannot itself sufficiently justify any right.

This problem can be solved only by arriving at criteria for ranking the sorts of reasons for action that we have been discussing. Later we try to identify grounds on which to give certain reasons for action a sufficiently high rank to justify according rights to act to satisfy them. In doing so we concentrate on what is in many respects the easiest (but also the most important) case, namely, rights in the sense of liberties. Before undertaking this task it will be useful to formalize aspects of our reasoning to this point by introducing the technical notation of prima facie good.

Prima facie, the foregoing reasoning suggests, it is good for A to have and to be in a position to act upon and to satisfy or achieve his interests and desires, objectives and purposes. The qualifier *prima facie* is necessary because it can be confidently expected that there will be occasions on which the Bs – and indeed the Cs and Ds – will properly be unwilling to grant that it is good or innocent for A to act upon or to satisfy particular interests or desires, objectives and purposes. A considerable part of the corpus of legal, moral, prudential, and other restrictions that societies impose on themselves embody such judgments. To take the most obvious example, if A's interest or desire is to murder a particular B, the latter is not likely to take the view that it would be good or innocent for A to act on or to satisfy that interest or desire.

Before pursuing this aspect of the significance of *prima facie*, however, emphasis should be given to the literal meaning of the expression, namely, "at first sight" or "on the face of it." On the face of it it is a good thing for the As to have, to be able to act upon, and to satisfy or achieve their interests and desires, their objectives and purposes. On the line of reasoning we are pursuing this is the principle with which the discussion begins. If someone contends that it is not a good thing for A to have, to act upon, and to satisfy a particular interest or purpose, it falls on them to show why, despite the prima facie good of A's doing so, it is not a good thing in this case. Until such a showing has been made, the foregoing reasoning requires the conclusion that it *is* a good thing. On the liberal principle, which is what we are explicating here, having and being in a position to act upon and satisfy reasons for action is the expected state of affairs, and objections to doing so require justification.

Such justifications can often be produced quite easily. Perhaps the easiest of them is the one implicit in the statement of the principle itself, namely, that we should not act on desires to meddle gratuitously in the affairs of other people. If I am inclined to do so, and if I recite the liberal principle as a justification for doing so, B can properly object that in fact the principle condemns the action I am contemplating.

This justification for objecting to acting on interests and desires can be rested upon a notion of logical consistency that is agreeably difficult to controvert and that can be extended so as to apply to types of cases beyond the simple one just mentioned.[9] I cannot use the principle as a justification for acting in a manner that in effect denies it to other persons. Or rather, and the difference is of great importance, I cannot do so without finding reasoned grounds on which to differentiate my case from the cases of other persons.

Unfortunately, there is no way to make such differentiations without going into the substance of the reasons for action in question in a particular case.[10] If I object to your having and/or acting on a desire to kill me, I am implicitly defending my desire to act on interests of mine – for example, my interest in denying you your desire and its satisfaction. Unless I undertake the hopeless task of showing that my interests are more valuable than yours simply because they are mine (hopeless because the same argument is equally available to you), I must show that my interest is more valuable than yours.

In the example in question it is tempting to say something like "My interest in denying your liberty to act on your desire to kill me is intrinsically or naturally superior to your desire to kill me." Or perhaps "Your interest in killing me is intrinsically without value, indeed is intrinsically evil." If such a position is defensible, especially in the second formulation, it would follow that your interest in killing me merits no consideration whatever. If so, there would be no question of comparing the value of your interest with the value of mine. It would also follow that we would have to qualify the liberal principle. There would be some interests (in addition to those condemned by the principle itself) that it would be prima facie worthless or even bad for people to have, act upon, and satisfy. At most we could say something like "It is prima facie a good for people to have, act upon, and satisfy all interests except the following" or ". . . all interests save those with the following characteristics."

There are of course many reasons for action that most of us would think should seldom if ever be acted upon. Perhaps for this reason the position that some interests and purposes, some actions, are intrinsically bad or evil seems to be descriptive of widely held views. It is important to note, however, that lists of interests and purposes that are said to be *malum en se* are typically drawn up in generic, abstract terms, terms that require a good deal of interpretation to be applied to particular actions.

This interpretive task is (or at least should be) highly influenced by contextual considerations. The prohibitions of the Decalogue, the relevant items of which form a representative list of actions thought to be wrong in themselves, employ such terms as killing, bearing false witness, and stealing. Judgments about the first of these are obviously context dependent in that there are many kinds of killing that are not only approved but encouraged. (See, for example, the chapters that immediately follow the announcement of what has come to be known as the Decalogue in Exodus!) The specific kind of killing called murder, bearing false witness, and stealing are seldom, if ever, approved as such in societies that have these concepts. They are, however, sometimes *excused* and even *justified* in the sense of saying that the person who committed them must be excused because of some feature of the circumstances or justified because the good done or the evil avoided outweighed the evil of the act. Moreover, the task of deciding whether an action was in fact murder or stealing is often enough no simple matter. Highly intricate questions about intention, about degree of choice available, and about consequences for others must be canvassed before these concepts can be applied to an action. Use of these concepts in making legal and moral judgments allows of, or rather *requires,* the making of subtle differentiations of degrees of offense.

These last remarks are not intended to deny that when *A*'s interest or objective is to steal or kill or bear false witness there is a strong, almost always a conclusive case against his pursuing his objective or acting on his interests. Nor are we suggesting that it is never possible to settle the question of whether such concepts properly apply to a person's objectives, interests, or conduct. All of us apply these concepts to ourselves and to one another with great frequency. As Phillipa Foot has argued in several important papers, when all the relevant considerations have been examined it will often be the case that the question whether the concepts apply to a particular action is settled in a very strong sense.[11] Our point, rather, is that identifying and assessing the relevant considerations is a complex activity that ought to be carried on in a manner sensitive to subtle differences among persons and situations.[12]

There is no denying the fact that certain forms of action, and the interests, desires, and purposes that lead to them, are widely, regularly, and properly disapproved. But it does not follow that it is advantageous to think of these forms of action and these interests and purposes as intrinsically or naturally evil. Quite apart from the epistemological and even metaphysical questions raised by it, such thinking diminishes the sorts of sensitivity just discussed. It also threatens to deprive individuals of pleasures and satisfactions that may in fact be innocent or even positively good in many manifestations; it generates guilt and self-contempt on the part of persons who have the allegedly unnatural, evil, or vulgar interests and desires; and it retards a flow of initiatives and experimentation that may be socially valuable. Above all, it too readily legitimates the dispositions of ascetical, puritanical, and other moralistic meddlers, licensing them in their well-documented tendency to dismiss the interests and desires of other people and to put the latter down in the name of values and concerns asserted to be *bonum in se*. The liberal principle contends that all interferences and restrictions be justified in the light of the fact that they eliminate or diminish a prima facie good. The principle, of course, is hardly a sufficient obstacle to the mischiefs just mentioned. It must be supplemented with reasoning concerning the kinds of justification that will, and will not, warrant interference with actions taken to serve interests and satisfy desires. Because the decision to accord a right is a decision to warrant such an interference, reasoning about rights must be addressed to this problem. But the liberal principle does exclude justifications that are commonly advanced and it does place the burden of justification where it belongs in an individualist society, namely, on those who wish to deny or limit the satisfaction of individual interests and desires, the achievement of individual objectives and purposes. For this reason, and despite the difficulties that are posed by it, it is better to begin reasoning with this principle and then proceed, cautiously, to enter the necessary qualifications to it than to begin with the notion that some reasons for action are intrinsically or inherently evil and then move to qualifications that allow action on them under certain specified conditions.[13]

Two further comments on these contentions are immediately in order. First, we noted earlier that a difficulty with the view that there is a natural right to equal freedom is that the principle in terms of which judgments are to be made, the principle of equal freedom, can be claimed by all parties to any dispute, can be used to support all positions that are under consideration. When it becomes necessary to justify limitations upon or interferences with the alleged right to equal freedom, the principle of equal freedom is not and cannot be of assistance. The principle that it is prima facie a good thing to satisfy desires, serve interests, and so on, does not suffer from this defect. In the present context it is particularly important to note that the principle does not say that there is a right – even in the sense of a liberty – to the satisfaction of desires or to act to satisfy desires. It says that these are prima facie goods and hence that any action or policy that conflicts with the principle must be justified.

Interests and desires, objectives and purposes, are rankable and are in fact ranked by the individuals whose interests they are and by the members of their societies. It is a feature of their logic that judgments can be made as to which of them should be served when conflicts develop among them; as to which of the choices or policies, all of which would accord with the principle of prima facie good, would accomplish the *most* good, would be the *best* choice or policy in the circumstances at hand. Hence it would also be a feature of a theory of rights grounded in this principle that it would be possible to make judgments as to which interests, desires, and so on, should be protected by rights and which should not, as to which of those rights should be sustained if a conflict should develop among or between them, and as to when rights might justifiably be violated if a conflict develops between respecting them and acting on some other precept.

Because all the types of situations just mentioned do in fact develop, because the types of choices and judgments just mentioned are in fact made, it is well that a theory be able to accommodate and account for them. It will be objected, however, that the theory we are developing accommodates such decisions all too easily. More specifically, it will be objected that employing this reasoning in a theory of rights wipes out the distinctively rigorous or stringent character of the latter. Rights are to be respected. To have a right to do X is to be warranted in doing X. Period. Or at least this is how it should be.

To begin with the latter point, the present reasoning does not eliminate the possibility of a right being as rigorous or absolute as you please. The reasoning allows of the judgment that certain interests or purposes are so valuable, so important, that in fact it would always be wrong to qualify them in any way, always wrong to violate them in any way. The view that rights are grounded in reasoning concerning interests and purposes that are rankable does not itself dictate any particular ranking of them or the rights established to protect them. What it does is to provide a theoretical basis on which to recognize what will in any case be the fact, namely, that the importance accorded to any particular right is a matter of judgments on the part of those who participate in the practice of rights in question, not something given or dictated by nature or some other alleged extrahuman agent, agency, or source.

The second comment points forward to a later topic on the agenda. We have suggested that rights in the sense of liberties are the easiest to justify on the mode of reasoning we are pursuing. This is because so little has to be added to our reasoning concerning the liberal principle in order to cover the decision to accord A a liberty to do X. From an individualist perspective, however, it is at least as important to emphasize that liberties are comparatively easy to justify on this mode of reasoning because according them places minimal restrictions upon the Bs and minimal responsibilities on the Cs and Ds. According A a liberty to do X raises in a compartively limited way the hard question of ranking different interests and desires and choosing which among them should be warranted and pro-

tected – questions that are raised in more complicated ˙ways by
the decision to accord rights s.s. and the other types of rights we
have discussed.

The important similarity between the present argument and
the natural rights arguments lies in the fact that both demand
that reasons for action be given consideration; that all interferences with having and acting upon reasons for action be
explicitly justified. There are, to sum up, several differences.
First, the present argument does not claim that the liberal principle is "natural" in standing. It attempts to derive the principle
from conventional arrangements as manifested in conceptual
facts and to defend it in terms of the anticipated consequences
of accepting and acting upon it.[14] Second, the liberal principle
does not itself yield a right of any of the Hohfeldian types to
have or do any particular X. It says that it is wrong to interfere
with A's actions without justification but it makes no attempt
to identify a set of Xs, interference with which could in principle never be justified. Third, consideration is owed not to
some natural or primitive inherent value but to reasons for
action that are meaningfully identifiable in a conceptual scheme
that is part of a pattern of social life. Fourth and most specifically at odds with H. L. A. Hart's formulation, considerations
concerning the goodness and badness of the consequences
of interference – that is, broadly utilitarian considerations – are
treated as relevant to the decision of whether such interferences,
including the sort of interference represented by according a
right in one of the Hohfeldian senses, are justified. Given that
consideration must be given to all reasons for action – that is,
given that all interferences must be justified – the question of
justifying an interference is treated as a question of making a
ranking of the various reasons for action at issue. Freedom has
special standing or significance in this justificatory process only
in the sense discussed in Chapter 7; that is, only in the sense in
which it is intrinsic to the notion of human action itself.[15]

9

Rights and community

The basic moves from the propositions discussed in the previous chapter to a defense of the practice of rights are evident from the analysis of the generic features of rights. Rights are a particular type of warrant for and protection accorded to certain types of actions. By establishing a sphere of special protection in which the individual can act, rights make possible and otherwise encourage the individual to develop, express, and satisfy or achieve his interests, objectives, and so on. By providing a distinctive type of warrant for particularly valuable actions within that sphere, and sometimes by additional modes of support as well, rights increase the likelihood that the latter process will be satisfying and rewarding rather than frustrating or debilitating. In doing the things just mentioned the practice also injects elements of stability and predictability into relationships that, given the rapidly changing and difficult to predict processes through which interests, purposes, and so on, develop, might be unsettling to individuals and to social arrangements. Having a practice of rights connects the present with the past and helps to tie down the future by providing assurances that it will be possible to act in certain desired ways.

However plausible it may be, the foregoing reasoning is not a sufficient justification for the practice of rights as we have analyzed it. There are two broad reasons for this. First, in according rights a society does not merely warrant and protect interests and purposes of individual members, it warrants and protects some of the interests and purposes of its members at the expense of others. This problem is our concern in Chapter 10. Second and yet more broadly, the very existence of the practice affects other social arrangements; the latter must, as it were, share the social landscape with the practice of rights. To mention only one example, the existence of the practice of rights has profound consequences for the character and operation of authority.

The first of these broad-gauged problems – that rights interfere with at the same time that they warrant and protect individual action – arises in respect to rights of all the Hohfeldian types. But the forms the problem takes differ importantly among the several types of liberties and rights we have discussed. If there are solutions they will also differ significantly among the major types of rights. For these reasons we will postpone discussion of this problem until we begin to elaborate the preceding reasoning in respect to the type of rights – that is, civil liberties – with which we are most concerned.

Our immediate task arises from the second problem, from the fact that objections can be brought against the effects of the existence of the practice of rights qua practice. Many of these more categorical objections can be conveniently collected under the rubrics of antiindividualism and advocacy of community. In its most general form the objection is that the practice of rights is based upon and fosters an excessive, egoistic individualism, an individualism that is destructive of the most desirable forms of human relationships – namely, those involved in and fostered by a high degree of community. Prominent in conservative reactions against the Enlightenment and the French Revolution and characteristic of much continental social theory in the nineteenth century, this objection was echoed in modified form in Marx and later Marxism and has been picked up by Left, Right, and apolitical critics of liberalism and the self-proclaimed liberal societies of the twentieth century. It is the basis of the most persistent and unqualified criticisms that have been leveled against the practice of rights.

The notion of community is, notoriously, one of the most protean of the concepts of social and political thought. There is, however, a cluster or family of concerns and values that recur in connection with its use, particularly its use as a fulcrum for attack on the sort of individualism alleged to be both presupposed and generated by the practice of rights. These values and concerns are signaled by such terms as fellowship, integration and cooperation; deep, intense, and intimate ties and relationships; interdependency and solidarity; immersion in and subordination and sacrifice to an organic whole; permanent and otherwise unreserved commitment to an entity larger than oneself. In a genuine community the statuses and roles of participants are defined, interpreted, and enforced by norms and processes directed toward objectives of the corporate whole. Membership in such a community is thought to provide participants with forms of support and sustenance held to be essential to material, psychological, and spiritual well-being and development. Human relationships in a community are said to be full, intense, cohesive, and continuous, whereas the individualistic sorts of association with which communities are (unfavorably) contrasted produce relationships that are partial, either flat and uninteresting or destructively competitive, and stacattolike in their discontinuities. Whether this conception of community bears any relationship to actual aggregations of human beings, it continues to be influential. It provides a grounding, at least in thought, for criticism and rejection of the practice of rights.[1]

A recurrent strain in communitarian thinking is that an emphasis on individual rights fragments human relationships in a manner and to a degree that renders genuine community impossible. It would be difficult to show that this judgment is entirely mistaken. Individual rights warrant and protect self-directed and even self-serving action. Although we have emphasized ways in which individual action is logically and practically dependent on a social context, there is no doubt that the pursuit of individual interests and desires, objectives and purposes is at odds with, if not simply and directly destructive of, some of the kinds of relationships that proponents of community have valued. Justifications for the practice of individual rights are therefore inevitably arguments against some forms of community or at least arguments for limitations on communitarian relationships. The controversy between de Bonald and de Maistre, Burke and Frederich Gentz, the New Left and the Radical Right, on the one hand, and Paine and Condorcet, J. S. Mill and Henry Sidgwick, the American Civil Liberties Union and the League for the Defense of the Rights of Man, on the other, although often overdrawn and exaggerated, is a genuine controversy. It is a controversy between differing models or conceptions of what human societies and human relationships should be like.

As such writers as Hegel and Constant, Hume and Tocqueville remind us, however, the issues need not be so sharply drawn, indeed are not properly drawn, in quite the way that de Bonald's polemics against the revolutionaries or Paine's polemics against Burke might lead us to believe. The distinctions between a community and an aggregation, between an individualistic, rights-oriented association and a communitarian collectivity are valuable and important. But they are distinctions within the more encompassing category of the social or society; they identify species of the generic form known as society. Briefly reminding ourselves of some of the ways in which rights is a social practice will help to delineate the fundamental issues that must be faced.

The practice of rights is individualistic and individualizing but it is not fairly described as atomistic or atomizing. First, there are the many respects in which the practice involves language and hence the shared rules, judgments, and so on, that a common language involves. Second, we have noted the several respects in which the practice presupposes and indeed is constituted by rules, involving but going beyond rules of language, that must be accepted and on the whole followed by most participants. Participation in the practice of rights enmeshes individuals in and makes their actions both logically and practically dependent upon an elaborate network of social rules and the shared beliefs, values, assumptions, and so on, that an accepted set of rules involves. Thus there is a very important sense in which participation in the practice of rights enmeshes individuals in a network of social relationships and a social structure. The autonomy of action that rights warrant and protect is autonomy within that network.

Third, and already partly implicit in the previous two points, the practice of rights necessarily involves the existence and acceptence of authority, and participation in the practice presupposes acceptance of and some degree of subordination to authority. The broadest sense in which this is true is the sense in which all the types of rules discussed earlier are authoritative – namely, that they are viewed as considerations that should be attended to in making decisions concerning the modes of action to which they apply. Even instruction-type rules, which are authoritative in the weakest sense of the several type of rules we have examined, are authoritative in this broad sense. Such rules embody, are abbreviations of, the experience of persons who have engaged in the type of actions they cover. They are authoritative in the sense that some number of people accept them as abbreviating the lessons taught by that experience. No one is legally or morally required to act in the manner such rules suggest. But if *A* pays no attention to the rules – for example, acts contrary to them without explaining why – other persons are likely to regard him as thoughtless, imprudent, and so on. Other types of rules are authoritative in the further and stronger sense that they are viewed by participants as defining legal or moral obligations to act in certain ways. Of course legal rules presuppose authority in the yet more specific sense of formalized legal authority. To exercise a legal right is to accept, at least for the purposes of that action, formal political authority. Rights, and especially legal rights, do place limitations on authority. But in the very process of so doing they presuppose and hence affirm authority. The charge that rights are atomizing and fragmenting in the sense of removing the individual from authority structures and from relationships governed by authority is simply not cogent.

Fourth, the exercise of rights in the strict sense and in the sense of powers and immunities enmeshes the parties to the interaction in that highly structured type of relationship that involves mutual obligations. If Jones and Smith make a contract with one another they acquire rights that warrant and protect particular modes of action on the part of each. But the very process of acquiring those rights makes Jones and Smith dependent on one another in ways that limit the autonomy they had prior to acquiring those rights. In its concrete manifestations the practice of rights consists of an elaborate and extensive pattern of such interdependencies. It is quite possible to object to the tone or quality of the relationships of which the pattern consists, but it is, once again, simply not cogent to argue that the practice of rights isolates participants from one another or is categorically destructive of social relationships.

In all these ways the practice of rights involves participants in patterned interrelationships and interdependencies. Claiming and exercising rights is a way of seeking protection against the society and the polity of which one is a part. But the protection against society and polity is sought *from* the society and polity themselves. Someone who *desired* an atomistic, isolated, or anomic condition might properly object to the practice of rights on the ground that it makes such a condition impossible for participants, but it is not cogent to object to it on the grounds that it fosters such a condition.

These same points can be usefully restated from the slightly different perspective yielded by so-called mass society theories.[2] Conservative critics of the practice of rights have charged that it is based on a conception of the individual so abstracted from history, society, and politics as to be positively metaphysical in character. This conception of the individual, the argument continues, has tended to be self-realizing; it has tended *to produce* individuals who, though hardly abstractions, are faceless and characterless in their uniformity. Such individuals contribute little to the development of a tough, resilient social pattern because their very interchangeability ensures that they have little to offer one another and hence little reason to enter into cooperative, mutually beneficial relationships. Thus in their very characterlessness they are weak individually, and this same attribute means that such social fabric as exists among them is also weak. It is in these circumstances that the distinctively modern forms of tyranny have arisen and have flourished.

There is no denying that some theorists of individual rights, particularly those belonging to the natural rights school of thought, have conceived of both the individual and individual rights in a manner vulnerable to the criticisms just sketched. Rights attach to the individual *as such,* to the individual as he is alleged to be or to have been apart from historical influences and social relationships. Because individuals are equal (i.e., the same) in those respects that warrant their being holders of rights, everyone should have the same rights. Moreover, many of these same theorists, particularly Rousseau and leaders of the French Revolution such as Robespierre, argued that activities or social relationships that encourage differentiation (e.g., the development of groups or associations with distinct objectives and purposes) are evil and should be prevented. It may well be that an individualism and a practice of rights conceived in this manner would foster anomic, faceless, and politically vulnerable individuals.

Unless the analysis presented in this book is totally mistaken, however, there is a great gulf between the conception of the individual and individual rights advanced by natural rights theorists and the practice of rights as it operates in contemporary Western societies. As we have just reemphasized, rights as we know them would be impossible in the absence of a rather elaborate array of arrangements and structures, an array totally at variance with so-called anomic or mass society. What is more, it is in and through these arrangements and structures that individuals develop interests and purposes and acquire rights to act on them. Rights provide the individual with at least some of the elements of a *place,* an *identity,* a *role* in the social milieu. The present writer personally finds unconvincing the picture of modern societies as undifferentiated, unstructured, anomic. But if this picture is at least partially accurate, if contemporary societies have less differentiation of role, function, and so on, than the medieval societies (or the idealized portrayals, of medieval societies) with which they are sometimes unfavorably compared, then the practice of rights as we have analyzed it emerges as a differentiating factor, as a source and guarantor of distinctness, differentiation, and individual identity. Who am I? A participant in a practice of rights can at least answer, "I am the bearer of the following rights; I am subject to the following obligations." And to say these things is also to say, "I am a person with the following interests and desires, purposes, and objectives; and I am a person who interacts with others in attempting to serve those interests, to realize those objectives."

The foregoing arguments do not show, and are not intended to show, that communitarian objections to the practice of rights are without foundation. The considerations we have rehearsed suggest that the practice is consistent with and is productive of complex, differentiated, and structured and structuring social relationships and arrangements. They do not suggest that the practice fosters relationships that have what we might call the tone, quality, or intensity that communitarians have valued.

Rights involve a certain holding back, a certain reserve, in relationships with other people. The participants in the practice are explicitly and in very substantial respects parties to such relationships, but they enter into them, as it were, on condition. An area of action remains with the participant. Although the relationships of which the practice consists are cooperative in vital respects, they are also, at least typically, significantly competitive. Shared interests, concerns, and values must be present; otherwise there would be no reason to enter into or act to maintain the cooperative practice. But the at least implicit assumption is that the shared concerns remain within definite limits, beyond which the parties may want to compete for the resources available rather than share them or even cooperate in dividing them up.

One way to appreciate these characteristics of the practice is to notice the range of concepts that are odd or even definitely foreign to discourse within the practice of rights. We have already noted that concepts such as gratitude and thankfulness, on the one side, and generosity and charitableness, on the other, have little or no place in such discourse. A's doing and having the Xs the practice accords him is *by right,* not because of the generosity of the Bs or Cs. A will properly be irate, offended, and so on, if B or C does not respect his rights, but he will not be grateful or thankful to them for doing so. (He might be thankful, in the always almost religious sense, for the fact that he lives in a society that accords and respects rights.) B or C will properly feel guilt if they violate A's rights, but it is inappropriate for them to congratulate themselves on their generosity if they respect those rights. Similarly, the exercise and the respect of rights is not properly thought of as a matter involving loyalty or friendship. Short of extreme hazard in doing so, one cannot prove himself to be loyal to other persons or to the society or group by exercising or respecting rights. (Defending rights against generalized attacks or defending the rights of a person under particularly heavy attack might be evidence of loyalty.) We expect our friends to defend our rights against the attacks of others, but asserting and respecting rights against one another is surely not, as such, a feature of relationships among or between friends.

If *rights* goes badly with talk of generosity, gratitude, loyalty, and friendship, it is positively incongruous in respect to yet more personal, "deeper," and more emotionally intense relationships involving fraternity and especially love. In the precincts of these concepts the reserve, the self-concern and self-protectiveness, the competitiveness characteristic of rights gives way to an openness, a completeness, if necessary a willing and even joyful subordination and sacrifice of self.

All these concepts – gratitude, thankfulness, generosity, loyalty, sacrifice, friendship, fraternity, love – are prominent in communitarian theory and parlance. The kinds of relationships to which they refer are commonly thought to form the essence of a true community. Such relationships provide definition, strength, support, and sustenance to the members of a community and give their lives meaning and significance. These concepts have little or no place in the idioms of the practice of rights. This is solid evidence that there are important differences between that practice and the model of human relationships that has been associated with the concept of community. In the terms of the now classical nineteenth-century distinctions between *gemeinschaft* and *gesselschaft,* traditional and modern, status and contract, *community* goes with the former terms and *rights* with the latter. The practice of rights is not disassociating, fragmenting, or anarchistic if those terms are used to imply a lack of structured and structuring rules, institutions, and relationships. The practice of rights, as we have insisted from the beginning, is a social practice. But it is disassociating and fragmenting *by comparison with* the model of society that communitarians have projected and preferred.

We have not, however, completed the task of identifying the issues between communitarianism and rights-oriented individualism. We have been discussing these modes of thought as comprehensive and undifferentiated models of human relationships. Considered in this fashion the differences between them are striking, important, and seemingly irreconcilable.

But if we shift our focus from abstract modes of thought to actual societies and the place of rights and communitarian relationships in them, the picture becomes more complicated and the contrasts less distinctly drawn. The practice of rights has not been a sufficient or all-encompassing mode of social and political organization. Rights infect a great many aspects of life in numerous societies, but it is very far from the case that all human interaction in any society takes place in terms of them. If the practice of rights were all-encompassing we could, and presumably in time would, dispense with all the other comparable conduct-guiding concepts that now figure in social and political interaction except insofar as they are internally related to rights. We would speak of justice only in respect to distributing and respecting rights, freedom only insofar as it is a right or is involved in the exercise of rights, authority only with regard to the rules and rule-making processes that establish and enforce rights. Most directly to the point here, the concepts we just surveyed (e.g., gratitude, generosity, friendship, and love) would certainly disappear (except as used to discuss other so-

cieties or other historical periods). The fact that these and many
other concepts continue to be prominent in our discourse is a
good indicator that a critique of the practice of rights will be
very far from an all-encompassing critique of a society of which
it is part.

In some of its uses, *community* is a broader, more inclusive
concept and it is more plausible to think that the relationships
and values associated with it could characterize virtually all
aspects of an entire society. Accounts of medieval societies by
some nineteenth-century writers seem to suggest that this was
the case in those societies.[3] Whether these accounts are accurate
is, fortunately, not a question at the center of present concerns.
Assuming that they are accurate, what seems clear is that we
will not soon return to societies of the kind those accounts
describe. The concern with privacy and autonomy, the inclination to competitiveness and even conflict that have been so
prominent in the West at least since the seventeenth century
can be softened, modified, and combined more effectively with
the service of other values; neither they nor the social practices
and arrangements of which they are an integral part are likely
to disappear.

The point is that we are not presented with a simple choice
between rights-oriented individualism and community. We are
presented, rather, with a complex admixture of practices, arrangements, institutions, and values and with choices as to the
ways in which that mixture should be preserved and/or altered
in particular respects. From this perspective there are respects
in which the values of the practice of rights and those of community, however irreconcilable they may be in abstract formulation, can be not merely compatible but complimentary and
mutually supportive. If it is difficult to find the sort of relationships that communitarians have valued at the encompassing
level of the modern nation-state, such relationships do continue
to manifest themselves in the more circumscribed context of
the family, the workplace, and the various other groups and
associations that bring people together for specific purposes.
These contexts do not engender or even permit the totalistic,

unreserved, life-purpose-defining relationships that communitarians at their most rhapsodical have idolized. But they do permit deep friendships, self-subordination, and love among those persons who desire them and are capable of them.

In a society that includes the practice of rights these partial relationships and associations may permit realization of at least some of the values of community without engendering the consequences that many observers have thought endemic to unqualifiedly communitarian societies. The following passage from Karl Marx, a thinker who defies easy classification in respect to the individualism-communitarianism dichotomy, is a good sample of the concerns of the type of commentator we have in mind. Speaking of the impact of British rule on life in the then sometimes idealized Indian villages, Marx commented that, "sickening as it must be to human feeling to witness those . . . patriarchal and inoffensive social organizations disorganized and dissolved into their units . . . we must not forget that these idyllic village communities, inoffensive though they may appear, had always been the solid foundation of Oriental despotism, that they restrained the human mind within the smallest possible compass, making it the unresisting tool of superstition, enslaving it beneath traditional rules, depriving it of all grandeur and historical energies. . . ." Rather than "elevating man into the sovereign of circumstances," life in these communities "subjugated man to external circumstances and . . . transformed a self-developing social state into never changing natural destiny. . . ."[4] Analogous assessments of "traditional" societies had earlier prompted Rousseau and French revolutionaries influenced by him to want to dissolve substate associations altogether and to prohibit their being reformed. Thus the *Loi le Chapelier* passed in June 1791, decreed, "There is no longer any corporation within the state; there is but the particular interest of each individual and the general interest. . . ."[5]

But Marx's critique of traditional communities does not entail the Rousseauist solution to the problems created by such communities. It is one thing to be caught in the communitarian

embrace of an entire society – an embrace from which escape
cannot even be imagined – decidedly another to have a right to
enter (and to leave) a group, association, commune, or even
family in which those who desire them may find deeper and
more sustaining relationships than are available in the larger
society of which the commune is a part. It is one thing to
enter, or to be born into, an association when doing so means
placing oneself unqualifiedly at its disposal, quite another when
the larger society subjects the conduct of the association to
limitations designed, among other things, to protect the individual rights of the members should they choose to exercise
them.[6]

Rights of ingress and egress and other rights of the individual
against the family, corporations, associations, and so on, clearly
distinguish them from the traditional entities that Marx attacked and that have been the favorites of communitarians. But
it does not follow that such associations must lack the characteristics, could not achieve many of the objectives, that *community*
implies. The views of such writers as Hegel, Tocqueville, and
proponents of the several varieties of pluralist social and political theory in the twentieth century are relevant in this connection.[7] These commentators shared the concern of full-fledged
communitarians that rights-oriented individualism will frag-
ment, isolate, and render defenseless the very individuals it had
freed from the narrowing and finally enslaving embrace that
Marx attacked. For this reason they rejected the Rousseauist
model of political and social relationships. But they also shared
Marx's doubts about all-encompassing communities. Thus (in
ways that vary substantially from thinker to thinker) they urged
upon us a more complicated model of society and politics than
either the extreme individualism of Rousseau and the French
revolutionaries or the extreme communitarianism of the critics
of the latter. There should be a practice of individual rights
and it should be a respected part of social and political arrangements. But prominent among these rights should be the right
of numbers of individuals to form families and other groups
and associations of various sizes, kinds, and purposes; to dis-

tinguish themselves from the bulk of the members of their society in order to pursue objectives that are peculiar to themselves. Such values and objectives as dignity, privacy, and autonomy are to be the hallmark of those relationships characteristic of the practice of rights, a practice that in fundamental respects is to include all members of the society. Those values and objectives that are strongly associated with the concept of community – for example, friendship, love, and subordination and sacrifice – are primarily to be served in the smaller, more intimate contexts and confines of subsocietal groups and associations. The former sphere is to protect the individual not only from the state but from the kind of tyrannizing that Marx found to be characteristic of Indian villages and medieval guilds. The latter is to make possible, for those who seek them and for as long as they can tolerate them, deeper, more intense relationships than are encouraged by the practice of rights.

We have suggested that this more complicated vision is in fact descriptive of modern Western societies to a greater degree than either the strict individualist or the encompassing communitarian conception. It certainly has more to recommend it as a conception of how societies ought to be arranged. Both the individualist and the communitarian conceptions partake too much of the monolithic; give too little heed to the diversity of human interests and desires, objectives, and purposes; allow too little scope for the creation of social institutions and practices responsive to that diversity. A person may like to maintain a certain distance in respect to people he or she does not know well (and may perhaps have no desire to know any great number of people really well) and may find a degree of competitiveness and conflict with such persons bracing and invigorating. But the same person may have strong desires, for close, intense, unguarded relationships with some number of people with whom disposition and continuing interaction have produced deep commonalities of purpose and spirit. A person may place high value upon membership in a political society and yet be very far from wanting that membership to be a dominant, all-pervasive dimension of his life. Indeed membership may be valued in part *because* it is not a pervasive or dominant dimension of life.

It is true that in practice as well as in theory tensions develop between these sets of preferences. Both rights-oriented individualism and communitarianism are value-infused mentalities, not just lifeless arrangements or mechanistic patterns of behavior. The tendency of individualistic and communitarian theorists to press these mentalities to an extreme that renders them incompatible is observable in the ebb and flow of practice as well as in the heavy volumes of social and political theory. The much-discussed difficulties that Western societies have had in maintaining (even) the nuclear family are perhaps the most striking case in point. Persons who adopt an individualistic, rights-oriented mentality, and societies that reinforce such a mentality through social arrangements and practices, do indeed experience difficulties in sustaining arrangements in which individual interests and desires must regularly be subordinated. But difficulties are not impossibilities. For all its vicissitudes, and in spite of the great volume of pessimistic writing concerning it, the nuclear family (and many other more or less communitarian institutions) survives as a key social institution in Western societies which have been marked by a vigorous rights-oriented individualism for several centuries. If it gives way or if, as is most likely, it continues to undergo modifications, this will be not because the practice of rights and significant communitarian-type relationships are incompatible as such, but because human beings have ceased to value one or the other or both. It is a question not of logical or any other kind of necessity, but of choice and action to effectuate choice.[8]

To sum up, in important respects the rights-community dichotomy has been exaggerated and misrepresented. The practice of rights involves differentiated and structured relationships among participants and provides individuals with place, role, and identity. These relationships do not commonly have the tone or quality that communitarians have desired, but the existence and even the prominence of the practice of rights is not incompatible with relationships that have that tone and quality.

These are encouraging conclusions. A social system without friendship, love, generosity, and gratitude would be an unpleasant, perhaps even an unlivable, affair. (This much is perhaps evident from Hobbes' attempt to describe a society in which these qualities are accorded no significant place.) At the same time, a social system that did not respect and protect autonomous spheres of action, privacy, and competition of various kinds would also be an unpleasant, perhaps by now an unlivable, affair. That the two sets of values are compatible and even complimentary in important respects is no small thing. Evolving understandings and arrangements in which they can coexist is by no means the least of the achievements of Western societies since the seventeenth century.

But none of this is to say that their continued coexistence is assured or that there are no issues between communitarians and rights-oriented individualists. Their continued coexistence depends on the choices and actions of the members of the societies in question. Because the modes of community we have discussed are circumscribed, qualified, and intertwined with relationships of a very different sort, it would be unrealistic to expect that the choices and actions of committed communitarians will be strongly supportive of them (although there is, again, some evidence that seekers for – as opposed perhaps to theorists of – community are content with or at least reconciled to the much less than societywide communitarian relationships that obtain in a context that includes the practice of rights). Nor are such phenomena as the widespread hostility of "Middle America" to the "counterculture" reassuring as to the willingness of rights-oriented individualists (of which "Middle America" seems largely to consist) to accept that J. S. Mill called "experiments in living" that are communitarian in sometimes novel ways.[9]

The appropriate response to rights-oriented individualists who are intolerant of communitarian experiments is surely that consistency with their own position and values requires a more accepting, even welcoming posture. If their individualism is grounded in the notion that it is good that human beings have and act effectively to satisfy interests, objectives, and so on, such experiments in living are to be welcomed until it can be shown concretely that they are harmful in unacceptable ways. Much of the appropriate response to the crusading communitarian conception of human society is along the same lines. This conception will be attractive to anyone who values intense, closely knit, emotionally deep and supportive relationships. But first, for better or for worse, and for whatever reason, not everyone who values such relationships does so to the same degree. Some among us, moreover, find them exhausting and difficult to bear. Second and most important, if such relationships are imposed upon us they become not only exhausting and difficult to bear but overwhelming and simply oppressive. In such circumstances the values attributed to them cannot be realized. Rather than sustaining individuals by giving them identity, purpose, and the sense of significance that sometimes comes with participation in entities larger than the self, they reduce, restrict, and finally enslave. Admitting that there are anachronisms intrinsic to it, Marx's assessment of often idealized communities of the past points forcefully to these dangers. Given that the overwhelming majority of human beings are like Indian peasants in the crucial respect that they have no realistic alternative to living their lives in the societies in which they are born, a substantially more encompassing communitarianism than now obtains in Western societies would still pose the dangers Marx signaled. The practice of rights is no guarantee against those dangers and it is by no means the only barrier to them. The fact that it is one such barrier is no small part of the justification for it.

10

Individual liberties in a liberal society

We now return to the first of the two problems noted at the beginning of Chapter 9, the problem of justifying A's right, knowing that it has direct and commonly adverse effects for other persons. As indicated, our treatment of this problem will focus on the case of liberties and particularly emphatically political liberties such as freedom of speech, press, and association.

If communitarian objections are discounted, the three propositions discussed in Chapter 8 and formalized by the liberal principle make the idea of these liberties highly attractive. From the perspective of the preceding reasoning concerning the liberal principle, the decision to accord liberties can be viewed as a way of recording societal commitment to that principle. Doing so provides reminders of and reinforcements for the principle, reminders issued in respect to cases in which reason and experience have taught that disinclination to act on the principle is particularly likely and especially unfortunate.

For reasons already canvassed, however, the liberal principle cannot itself provide a sufficient justification for according a liberty. Liberties go beyond the liberal principle. They single out particular classes of interests and desires, objectives and purposes and accord special preference to them. Acting on these preferred reasons for action is specifically protected against a more or less definite range of potential interferences. In the case of liberties that have legal standing, this protection takes the form of limitations on state authority and hence leaves conflicting interests devoid of the support of such authority. For these reasons the justification that the liberal principle supplies for liberties must be supplemented by criteria that support preferring and protecting particular actions against those that conflict with them. The criteria used to select and justify liberties, in other words, must yield a result that the liberal principle itself cannot yield – namely, a ranking of actions sanctioned by the principle.

The criteria used for this purpose must be consistent with the liberal principle but also must have the latter's standing as a source of justifications for actions and policies to which some affected individuals object. The liberal principle celebrates individual action. At the same time, it is a barrier against individual actions that violate the principle itself. It takes its point as a principle from the conjunction of these two features. The criteria that rank reasons for action for purposes of according individual liberties take their point from a conjunction of three closely related features. (1) They must justify giving particular preference to those individual actions to which the liberties are accorded, and (2) they must erect particular barriers against actions that interfere with liberties. (3) If they are to do the first two jobs in a manner consistent with the liberal principle itself, they must not abandon the fundamental idea that it is a prima facie good for individuals to have, act upon, and satisfy their interests and desires, their objectives and purposes. The rankings must be rankings *of* individual interests, desires, and so on, not something else. The criteria that yield the rankings must be constructed and applied in awareness that all interferences with individual action are suspect because of their adverse effect on a prima facie good.

These considerations require that we reject at the outset any and all criteria that render the individual's own understandings of his reasons for action irrelevant to decisions to accord or withhold liberties. Theories that generate such criteria are attractive precisely because such criteria are used to impose decisions on persons who judge them to be disadvantageous to their own interests and desires. If the judgments of those individuals are dismissed as irrelevant, the imposition of the decisions will appear to be a much easier matter. The difficulty, of course, is that it is anything but clear in what sense an imposition has been justified if the arguments for it ignore the objections of those against whom it has been imposed.

Particularly attractive in this regard are theories that give an appearance of taking something like the liberal principle seriously but that in fact allow it to be set aside. The most prominent examples of such theories assert that the criteria they propose give preference to the interests and objectives that the individuals affected *would* rank most highly *if* they were fully informed and thought clearly and rationally about the matter. So-called false consciousness theories and numerous versions of rational-man theories exemplify this pattern of argument. They encourage us to set the actual, the expressed, interests and desires of human beings aside and yet to go on claiming that the authorizations and requirements they impose serve interests and desires. If the present analysis of the practice of rights is correct, argumentation of this sort is irrelevant to it. Rights serve the interests of the *A*s as *they* understand them, and they must be justifiable despite disserving the interests of the *B*s as *the B*s understand them.

What, then, would be an appropriate set of criteria for selecting and justifying political liberties? On what conception, what set of values, could a society or polity, especially one committed to the liberal principle, justify the impositions that political liberties involve? We try to deal with this question by considering two prominent modes of individualism that have definite but significantly different implications for rights in general and for political liberties in particular. The two are private individualism and public or civic individualism.

I.   Private individualism

The Stoics, Hobbes, to some extent Locke, and laissez-faire economists and political theorists such as Herbert Spencer, Milton Friedman, and Robert Nozick are good representatives of private individualism. Aristotle, Machiavelli, Harrington, Rousseau (in very distinctive ways), and Hannah Arendt among recent writers have expressed the characteristic ideas of the civic variety.[1] Both modes of thought place a high value on personal independence and spheres of autonomous individual action and hence are not to be placed in the category of communitarian theories. But the reasons for which they value individual autonomy of action, the purposes they hope to achieve by protecting such action, and the conceptions they project of the proper relationship between the individual and the sociopolitical order differ greatly.

Private individualists want to protect the individual from the social and particularly the political order. They want to do so primarily in order to facilitate satisfaction of those interests and desires that are highly personal in the sense that the benefits of satisfying them are intended to accrue primarily if not exclusively to the individual. Private individualists concede that a social and political order is necessary to the individual for certain purposes and they recognize that pursuit and satisfaction of individual interests may benefit or have other consequences for that order. But they want to keep the impact of society and especially politics on individual action to a minimum and they discourage any very deep attachment to, identification with, or most important, participation in political activities. In particular, they deny that participation in political life is in itself morally elevating, ennobling, or enriching. Such notions as nobility and morality are not, to begin with, especially prominent in this tradition. When they do occur they are accompanied by the assumption that people have within themselves the capacities sufficient to act in a morally satisfactory manner; that they do not need assistance from the political order to do so. Indeed the political order, although recognized as necessary for certain limited purposes, is thought to be a distraction if not actually an intrusive and corrupting force.[2]

These assumptions, and particularly the assumption that the political order is intrusive, cohere easily with the notion that the most important of the individual's interests and purposes are personal in character. If this is true, interested or purposive action will ordinarily be self-interested action. Hence there is good reason to expect that those who possess political power and authority will use it to advance their own interests. If their interests conflict with mine, their actions can be expected to disserve my interests. This line of thought was one consideration leading Hobbes to the conclusion that monarchy is the best form of government; the interests of one ruler can be satisfied at less cost to the subjects than the interests of a number of rulers.[3] When allied to this mode of individualism, rights take on the character of devices for protecting activities that serve the purely personal, often the personal economic, interests and objectives of those to whom the rights are accorded. The right to property and associated rights of contract are the classic and most obvious cases in point. Efforts have also been made to defend what are sometimes called the Great Rights in terms of this conception of individualism, but this is a much more problematic enterprise. (The Great Rights include freedom of speech, press, and association; habeas corpus; and perhaps the right to free and equal suffrage.) Exercise of these political liberties projects the individual into interactions concerning questions of interest and concern beyond those distinctive of his personal affairs. That is, they project the individual out of the realm that private individualists regard as the only one that is finally of genuine importance. Because the activities that the exercise of these liberties involve are held to be of little or no importance – even, as in Hobbes, positively distasteful and detrimental – there seems to be no very forceful reason why they should be accorded and respected. If such liberties are to be maintained it is primarily for defensive reasons. Political society and the authority and power it involves is necessary but dangerous. However distasteful political activity may be, it is sometimes necessary to engage in it in order to prevent those with authority and power from using them to the detriment of the private life of the individual. Thus the need to engage in the activities in question is an indication that the political order is functioning in a (predictably) unfortunate manner.

Private individualism does offer a possible justification for political liberties. The Bs should accept the disadvantages liberties impose upon them in order to keep the Cs under constraint. The Bs trade a measure of their freedom of action vis-à-vis the As for protections against the more dangerous threat posed by the Cs. Clearly, however, the justification is less than spirited or powerful. If B sees a possibility of protecting his more valuable interests despite his refusal to respect A's liberties, the arguments for the latter will be little, if any, barrier against doing so. The justification, in other words, is an invitation to parasitical, or "free rider," conduct on B's part. Again, the Ds in a society of private individualists are given no very strong reason for coming to the defense of the liberties of the As. The justification does not rank the liberties high enough to warrant sacrificing more purely personal interests and desires to them.

II. Civic individualism

Public or civic individualism does not deny the value or the significance of the primarily personal interests and desires on which private individualists lay so much emphasis. Satisfaction of at least the most fundamental of these interests – *needs,* as they are likely to be called in this context – is necessary to life itself and hence is, in at least this sense, a necessary condition of the satisfaction of other interests. But from Aristotle forward civic individualists have insisted that there are interests and desires, purposes and objectives that cannot be served or satisfied apart from the public, political realm.[4] The activities that satisfy these latter interests are intrinsically or necessarily public in character; they are directed to ends and objectives shared among persons as members of a political order and they can only be pursued through interaction among persons so identified. These interactions redound to the benefit of individuals, but to individuals in their character as members of a political order, in their character as citizens.

In particular, the thinkers in this tradition have insisted on the very point that private individualists have been anxious to deny, namely, that the individual requires the kinds of interactions distinctive of the public realm in order to develop his capacities for moral virtue and the moral life. Even in its most insistent forms, as presented by Aristotle, Rousseau, and Arendt, this conception does not characterize the private realm as immoral. But it does view that realm as amoral, nonmoral, or, at best, the arena of an inferior, less elevating form or mode of morality. It is only when the individual enters into interactions concerned with issues and objectives common to participants in the *vivere civile* that moral choices are presented in a fully developed and significant form.

When allied to this conception the notion of individual rights, and especially the Great Rights, takes on a significance very different and very much greater than that which it carries in private individualism. Having such rights is important not merely to protect individuals in what they now are and in what they now have, but also to make it possible for them to develop to a level they have not yet achieved and could not achieve without engaging in the activities that the liberties protect. The political order is thought of as an opportunity, not a threat. The citizen (a term very prominent in civic individualism but with no great resonance in the private variety) welcomes it and enters into its activities with enthusiasm. Participation in political life contributes to the political order and to the development of the individual at one and the same time, and it is to be welcomed and valued for these reasons. Rousseau's formulation, that the citizen should give himself "without reserve" to the life of the polity, is only the most unqualified of many civic individualist statements in this respect. Citizens pursue their most important interests and purposes not by holding themselves apart from the political order, but by involving themselves in it. Indeed, and this is a point that will have to be discussed again later, the distinction between the well-being of the polity and the well-being of the citizen all but disappears in Rousseau's *The Social Contract* and is anything but prominent in the works of civic individualist writers in general.

This feature of civic individualism serves to place the greatest possible emphasis on the activities that political liberties protect. As noted, one of the key concepts in civic individualism is *citizen*. It is the citizen who participates in political life. Concretely speaking, this participation consists of the activities that are the Xs now protected by the Great Rights; it consists of speaking and writing about issues of public concern, of associating with other citizens in the course of acting in the public realm. If no one could engage in these activities there would be no citizens and the political society would not accord with the model proposed by civic individualists. As Aristotle insisted, on this understanding of politics, engaging in these activities is the defining characteristic of the citizen.[5]

It is evident from these brief remarks that the conception we are calling civic individualism carries potentially important advantages for anyone interested in justifying the political liberties that make up the Great Rights. We will try to develop these advantages further. Before doing so, however, we must attend to a historical objection that is certain to be prompted by our attempt to draw upon such writers as Aristotle and Rousseau in developing a justification for these liberties. The objection is that, for all their emphasis on the activities protected by these liberties in modern practices of rights, the theorists in question made no use of or were actively hostile to the notion of a right to such activities. This objection is particularly serious because the ideals that inform civic individualism have lost much of their resonance in contemporary societies. If we are to draw on them as a basis for thinking about political liberties we are necessarily led back to earlier, more optimistic formulations. But if hostility to such liberties is deeply ingrained in those earlier formulations, the attempt to draw on them for this purpose is bound to fail. Thus the objection is of more than historical interest.

Given the importance assigned to political participation by civic individualists and given that the Great Rights purport to protect such participation, five possibilities suggest themselves as explanations for the fact that writers in this tradition have not emphasized such rights: (1) The idea of a device such as rights had not developed and was not available to them; (2)

they felt that such a device would be objectionable because, although a possible source of protection for political participation, it would bring with it other effects that would subvert or weaken the kind of political society they favored; (3) they believed that the device was unnecessary because the activities in question would be sufficiently protected without making use of it; (4) they judged that the device would be ineffectual as a protection for participatory activities; (5) some combination of items 2 through 4.

Explanation 1 clearly holds for much of the civic individualist tradition. The concept of a right as we know it seems not to have become an identifiable part of Western social and political thought and practice until well into the seventeenth century. Hence in respect to such writers as Aristotle, Machiavelli, and Harrington the question is whether there are features of their thought that would militate against reliance on the device of rights if it had been available to them. Fortunately Rousseau rescues us from the necessity of such hypothetical and anachronistic reasoning; he was familiar with but apparently unenthusiastic about rights. For this reason the following discussion emphasizes Rousseau's thought.

The tactic of focusing on Rousseau maximizes the plausibility of item 2 as an explanation for the fact in question. As numerous interpreters have insisted, Rousseau can be construed as a communitarian (some make him out to be an incipient totalitarian) who would deprive the individual of all autonomy and even distinctive identity by melding him into an encompassing sociopolitical order that would pervade every aspect of the lives of its members. On this interpretation of Rousseau's thinking, the notion of individual rights would indeed be objectionable to him.[6]

This interpretation, of course, takes Rousseau altogether out of the tradition of civic individualism. As with all the writers in that tradition, Rousseau placed far more emphasis on the individual's relation to the political order than did such private individualists as Hobbes, Locke, and Spencer. But only a bias toward the private mode of individualism requires the conclu-

sion that he (and other writers in the civic tradition) is therefore no individualist at all. There is no denying that Rousseau
hoped for deep involvement in and commitment to the political
order. But as we read him (and of course we cannot adequately
defend the reading here) it was not his intention that the individual be submerged in or lose his identity to that order. If
rights were necessary' and/or useful to protecting individual
political action, he would have favored them.

For Rousseau (and for earlier civic individualists if we choose
to raise the anachronistic question) the rejection of rights is best
explained by (5) with heavier emphasis on (3) than on (2) and
(4). The fundamental point seems to be that protective devices
such as the Great Rights would not be necessary in the political
society depicted in *The Social Contract* because the chief threats
to individual participation would be eliminated in other ways.
The corollary to this point is that in a society in which the chief
threats remain, rights (and other moral and juridical devices)
are not likely to provide effective protection.

According rights to the activities that constitute political participation in the society described in *The Social Contract* would
be like according a right to Canadians, Swedes, or Americans to
plant violas rather than geraniums in their gardens. We do not
accord, exercise, or protect such rights because it is unlikely that
anyone would ever be prevented from doing these things. As we
argued earlier, the notion of having a right to X has application
only if there is, at least often, some B or C who thinks that he
will be disadvantaged by A's having or doing X. Rousseau's
view seems to be that no one in a truly civic individualist society will feel disadvantaged by the political activities of other
citizens and hence the notion of having a right to engage in such
activity will be irrelevant.

Given the historical record concerning limitations upon and
interferences with political participation, a record with which
he was fully familiar, we can hardly avoid asking how Rousseau
could possibly have entertained such an expectation. We must
of course grant that a right will not provide effective protection
for an activity unless some substantial part of the populace in

question values that activity, values it not because rights should be respected but because the activity in question is believed important and should be welcomed and encouraged. But this is far short of the expectation that there would be no interferences or the denial that interferences would be easier to fend off if a right to the activity were established.

Two assumptions seem to be of primary and distinctive importance in fostering these hopes. The first connects with the classical idea that politics and political life are the realm of the moral as opposed to the pre-, sub-, or amoral. It is in the course of political activity that genuinely moral questions arise and are debated and resolved. It is primarily in the course of debating and resolving such questions that an individual's capacities for moral discourse, decision, and judgment are developed. As Rousseau put it in one of the more rhapsodical paragraphs of *The Social Contract,* "The passage from the state of nature to the civil state produces a very remarkable change in man, by substituting justice for instinct in his conduct, and giving his actions the morality they formerly lacked. Then only, when the voice of duty takes the place of physical impulses and rights of appetite, does man, who so far had considered only himself, find that he is forced to act on different principles, and to consult his reason before listening to his inclinations."[7] In short, the thought that a proper political society is the realm of the moral as opposed to the amoral seems to have given rise to the thought that such a society is also the domain of the moral as opposed to the immoral. The "remarkable transformation" of which Rousseau speaks ensures that citizens do not harm or improperly interfere with one another, particularly with those activities distinctive of the role of citizen. For this reason the device of rights is unnecessary in such a society. If *right* conduct is assured, there is no need for the sorts of protections that *rights* are intended to afford.

This assumption (speculation) would be of particular relevance to the Great Rights if extended to the conduct of those who hold political authority. Suspicion of persons in authority has been prominent in the tradition of liberalism and in that tradition and beyond it has been a major impetus to establishing and insisting upon rights held against authority. If such suspicion is groundless one reason for having the practice of rights loses its cogency.

On some versions of civic individualism, moreover, the whole question of the rectitude and trustworthiness of persons who hold authority ceases to be relevant. This is because of the second of the two assumptions just alluded to, namely, that political authority in the sense of a right of decision and command invested in a limited number of persons occupying designated offices is all but unnecessary in a civic individualist political order. One again Rousseau's argument in *The Social Contract* is the leading case in point. Leaving aside the puzzling case of the "Legislator" who founds the political order, the role of authority in the preceding sense is sharply minimized. Rousseau does speak of "government" and of "magistrates" who administer the decisions of the citizenry, but it seems to be his thought that laws will be adopted by action of the entire citizenry.[8] If this intention were realized it could be contended that there would be no authorities in the preceding sense to distrust, or to hold rights against. Nor is Rousseau the only theorist to have projected this vision. Aristotle's view that all citizens are equal in that they "rule and are ruled in turn" does posit distinct offices in which authority is invested.[9] But the easy and frequent exchange of roles, together with the emphasis on active participation by all citizens, renders it difficult to think of those in office as importantly distinct or as distinctively suspect. Similarly, Marx, who bears some of the insignia of the civic individualist, apparently held out the hope that authority could be all but dispensed with in the communist society.[10] On these conceptions of politics the notion of rights necessitated by the likelihood of abuses of authority is simply not credible.

Because civic individualism provides a powerful argument for the activities that the Great Rights protect, the next question is whether the assumptions that explain the bias against such rights are viable or plausible – whether we ought to adopt those assumptions and hence decide that the practice of rights is unnecessary in respect to these activities. The answer is pretty clearly that the assumptions are implausible and that we should reject them.

The assumption that the members of a civic individualist polity, whether in authority or not, will not misuse or interfere with one another presumes that we can both identify and instantiate the sufficient conditions of satisfactory conduct in these respects on the part of an entire society. One can readily agree that the ethos that would pervade a society of civic individualists could contribute significantly to the character and quality of the relevant relationships among the members. Persons who accept and act upon the precepts characteristic of this tradition would respect political activity and would have a degree of concern for shared problems and arrangements that is simply not encouraged by private individualism. But there is no reason to think that acceptance of these or any other precepts would completely eliminate conflict among or interference with citizens, nor is there any reason to think that all of the members of such a society will accept and/or always act on these or any other set of precepts.

As to the elimination or virtual elimination of centralized, hierarchical political authority, if this is a precondition of a participatory, civic individualist society, we must give up not only rights that protect participatory activities but those activities themselves. As is well known, most theorists of this tradition insisted that their visions would be realizable, if at all, only under conditions that are now scarcely imaginable. The small size, the comparative simplicity of social and economic structure, the homogeneity that they posited are not even approximated in contemporary political societies. And as size, complexity, and heterogeneity has increased, centralized authority, as a generalization, has increased with them. Moreover, contemporary societies have made extensive use of a further device – namely, representation – that many civic individualists have specifically rejected as inimical to politics.

Nor were these theorists obviously mistaken in thinking that the objectives they sought could be achieved only if authority and representation were narrowly limited and only if the citizenry welcomed one another's political activities. Confidence on the latter point undoubtedly encourages the kinds of individual initiatives and cooperative interactions of which a strongly participatory politics consists. As such confidence has declined and as the prominence of centralized authority has increased, the attractiveness of participation in political life has certainly diminished. Thus it has been tempting to retreat more and more to private concerns and seek protections against the political realm. It is no accident that private individualism and the large, centralized nation-state have flourished together, nor is it likely that the model provided by civic individualism in its purer forms will be descriptive of political life in the nation-states that dominate the world in our time.

It does not follow that we must discard the civic individualist conception altogether; in particular, it does not follow that we cannot draw upon that conception in thinking about the proper place of individual liberties in our politics. Citizens are indeed likely to interfere with and otherwise mistreat one another from time to time. But this fact no more supports the inference that one should shun the citizen's role than does the fact that entrepreneurs mistreat one another support the inference that one should shun the marketplace. The fact is that people mistreat people, and the one sure way to shun the "people role" does not recommend itself to most of us. Again, we must recognize that those holding positions of leadership and authority play a vastly more important role in our politics than envisioned by Aristotle or Rousseau. Such recognition does not support the inference that participation in politics is a waste of time for those who are not in positions of authority. To begin with, participation is the route to positions of leadership and authority and the greater advantages that holding them can yield in our politics. Moreover, there are many human activities in which representation, leadership, and authority have prominence as great as or greater than they have in politics. The conductor of an orchestra or chorus, the quarterback of a football team, the coxswain of a crew all typically dominate decision processes in those activities. It is not, however, widely thought that they alone can derive significant benefits and satisfactions from participating in them. Of course the notion of participation does not work the same in the activities just mentioned as it does in politics, and particularly as the latter has been understood in the tradition of political thought we are discussing. To mention only one point, we do not ordinarily join orchestras and crews in order to take part in discussion and decision making about issues of high moral or other collective import. But we do sometimes have these (among other) objectives in view when we participate in labor unions, professional associations, churches, university faculties, and avocational associations. We do so despite the fact that shop stewards, secretaries-general, deacons and ministers, provosts and deans are conspicuous in the affairs and processes of such entities. Active participation in the political life of the modern nation-state is not likely to have all the dimensions or yield all the benefits hoped for by Aristotle or Rousseau. It may nevertheless add valuable dimensions to the lives of those who engage in it (to say nothing of the consequences, other than the loss of the unique benefits, of eschewing it altogether).

One of the inferences that *is* supported by a recognition of the realities we have been discussing is that it will be advisable to take precautions to protect the citizen's role against *avoidable* interferences and diminutions. There is no certain or even best way to do this. But according rights, and especially rights in the sense of liberties, is a device that has proved to be valuable in this regard. Rousseau was certainly correct in thinking that a participatory political society presupposes widespread belief in the value of such a society and hence belief in the value of the activities of which such a society distinctively consists. Juridical and moral devices such as rights will not long protect inveterately controversial modes of action if there is no conviction that those modes of action are valuable. But even leaving aside the enforcement aspects of the practice, there is more than a little value in registering or enrolling such convictions in a public way. Persons who hold a conviction sometimes lose sight of it in the hurly-burly of day-to-day interactions. To accord a right, especially a legal right, is to make a record to which reference can be made in such moments. When A says to B or C, "But I have a right to do X," he says, among other things, "I remind you that this society, of which you are a member, has made the judgment that doing X is valuable and important." In the first instance at least, this is an appeal to B or C to reflect whether, admitting that they will be immediately disadvantaged by X, they do not think that the judgment that the right records is correct and should be sustained. That such appeals are not always successful does not imply that making them, and hence that devices that allow us to make them, does not contribute to maintaining the conviction that the activities are important and to transmitting those convictions to new generations.

Recognizing as we must, then, that writers in the civic individualist tradition have not been proponents of individual liberties in the Hohfeldian sense, there are substantial grounds for thinking that such liberties are compatible with the basic values and purposes of that tradition. There are also grounds for arguing that such liberties may be advantageous, if not simply necessary, if the values of that tradition are to be realized in the political conditions under which we live. Hence we must return to the question of how the modified civic individualism that has evolved in the course of our discussion contributes to solving the problem that led us to discuss it, the problem of justifying the decision to accord a right to X when doing so disadvantages some B or Bs, C or Cs.

(The preceding discussion signals one of the tensions implicit in any attempt to justify civil liberties and particularly in any such attempt that draws significantly on civic individualist values and assumptions. The latter assign great importance to politics and to participation therein. They depend upon the belief that political participation contributes significantly to the quality of human life. Because civil liberties protect such participation, it is not only plausible but attractive to draw on civic individualist assumptions in arguing for them. But civil liberties are also a protection against and an attempt to place limitations upon politics and the political process. In this respect the judgment that they are important or even essential is an expression of a qualified faith in the very political process that the civil libertarian professes to esteem. In our judgment this tension is inescapable in the political societies in which we live and is a chief source of many of the practical problems that arise in the day-to-day practice of rights.)

At one level of analysis it contributes by proposing a ranking of the value, to the individual, of various recurrent interests and desires, objectives and purposes. It contends that the interests and objectives satisfied by participation in public life are more elevated and elevating, even more noble and ennobling, than those satisfied by activities in what it classifies as the personal or private realm. If accepted, these rankings would provide a basis on which to accord special protections to activities that serve these especially valuable reasons for action, protections not accorded to activities that satisfy the allegedly less valuable varieties. (This is not to say that, for example, those interests alleged to be of less value are of *no* value. Serving the less valuable interests remains a prima facie good. But the prima facie good of serving them ordinarily is outweighed when doing so conflicts with serving those judged to be more valuable.) It does not follow that every individual is required (if only on pain of being guilty of false consciousness or irrationality) to act on the rankings in the sense of preferring those reasons for action designated more valuable whenever acting on them conflicts with those designated less valuable. To accord a right is ordinarily to leave it to the *A*s to decide whether that right should be exercised. It follows that individuals are expected to treat the rankings as providing sufficient grounds for not interfering in forbidden ways with someone else's attempt to act on the more valuable interests. *B* is wrong to insist on pursuing a less valuable interest or objective if doing so conflicts with *A*'s pursuit of a more valuable one.

In this last sense the argument is (potentially) of the "false consciousness" type. It could be viewed as a specification of the individual's highest interests and a claim that this specification must take precedence over, must be authoritative against, the individual's express judgments concerning his interests. In this respect the argument is objectionable because it tends to render the individual's assessments subject not only to rejection as a basis for decision about this or that right but irrelevant as a consideration in making such decisions. Individuals who do not accept the rankings the argument yields and/or do not cast their judgments and demands in terms of them thereby disqualify their views as proper considerations in the social or political decision-making process. But this would be a misinterpretation of the argument. It is indeed desirable that the members of a society be presented with this reasoning and it is desirable for them to accept the rankings it yields. But it would be contrary to the liberal principle to treat the reasoning as a basis for deciding that certain interests are irrelevant. *If* accepted in a society the argument helps to justify according liberties and imposing obligations; it does not justify disregarding the interests that are disserved by doing so.

It is misleading, however, to treat our modified civic individualist argument for the Great Rights as yielding nothing more than a ranking of the value of various interests and desires to individuals qua individuals. The argument effects a very close relationship between the individual and individual interests, on the one hand, and social and political arrangements, institutions and understandings, on the other. To begin with, the argument contends that it is, among other things, a good for the individual to participate actively in the political life of society. Such participation presupposes arrangements and institutions that are shared among the members of the society and open to the participation of the latter. Conversely, individual participation in those institutions and arrangements is necessary to their existence and operation. Thus participation not only benefits the individual directly but also benefits all members of the polity, including the *B*s, by helping to maintain the conditions under which they are all able to participate in political life and obtain the benefits of doing so. The person who acts to prevent an *A* from political participation prefers his interest in doing so not only to the interest or interests on which *A* is acting in the case at hand but also to the interest of members of the polity in maintaining the conditions necessary to political participation. When the polity makes the authoritative decision to accord and protect the Great Rights, and it is worth emphasizing that in one way or another it is the polity that makes this decision, the decision can be justified on grounds that go beyond the resultant or expected benefits to this or that *A*. The decision is not simply to serve the interests of particular *A*s rather than those of particular *B*s or *C*s, but to serve the interest that members of the polity have in maintaining certain types of political arrangements and institutions. If a *B* or a *C* objects to the right of free speech or association on the ground that its exercise disserves his personal interests, it can be responded that these liberties are justified not simply because *A*'s interest is more important to *A* than *B*'s is to *B,* but because the existence of the right serves very important interests of all members of the polity. Put a slightly different way, there can be no such thing as a civic individualist political society without free expression, association, and other modes of political action on the part of individual citizens. Hence arrangements that protect such modes of action find justification in the conception, in the ethos, of a society that models itself on this understanding of what a political society ought to be like.

This last way of stating the case for the Great Rights calls attention to further arguments for them. If the Great Rights protect the ethos of a civic individualist polity, they contribute to the protection of other features of the polity that depend upon that ethos. Consider the case of authority, a feature that we would ordinarily (and in some measure properly) think of as limited and perhaps weakened by these rights. Authority depends on the legitimating effects of shared purposes and understandings and is best maintained if those purposes and understandings are respected. In a civic individualist society this would imply that those in authority ought to respect and even welcome the modes of individual political participation that the Great Rights protect. It is perhaps this thought that prompted

Rousseau and other civic individualists to hope that these rights
would be unnecessary. If we are correct in thinking that Rousseau was overly sanguine on this point, the Great Rights are
important as protections of the citizen's activities and hence the
citizen's role. But in protecting that role they also help to keep
the actions of those in authority consistent with the values and
purposes of the society and in this sense help to maintain it. In
a civic individualist society the Great Rights are at one and the
same time limitations upon, protections against, and preservers
of authority. They serve the particular interests on which the
As act when they exercise them, they serve the interests of members of such a society in maintaining the citizen's role, and they
serve the interests of members of the society (including those in
positions of authority) in maintaining legitimate authority. In
Rousseauist terms, given the character and purposes of the society, in this case it is difficult to distinguish between serving
individual interests and serving the purposes and objectives of
the political society in which those interests and purposes develop and are pursued. In more emphatically individualist terms
the Great Rights serve and protect the interests of the Bs, Cs,
and Ds as well as the As – interests that develop in and take
their distinctive characteristics in large part from the character
and purposes of the society in which the rights are accorded.

Earlier we discussed some of the respects in which the notion
of having interests and purposes, desires and objectives – whatever their content – is, logically speaking, a social notion. We
argued that taking the defense of individual rights back to reasons for action such as individual interests and desires, objectives and purposes, and the prima facie good of having, acting
upon, and satisfying them does not put that defense into asocial
or atomistic terms. Drawing upon modified civic individualist
conceptions to defend the Great Rights gives more definite content to that argument. It does so because the latter conceptions
forge especially substantial links between reasons for individual
action and a particular kind of sociopolitical order and a particular kind of relationship between the individual and that order. This does not mean that the civic conception ceases to be

a mode of individualism. Individual interests and purposes and the actions taken to satisfy them are fundamental to the conception. If this point is not insisted upon, civic individualism can easily be transformed (as admittedly tends to happen in Rousseau) into a species of communitarianism. (An alteration sometimes effected by tinkering with the concept of participation.) But because certain of those interests and purposes cannot be served, indeed cannot be conceived or understood, apart from shared social and political arrangements, reasoning concerning what might serve them must necessarily make substantial reference to arrangements that involve more than individuals taken as atomic entities.

III. Concluding remarks

This last point leads conveniently into a summary and extension of the argument we have been developing. We have stressed the ways in which rights are a social phenomenon, the ways in which the practice of rights is a social practice. In earlier chapters this point was made primarily by reference to what could plausibly be regarded as generic features of the concept of a society – for example, shared language and various kinds of shared rules. But there are many species of the genus *society* and they differ greatly one from the other. For this reason the practice of rights cannot be fully derived from or defended in terms of the concept of society as such. The characteristics of the practice cannot be fully appreciated or evaluated apart from the ways in which the practice fits into and contributes to the mix of rules, values, purposes, and institutions that constitute this or that society. Because we have not analyzed any particular society in detail, present discussions do not permit a full understanding or assessment of any example of the practice.

But the species of which the genus *society* consists can be classified into groups or types (phyla) according to clusters of characteristics that are common among a number of societies but not common to the genus as an inclusive class. Social analysts have evolved and employed numerous such classifications,

and theorists have utilized them in projecting normatively ori-
ented conceptions of the sociopolitical order. The conceptions
that we have called communitarianism, private and public or
civic individualism are examples of such analytic classifications
– cum-normative projections. They sketch the characteristic features of at once ideal-typical (in the Weberian sense) and idealized (in the explicitly normative sense) sociopolitical orders.
They are not sufficiently descriptive of any past or present society to allow us to offer detailed evaluations of the practice of
rights or alternative arrangements in concrete historical manifestation. They do help us to reflect about rights as they relate
to the mix of values, purposes, and institutions distinctive of
the conceptions in question. Hence they allow assessments and
evaluations of rights that would be impossible if the practice
were discussed altogether in isolation or at the very high level
of abstraction of the generic concept of society.

It was to make such assessments of certain political liberties
possible that we turned to the models of private and civic individualism. Finding the civic model consistent with the fundamental evaluative premises with which we began (premises
that take both their strengths and their weaknesses from the
fact that they are at the level of abstraction of the generic concept of society) and more attractive than private individualism
and communitarianism on other grounds, we were constrained
to note that in its major historical forms that conception is at
variance with prominent characteristics of most, if not all, contemporary societies – at variance, moreover, in ways directly
relevant to the problem of justifying the Great Rights. We then
modified the conception so as to reduce somewhat (albeit not to
eliminate) the discrepancies between it and contemporary political societies and we argued that, so modified, it contributes importantly to the case for according and respecting the Great
Rights. The resultant justification for these rights is that they
serve important interests of the individuals who exercise them
and also protect arrangements, institutions, and norms important to all members who value a sociopolitical order of the type
in question. For the latter reason the argument provides grounds

on which to justify A's doing X despite the fact that the action carries disadvantages for B or C.

Needless to say, the merits of this argument depend heavily on the attractiveness of the modified civil individualism in which we have set it. Above all it depends upon the belief that the possibility of active individual participation in the processes by which political decisions are made, and hence the availability of arrangements that encourage and support such participation, is valuable to individuals both as such and as members of a sociopolitical order. If we follow Hobbes and other private individualists in rejecting this belief or if we conceive of participation in less individualistic, more communitarian ways, we will reject the conception as a whole and the argument for the Great Rights that it yields.

We have not presented, and we cannot here present, a full-dress defense of this conception. But we can amplify somewhat themes available in the foregoing discussions. Doing so will lead to yet further modifications in civic individualism, which will show that the distinction between it and private individualism is for present purposes (however important it may be for historical analysis) a convenience that can now be largely left behind.

The vision of human affairs that civic individualism projects is one of substantial politicization. The lives of the citizens in such a society would be linked together at least in the sense that the activities of this or that citizen presuppose comparable or corresponding activities on the part of their fellow citizens. In the purest versions of the vision this is particularly and distinctively true of the moral dimensions of life. A morally virtuous life on my part depends not only on my own actions but on those of the actions of my fellow citizens that constitute and sustain the political realm that is a necessary condition of the pursuit and exercise of moral virtues in its most important forms.

For all its many attractions this position insists on a rather sharply hierarchical and narrowly limiting conception of morality in particular and of what is valuable to human beings in general. The contours of the moral and the valuable are very strictly defined by the conception; beliefs, actions, and practices that depart from the conception are thereby denied these labels. In this respect the conception is at variance with the much more latitudinarian assumptions with which we began our argument in these last chapters, the assumption that it is prima facie a good thing for individuals to have, to act upon, and to satisfy or achieve their interests and desires, their objectives and purposes.

Through much of its history the restrictive features of civic individualism have been defended on the basis of a notion that man has a distinctive nature, purpose, or *telos* that provides the criterion of what is moral and what is valuable and that identifies the kind of sociopolitical order in which man must live if the *telos* is to be realized. Although supported by an elaborate body of argumentation, for many (including the present writer) this notion now appears as a piece of dogmatic and even unintelligible metaphysics.

Fortunately the metaphysic is not essential to (an admittedly somewhat circumscribed) civic individualism that urges political participation and yields a strong argument for the Great Rights that encourage and protect such participation. We do not need the help of the Aristotelian notion of a nature or *telos* to recognize that few of the patterns of action and interaction in, by, and through which individual interests and purposes take shape and are pursued can be understood apart from political arrangements and practices. Nor do we need the assistance of a teleological metaphysic in order to argue that it is desirable for individuals to be in a position to act within and upon those arrangements and practices. If it is true that our lives take much of their shape and meaning from the political context in which they are lived, it is not an inordinately difficult step to the conclusion that it is desirable that we be in a position to influence the character of that context.

The phrase *to be in a position to* is of the utmost importance here. In the Aristotelian version of civic individualism this phraseology would of course be entirely inadequate. Citizens

not only must be in a position to participate in political processes and decisions but must in fact participate. If they do not
they are not citizens. If there are no citizens the political society
is not a genuine *polis* and the members thereof cannot achieve
their distinctive end, or *telos*.

The idea that the citizenry should be encouraged to participate in political life is altogether unobjectionable. This can
and should be done by education, by exhortation, and by example. And if some success is achieved with these devices, it can
and should be done by establishing the right to do so – that is,
among other things, by recording the conviction that such
participation is not only a defensible but a desirable thing. It
can be done on the grounds we have been discussing, namely,
that it will be to the personal advantage of individuals to participate and that their participation will contribute to the quality of the lives of their fellow citizens as it contributes to their
own. But such exhortations need not be based upon and need
not amount to acceptance of the restrictive view that political
participation is a necessary condition of a moral life or of a life
that pursues the one (and only) *telos* that is uniquely human.

In this perspective one of the distinctive features of the logic
of *rights* – namely, the "self-administered" character of the
moral and jural attributes that deserve this term – is of great importance. To say that individuals have a right to such modes of
political participation as speech, association, and voting is exactly to say that they are *in a position* to act within and upon
political processes if they so choose. They are in such a position
in the specific and strong sense that as a matter of right they
may engage in these activities if they decide to do so. It is also
and equally to say that they may forego such activities if they so
choose. Thus the decision to accord and maintain the Great
Rights is consistent with the broadly individualistic value premises with which we began, with a recognition of the ways in
which individual interests and desires, objectives and purposes,
in all their magnificent diversity, are influenced by the ineluctu-
bly social and political character of our lives, and with the fact

that life in a sociopolitical order requires authoritative choices as to which modes of conduct are preferred when interests and purposes conflict. For these reasons the practice of according, respecting, and protecting the Great Rights is an eminently defensible part of our arrangements.

APPENDIX

The right to
private property

Beginning with Aristotle, many of the arguments for civic individualism have included one or another version of the contention that a substantial degree of individual independence or self-sufficiency in respect to the economic or material requirements of life is a necessary condition of effective (later responsible) participation in political life.[1] On one version of this contention it is argued that persons who must constantly exercise themselves to satisfy material needs will lack both time and the elevation of mind and spirit that freedom from such concerns makes possible. Lacking these qualities, such persons will be incapable of meeting the responsibilities of citizenship. Other versions have it that a substantial degree of economic independence is necessary to the exercise of uncorrupted judgment about political issues. A third variant, closely related to the second, treats an economically independent citizenry as the most efficacious barrier to excessive power in government – power likely to be used to cow and even render servile a citizenry that falls into economic dependency upon it.

In all its versions this line of argumentation has involved an at least implicit defense of some form of the institution of private property. Whether in slaves, land, money, or some other desideratum, the existence of this institution guards individual wealth against various threats and thereby protects the independence of political thought and action that possession of such wealth makes possible. Insofar as the institution of private property has involved something approaching our notion of a right s.s., it would appear that the values of civic individualism (as well as the private variety) have been served best in societies that include not just the liberties we are calling the Great Rights

but rights s.s., and particularly rights s.s. to private property.
Such a conclusion is not obviously inconsistent with the contentions of our last three chapters. The notion of civic individualism, especially when interpreted to include the liberal principle, hardly excludes concern with personal or private interests; it only demands that there also be concern with shared interests and values and that some of the former be subordinated to the latter when the two conflict. Second, in the perspective we have just been discussing, establishing, maintaining, and respecting rights s.s. to private property is defensible not simply on the grounds that they contribute to the satisfaction of private interests, but also on the wider ground that they are necessary (or at least importantly contributive) to the realization of the shared interests and values distinctive of a civic individualist society. If rights s.s. to private property are necessary to (or the best means of) satisfying some private interests and if they also contribute importantly to realizing shared interests and values, then the argument for them is not only consistent with the contentions of our last chapters but commands the allegiance of anyone who finds those contentions persuasive.

We are not prepared to set ourselves categorically against this conclusion. Rights s.s. in general and such rights to various forms of private property in particular are manifestly a prominent feature of most of the contemporary societies that include the practice of rights in meaningful form. They are perhaps an even more prominent part of societies in which that practice includes vigorous exercise of and genuine respect for the liberties we are calling the Great Rights. Moreover, it seems impossible to deny that such rights have at times contributed significantly to realization of the values underlying both the liberal principle in general and the notion of a civic individualist society. Finally, and perhaps the most important reason for the present diffidence on this issue, there are a great variety of rights s.s. and a great many forms and manifestations of the institution of private property. Because the social, political, and moral consequences of this diverse array are by no means uniform, a well-grounded assessment of them would require a more detailed and differentiated investigation than we have attempted here. Considerations we have rehearsed in this work, however, do generate skepticism about the value of rights s.s. to private property as any very prominent part of political societies in our time. For the present we will rest with a sketch of the grounds for such skepticism as they emerge from the foregoing discussions.

We have noted some of the difficulties that rights s.s. pose for the justification of the practice of rights. In the abbreviation we have used several times, they do a good deal *for A,* but they also do a great deal *to B.* Although perhaps in principle justifiable on the ground that the *B*s in one situation can be the *A*s in another, in practice the availability of mechanisms that create such rights reinforces and augments sharp inequalities in wealth, status, and power. If this is the case, and taking account of the great advantages rights s.s. give the *A*s over the *B*s, it seems likely that the distribution and perhaps even the net "quantity" of such desiderata as individual autonomy of action will suffer from the availability of these rights and rights-creating mechanisms. This seems to be especially true in respect to property rights. Particularly in industrialized and postindustrial economies, such rights have facilitated and protected private accumulations of social goods vastly beyond what is necessary to the kind of individual autonomy or independence celebrated by writers in the tradition of civic individualism. These accumulations, moreover, adversely affect the possibility of independence on the part of the great numbers of people who do not themselves acquire them and who may in fact end up with less than they otherwise might because the accumulations are protected by the practice of rights. It seems difficult to deny that the gross and very well-protected inequalities of wealth in such contemporary societies as Canada, Great Britain, France, and the United States create powerful disincentives and pose significant obstacles to active political participation on the part of large numbers of people. When Aristotle argued that the citizen must be assured of the material necessities of life, he did not have in mind the incredible and indeed vulgar accumulations of a Ken-

nedy or a Rockefeller, a Macmillan or a Lord Home, a Roth-
schild or a Chaban-Delmas. Indeed Aristotle's discussions of the
destructive consequences of radical inequalities of wealth for a
civic individualist society remain among the most instructive
statements available to us.[2]

It would of course be superficial to suggest that the availability of rights s.s. to private property is the sole or even the
primary source of such inequalities or their consequences. But
features of the conception of a right as it has evolved in modern
political practice do complicate and otherwise augment the
difficulties we have been discussing. Some of the most prominent
features of the practice of rights – for example, the stringency
that attaches to the obligation to respect rights and the understanding that rights are self-administered – are important in
this connection. Massive, overbearing accumulations of wealth
are more difficult to reduce or even to regulate because doing
so involves an attack on a practice that not only comands wide
acceptance but seems to provide one of the most highly favored
and successful conceptualizations and political rhetorics.

Interestingly enough, recent tendencies to widen – indeed
inflate – the use of the concept of a right are paralleled by
modest developments in the direction of restricting and modi-
fying its use in respect to rights s.s. to certain types of private
property. There is now some recognition, for example, that
allowing a person, a corporation, a labor union, or any other
private party the kind of control that property rights bestow
over seashore or other recreationally attractive land has consequences for the lives of the entire populace that are simply not
acceptable.[3] Similarly, it has been recognized that works of art
and other irreplaceable treasures ought not to be unqualifiedly
at the disposal of private persons simply because they have
amassed sufficient wealth to acquire rights s.s. to them. In some
cases such lines of thought have led, quite rightly, to entirely
withdrawing the social goods in question from the realm of
private property – that is, to expropriation and public ownership. But there has also begun an effort to modify the use, and
hence the implications, of the notion of a right. Thus persons

can acquire a kind of ownership of treasured works of art, of sea or lakeshore property, and so on, but their rights in respect to these particular Xs do not include destruction, alienation to foreigners, control of access, and so forth to the degree that proprety rights s.s. have traditionally involved.

We will not attempt to describe or assess these developments in any detail. But one striking feature of the discussions concerning them deserves comment in the present context. So far as the present writer is aware, these discussions have thus far given little or no attention to the consequences of rights s.s. for the political arrangements and values that are prominent in civic individualism and that continue to cluster, albeit loosely and weakly, around the concept of citizenship. If rights s.s. should be restricted or modified in order to protect and increase access to art treasures and recreational opportunities or to protect the physical environment that we all must share, is there not a case for restrictions and modifications designed to protect, encourage, and facilitate the widest and most meaningful participation in the political dimensions of our lives together? Is not citizenship in something approaching the Aristotelian or Rousseauist sense a sufficiently significant value to justify alterations in the primarily economic and social aspects of the practice of rights?

The mere fact that the process of political decision making has such profound effects on economic and social arrangements suggests, at least from the perspective of the liberal principle, an affirmative answer to these questions. This suggestion is appreciably strengthened if the question is approached from a stance sympathetic to the central contentions of civic individualism – for example, that the activities distinctive of the role of citizen deserve to be placed among the most valuable aspects of membership in a social order. If the meaning and value of the role of citizen are now diminished by an institution (private property) originally justified because it enhanced them, anyone partial to the original justification will be disposed to seek modifications in present forms of that institution.

The great problem, of course, is to know just what modifica-

tions to enter. Democratic socialists have contended for a substantially enlarged sector of public ownership together with a
variety of strongly redistributive policies designed to reduce the
accumulations of those forms of wealth not actually taken over
by the state. Commonly accompanied by a strong emphasis on
the importance of citizenship and the liberties that protect the
citizen's role, at the theoretical level this position is clearly
consonant with the spirit animating many of the arguments of
this work.[4] Some considerable experience, however, has raised
serious doubts as to whether the accumulations *produced* by
following social democratic policies, accumulations directly
protected by the authority of the state rather than by individual
rights s.s. to private property, are in fact markedly favorable to
the values of the liberal principle and strongly participatory
citizenship. These doubts are yet better grounded as regards
more emphatically communitarian or otherwise collectivistic
recommendations.

Further experimentation with modifications in the concept
of a right s.s. to private property may hold promise, particularly
modifications that reduce without altogether eliminating the
control such rights give the *A*s over the *B*s. If combined with
tax policies and other measures that redistribute existing accumulations and limit new ones, such modifications might permit maintenance of the kind of individual material independence that civic individualists have always thought necessary
while avoiding the massive and destructive inequalities to
which the availability of rights s.s. to private property have
contributed.

These suggestions will not be refined or developed here. In
addition to the reasons for tentativeness already mentioned, it
is not obvious that a study of the practice of rights is a suitable
platform from which to launch prescriptions about such sweeping, intricate, and deeply contested issues. We have presented a
brief discussion of some of the issues in question because there
are important connections and reciprocal influences between
them and the practice of rights. More particularly, we have
taken these matters up out of the belief that the considerations

we have found most relevant to reasoning about the practice of rights are also highly pertinent to the resolution of yet wider questions concerning the distribution of wealth, status, and power in contemporary societies. Although these matters are by no means reducible to issues about citizenship, that role will certainly deteriorate further if questions about other forms of wealth, status, and power are decided without explicit concern for it.

Notes

Introduction

1 Robert Nozick, *Anarchy, State, and Utopia* (New York: Basic Books, 1974). This spirited work became available only after the main arguments of this book were completed. I will note a few parallels and disagreements, but I will not attempt to respond in detail to Nozick's formulations.

2 It is a somewhat surprising feature of Professor Nozick's work that the name of Hobbes – or this argument of Hobbes' – never makes an appearance in it.

3 See Sir Robert Filmer, *Patriarcha and Other Political Works*, ed. Peter Laslett (Oxford: Blackwell, 1949), pp. 185–231, 241–51; Peter Winch, "Man and Society in Hobbes and Rousseau," in Maurice Cranston and Richard Peters, eds., *Hobbes and Rousseau* (Garden City, N.Y.: Doubleday, Anchor Books, 1972).

4 See esp. Edmund Burke, *Reflections on the Revolution in France*, ed. Thomas H. D. Mahoney (Indianapolis: Bobbs-Merrill, 1955), pp. 30–9, 55–73, 98–120, 194–218.

5 See T. H. Green, *Lectures on the Principles of Political Obligation* (London: Longman, 1941), esp. pp. 1–25, 60–7, 121–53; F. H. Bradley, *Ethical Studies* (Oxford: Clarendon Press, 1876), esp. essays I, V, and VII; Bernard Bosanquet, *The Philosophical Theory of the State* (London: Macmillan, 1923), esp. pp. 60–78, 180–212, 296–334.

6 See Emile Durkheim, *The Division of Labor in Society*, trans. George Simpson (New York: Free Press, 1933), esp. pp. 329–52, 374–411; Emile Durkheim, *Suicide*, trans. John A. Spaulding and George Simpson, ed. George Simpson (New York: Free Press, 1951), esp. pp. 37–9, 297–320; George Herbert Mead, *Mind, Self and Society*, ed. Charles W. Morris (Chicago: University of Chicago Press, 1934), pp. 1–8, 222–26, 328–36.

7 F. H. Bradley, *op. cit.*, p. 174.

8 See, for example, Alasdair MacIntyre, *Against the Self-images of the Age* (New York: Schocken Books, 1971), pp. 282–83.

9 The second of these concepts is explained in Chapter 9, the first and last of these concepts are explained in detail in a discussion in Chapter 10.

Chapter 1

1 David Easton, *A Systems Analysis of Political Life* (New York: Wiley, 1965), esp. pp. 6–33, 471–91.

2 These latter concepts are among the most important and complex of those that concern us in this study. The discussion at this point will do no more than anticipate later more detailed treatments. See especially Chs. 5, 7, and 8.

3 For something of an exception in regard to logical necessities, see the discussion of constitutive rules in Chapter 5.

4 Aristotle, *Nicomachean Ethics*, trans. W. D. Ross, in Richard McKeon, ed., *The Basic Works of Aristotle* (New York: Random House, 1968), Bk. I, Ch. 3, 4. Also, Aristotle, *Metaphysics, ibid.*, Bk. E (VI), Ch. 1.

5 Ludwig Wittgenstein, *Philosophical Investigations,* trans. G. E. M. Anscombe (New York: Macmillan, 1953). For a discussion of language games see especially Part I, Sec. 21–24, pp. 10e–12e and Sec. 41–75, pp. 20e–35e. On forms of life see Part I, Sec. 19–23, pp. 8e–12e, Sec. 241, p. 88e, and Part II, p. 174e, 226e.

6 *Ibid.,* I, 23 p. 11e.

7 Ludwig Wittgenstein, *On Certainty,* ed. G. E. M. Anscombe and G. H. von Wright, trans. Denis Paul and G. E. M. Anscombe (Oxford: Blackwell, 1969) 204, p. 28e. Italics in original.

8 Ludwig Wittgenstein, *Philosophical Investigations, op. cit.,* II, XI, p. 203e.

9 The foregoing discussion draws directly and liberally upon the introduction to my *Concepts in Social and Political Philosophy* (New York: Macmillan, 1973).

10 See Peter Winch, *The Idea of a Social Science* (London: Routledge and Kegan Paul, 1958), esp. Chs. 1, 2.

11 Talcott Parsons, Edward Shils, et al., *Toward a General Theory of Action* (Cambridge, Mass.: Harvard University Press, 1959), pp. 28–9.

Chapter 2

1 Alexis de Tocqueville, *Democracy in America*, trans. George Lawrence, ed. J. P. Mayer (Garden City, N.Y.: Doubleday, 1969), esp. pp. 235–45, 676–700. Also, Judith Shklar, *Legalism* (Cambridge, Mass.: Harvard University Press, 1964), pp. 13–20.

2 Leo Strauss, *Natural Right and History* (Chicago: University of Chicago Press, 1953).

3 See, for example, Karl Marx, "On the Jewish Question," in Lloyd D. Easton and Kurt H. Guddat, eds., *Writings of the Young Marx on Philosophy and Society* (Garden City, N.Y.: Doubleday, Anchor Books, 1967), pp. 231–40. Also, Friedrich Engels, "Herr Eugen Duhring's Revolution in Science," in Karl Marx and Friedrich Engels, *Basic Writings on Politics and Philosophy,*

ed. Lewis S. Feuer (Garden City, N.Y.: Doubleday, Anchor Books, 1959), pp. 273–78.

4 See Wesley N. Hohfeld, *Fundamental Legal Conceptions,* ed. W. W. Cook (New Haven: Yale University Press, 1919).

5 Thomas Hobbes, *Leviathan* (New York: Collier Books, 1962), p. 103.

6 *Ibid.*

7 *Ibid.,* p. 104.

8 Readers familiar with H. L. A. Hart's important article "Are There Any Natural Rights?" *Philosophical Review,* Vol. 64 (1955), pp. 175–91 will recognize that the foregoing discussion of liberties is both indebted to and in disagreement with Professor Hart's argument. Hart distinguishes between *special* and *general* rights. The former are created by specific transactions such as contracts, promises, and so on. Most special rights are rights in the strict sense in the terminology of Hohfeld's schema and hence involve obligations on *B*'s part. General rights do not arise out of such transactions. They are held by all persons capable of choice and they are usually asserted defensively, that is, "when some unjustified interference is made or threatened" (*ibid.,* p. 183). General rights look most like liberties as we have interpreted the latter category, especially liberties asserted against private persons rather than persons in authority. If there is more than a terminological difference between Hart's analysis of the logic of general rights and the present analysis of liberties, it is that Hart argues that general rights do involve obligation on the part of the *B*s, namely, the obligation not to interfere with the exercise of such rights by the *A*s. If this way of talking means no more than that the *B*s have an obligation to respect these rights, I have no very strong objection to it. Care must be taken, however, to distinguish between the obligation (if that is the way to label it) to respect rights in all senses of the term and the specific obligations that correlate with particular rights s.s. There does seem to be an advantage to Hohfeld's distinction between the no-rights that correlate with liberties and the obligations that correlate with rights s.s. Hart's own analysis of *obligation* as a rule-dependent concept" (see his *The Concept of Law* [London: Oxford University Press, 1961]) would seem to recommend this conclusion. (On this point see also Ronald M. Dworkin, "The Model of Rules," *The University of Chicago Law Review,* Vol. 35, No. 1 [Autumn 1967]. Dworkin criticizes Hart for failing to distinguish between rules and principles. From this perspective there is a principle according to which it is morally incumbent to respect liberties and other rights; there are rules that define obligations that correlate with rights s.s.)

In regard to justifying rights, the differences between Hart's argument and the present one center on the differences between what we are calling the liberal principle and what Hart calls the natural right to equal freedom. Both would provide a measure of protection for autonomous individual action. The liberal principle does so in that it treats having, acting upon, and satisfying interests and desires, objectives and purposes as a prima facie good. On this view, any interferences with actions taken in the pursuit of interests, desires, and so on, need justification because they diminish the realization of the good that the principle identifies. Interference can be justified if it leads to a greater good than would be achieved by the action interfered with. This view presupposes that interests and desires, objectives and purposes can be ranked and that, for example, rights can be assigned, interpreted, and so on, on the basis of those rankings. All interests, desires, and so on, are valuable, but some are, as a generalization, more valuable than others and some are more valuable than others in particular circumstances. In all but the simplest situations, in other words, justifications for particular rights must consider the content of the interests, desires, and so on, that are in conflict. Hart's doctrine, by contrast, protects a realm of individual action by treating the freedom to act without interference as itself the most fundamental right. Justification for this right can properly make no reference to the characteristics of the particular action taken (hence make no reference to any alleged *good* realized by taking that action). Those interferences with freedom of action, effected by *A* in the course of exercising "special" rights, can be justified if and *only* if the "special" right is consistent with the natural right to equal freedom, and this condition is satisfied if and only if the special right is created by *B*'s exercise of the natural right, that is, only if *B* has in some way agreed to *A*'s special rights. Justifications for rights, in short, are entirely independent of the content (including therein the consequences) of the actions that they warrant; they refer exclusively to the procedures by which the rights are created.

The differences between the two arguments are instances of the differences between deontological and teleological theories. As with all natural rights and contractarian arguments, Hart's deontological position appears to have advantages in accounting for and defending two prominent features of rights and the practice thereof, their stringency and the powerful concern they display over the ways in which rights are and should be distributed among the individual members of whatever population is in question. The present, broadly utilitarian, version of a teleological argument has advantages in accounting for and defending the ways in which rights are in fact created, exercised, and interpreted, particularly the fact that rights are a social practice and that the creation, and interpretation of particular rights are activities performed by, and affecting, societies, not just individuals. We are concerned with the advantages and disadvantages of these competing views at various junctures in the following discussion. (See especially Chapters 7, 8, and 10.) It may emerge, however, that, properly understood, the differences between them are less dramatic and important than has commonly been thought.

9 For a helpful specification of the slippery term *correlate* see David Lyons,

"The Correlativity of Rights and Duties," *NOUS,* Vol. IV (1970), pp. 45–55.
For most commentators it is only usually the case, and not necessary to the
concept of a right s.s., that there be an established means of enforcing the
duty. Rights s.s. can be "imperfect," that is, lacking an established method
of obtaining a remedy for violations on *B*'s part. An example would be
rights against a foreign government such as to collect interest on bonds
issued by that government and held by *A*. *A* has a right s.s. to the interest,
and the government *(B)* has a legal duty to pay him, but there may be no
action by which *A* can obtain enforcement of *B*'s duty.

10 A moral analogue to legal powers might be the following: Jones hears
that Smith is going on vacation and is looking for someone to care for his
dog while he is away. Jones tells Smith he would be glad to do so. Smith
thanks him for his kind offer, says that he had hoped to find someone with
another dog to keep Rover company, but also asks if he may check back
with Jones if it proves impossible to find someone who meets the latter requirement. Jones then promises to take Rover if the need arises and if
Smith wishes. In such a case we might say that Jones' promise gives Smith
a power vis-à-vis Jones and puts Jones under a liability in regard to that
power. If Smith asks Jones to take Rover (i.e., uses the power), Jones'
liability is turned into an obligation. Smith could not have the power and
Jones could not have the liability if moral practice in the society did not
include the institution of promising and did not establish the possibility of
using that institution in the manner described. The moral system, of
course, does not provide for coercive enforcement procedures such as are
available in the law. But if Jones attempts to withdraw the power or
defaults on the obligation when Smith calls upon him to perform, Smith
is warranted in criticizing Jones, perhaps not trusting his promises in the
future, and so on.

11 How extensive powers are thought to be will depend in part on how we
choose to delineate the use of the concept. A narrow definition would be
that *A* has a power if and only if the rules establishing the jural or moral
attribute permit him to alter his own and some other person's or persons'
jural or moral relationships without specific consent or agreement on
their part. In our original example 3(a), for instance, *A*'s power to make
a will bequeathing *X* to *B* can be effectively used without *B*'s consent or
agreement (except perhaps his consent to the legal system in general and
the specific legal rules that establish the power to make wills). Again, in
some jurisdictions landlords have a power periodically to enter apartments
they have rented to *B* without *B*'s specific consent. A wider definition of
power would apply the concept to the right to make contracts that can
be concluded only with the specific consent of *B*. In the narrower sense *B*
is liable to acquire rights and obligations without his consent. In the wider
use *liable* would mean no more than that *B* is liable to have the offer of
a contract tendered but *A*'s tendering it, although it might obligate *A,*

would alter B's jural situation only if he accepted, agreed to, or otherwise consented to enter into the relationship proposed by A's offer.

So far as legal relations are concerned, it is clearly best to restrict *power* to the narrower use. (*Capacity* is sometimes used to mark the wider sense; I have the legal capacity to enter into contracts and similar relationships.) This policy may be best in regard to moral relationships as well, although practice is less uniform in this respect. If I receive an unsolicited invitation to dinner, particularly from a friend or even an acquaintance, I will usually think I have an obligation to accept or reject it. Thus it might be said that the rules of polite conduct (though not of morality in the more serious sense) give A a power to issue invitations and make B liable to receive and to be obligated to respond to such invitations. If this use of *power* and *liability* is accepted, the concepts might have application to a substantial range of interactions, especially among friends and acquaintances. One hopes, of course, that ordinarily B will not feel an obligation based on A's power but *pleasure* at the thought that A has thought to invite him. Any very wide use of *power* and *liability* outside the law would betoken rather formal and unattractive personal relationships.

12 In the Hohfeldian categories one can think of the citizens or subjects of a regime as having liabilities rather than obligations vis-à-vis the authority of the government. The government having authority to enact laws on a particular subject means that the citizens are liable to have their liberty of action (or more generally their jural situation) limited by the enactment of a law (or other form of authoritative measure). It is only when the authority has actually been exercised that the liability becomes an obligation to obey the command (or creates some other jural attribute; e.g., rights, power, or privilege). Describing the relationship in this way is a useful corrective to theories that treat obligation or duty as the invariant correlates of authority.

13 For a more systematic treatment of this line of argument than is appropriate here, see my *Political Obligation*, esp. Chs. 2, 6, 8 (New York: Atheneum, 1972).

14 Liberties form a special case, but even they are often defined by (constitutional) law that establishes limits upon authority and they are enforceable by court decisions.

15 More exactly, such laws are thought to involve rights only by persons operating with highly controversial political theories. On Hart's revised version of the social contract theory, for example, Jones' obligation not to violate laws against reckless driving is owed to the other members of the political society and the latter are said to have a right to Jones' discharge of that obligation (H. L. A. Hart, "Are There Any Natural Rights?" *op. cit.*, pp. 185–6). But note that Jones can be arrested and punished for reckless driving even if no A is harmed by or so much as witnesses Jones' violation. Thus on Hart's theory one must say either that Cs (policemen,

The practice of rights

judges, etc.) have a blanket authorization to exercise the rights of the *A*s on their behalf or that the element of "self-administration" that is usually part of having a right is simply not a necessary part of many of the rights that one has as a member of a political society. It seems preferable to say that Jones has the obligation under the law (as opposed to owing it to other citizens with a correlative right) and that the *C*s have both authority and a duty under law to arrest and punish Jones for his violation.

16 A distinction is often made between immunities and privileges. A privilege is commonly defined as an immunity that is held not by a named person or persons but by some class of persons that is usually of large but indeterminate size and that holds not for a single named or described case but for a class of cases. Thus in the United States the privilege against self-incrimination in criminal trials, barring waiver or grants of immunity to prosecution for the crime in question, is held by all citizens and is available in all criminal cases. On this usage (which is not uniform) immunities are granted to a particular person or persons in situations in which no general privilege is established. For further discussion and examples see Roscoe Pound, *Jurisprudence,* Vol. IV (St. Paul: West Publishing Company, 1959), pp. 126–43.

Of course both *privilege* and *immunity* have wider uses as well, uses that cut across the distinctions among rights s.s., liberties, powers, and immunities. The phrase *privileges and immunities* appears, for example, in Article IV, Section 2, and in Amendment XIV, Section I, of the U.S. Constitution. In the famous Slaughter-House cases (16 Wallace 36, 1873) Mr. Justice Miller interpreted this phrase to give citizens of the United States such "rights" as "to come to the seat of government," "to free access to its (i.e., the Nation's) seaports," "to demand the care and protection of the Federal Government over his life, liberty, and property when on the high seas or within the jurisdiction of a foreign government," and "the right to use the navigable waters of the United States." None of these items can plausibly be interpreted as privileges or immunities in the technical sense in which, following writers in jurisprudence, we are using those terms here. Thus our use of them, as with *rights s.s., liberty,* and so on, is technical, that is, intended to clarify distinctions operative in but not marked by distinct terms of ordinary language.

17 See Roscoe Pound, *ibid.,* pp. 144–7.

18 See Joel Feinberg, "Duties, Rights, and Claims," *American Philosophical Quarterly,* Vol. 3, No. 2 (April 1966), pp. 137–44.

Chapter 3

1 Many of the features of the practice in the international context are surveyed in Vernon Van Dyke, *Human Rights, the United States, and World Community* (New York: Oxford University Press, 1970). For the argument that the concept should be largely avoided in the international

context see, for example, Maurice Cranston, *What Are Human Rights?*
(New York: Basic Books, 1962).
2 See David Hume, *A Treatise of Human Nature,* ed. L. A. Selby-Bigge
(Oxford: Clarendon Press, 1951), pp. 487–91. Also, John Locke, "The Second
Treatise of Civil Government," *Two Treatises of Government,* ed.
Thomas I. Cook (New York: Macmillan, Hafner Press, 1947), Chs. V, IX.
3 Friedrich Engels, "Herr Eugen Duhring's Revolution in Science," in Karl
Marx and Friedrich Engels, *Basic Writings on Politics and Philosophy,*
ed. Lewis S. Feuer (Garden City, N.Y.: Doubleday, Anchor Books, 1959).
4 The question of the kinds of intellectual purchase the analyst can get
on established relationships such as that between *property* and *right* is a
part of large and important philosophical issues. There seems to be an
implication in some recent work that relationships of this type are necessary not only in the sense that, as our language now works, the concept
property implies the concept *right,* but in some deeper, perhaps metaphysical, sense such that this relationship must obtain in any and all
languages and practices. On this view the kind of conceptual analysis we
are attempting is expected to yield not merely accounts of concepts and
practices as they are used at historical times and places but necessary
truths about reality that cannot be questioned without lapsing into some
deep form of incoherence. In their general form the philosophical issues
raised by this view are immense and highly technical. We cannot deal with
them in an adequate manner here and we must rest with references to
examples, such as the example of Locke and Engels, that show that very
fundamental concepts have been coherently questioned and have in fact
changed over time. For a useful introduction to the philosophical issues
and major positions concerning them, see Richard J. Bernstein, *Praxis and
Action,* Part 4, esp. pp. 278–99 (London: Duckworth, 1972; Philadelphia:
The University of Pennsylvania Press, 1971). I have discussed examples of
such views in my *Political Obligation* (New York: Atheneum, 1972), Ch. 3.
See also my review essay "Nature, Convention, and the Study of Man,"
Journal of Politics (July 1973).
5 John Rawls, *A Theory of Justice* (Cambridge, Mass.: Harvard University
Press, 1971), esp. Chs. I–V.
6 David Hume, "Of the Original Contract," *Essays, Moral, Political, and
Literary,* Part II (London: Oxford University Press, 1963).
7 In his subtle elaboration of the contractarian position, Professor Rawls
concedes that social institutions, and an understanding of them, are presupposed by the reflections concerning justice and rights that yield identification of and "agreement" to the principles that provide the proper content
of those concepts (Rawls, *A Theory of Justice, op. cit.,* pp. 118–60). In this
sense he concedes the social character of rights and hence many of the
standard objections to contractarian theories do not apply to his version.
Rawls nevertheless insists that reflections about the principles of justice

and rights must take place behind a "Veil of Ignorance" concerning any particular set of social institutions and this or that person's relationship to them. One knows about society but not about this or that society or one's place in it. Of course much of the time we too are talking about the practice of rights in abstraction from details of particular social arrangements. But it is one thing to abstract from empirical detail for analytic purposes, another to treat such detail as logically or morally inappropriate to reflections about what the principles of justice and rights ought to be. Most generally put, a question that arises about Rawls' elaborate construct is whether, given the "Veil of Ignorance," the conditions necessary to the cogent use of such concepts as *rights, justice, social institution, self-interest,* and *good* are satisfied for discourse within it.

8 Third-party beneficiaries are persons who come to have a right by virtue of arrangements concluded among two or more parties other than themselves. To take a standard type of example, if Peters promises Jones that he will let Jones' colleague Smith live in his house while he (Peters) is abroad, Smith acquires a right to live in Peters' house. For a discussion of some of the complexities of this type of case, see H. L. A. Hart, "Are There Any Natural Rights?" *Philosophical Review*, Vol. 64 (1955), pp. 175–91; David Lyons, "Rights, Claimants, and Beneficiaries," *American Philosophical Quarterly*, Vol. 6 (1969), pp. 173–85; and Joel Feinberg, "Duties, Rights and Claims," *American Philosophical Quarterly*, Vol. 3 (1966), pp. 137–44.

9 See, for example, John Rodman, "The Ecological Perspective and Political Theory," The American Political Science Association, 1971; Christopher Stone, *Should Trees Have Standing: Toward Legal Rights for Natural Objects* (Los Altos, Calif.: William Kaufmann, 1974).

10 Reprinted in Maurice Cranston, *What Are Human Rights?* (New York: Basic Books, 1962).

11 Of course the preamble of the Declaration states that it is intended "as a common standard of achievement for all peoples and all nations" that is to be kept "constantly in mind" so as to "secure . . . universal and effective recognition and observance" of the rights declared in the document *(ibid.)*. Thus it appears that the Declaration, as perhaps has been true of other statements of human or natural rights, should be read as the enunciation of an ideal to which mankind should aspire. We may debate whether it is desirable to put the concept of rights to such a use. What is beyond doubt is that the logic of such uses is systematically different from the uses we have been explicating and that it is essential to understand the differences. Most important, in such uses the concept loses its stringency, that is, the clear implication that the *A*s are entitled to the *X*s in question and that it is wrong to fail to respect these rights.

12 For a more detailed discussion of this question, see my *Political Obligation, op. cit.,* esp. Chs. 2–5.

13 Jean-Jacques Rousseau, *The Social Contract,* trans. G. D. H. Cole, (New York: Dutton, 1950), p. 4.

14 *Ibid.,* pp. 15–19, 26–28.

15 J. Rawls, *A Theory of Justice, op. cit.,* pp. 111–4.

Chapter 4

1 The same situation sometimes obtains in domains that involve authority but not legal authority. For example, it is sometimes clear that teachers in private schools, union shop stewards, office supervisors, and so on, have a duty to intervene if the rights of one student, union member, or employee are threatened by another.

2 See James M. Ratcliff, ed., *The Good Samaritan and the Law* (Garden City, N.Y.: Doubleday, Anchor Books, 1966).

3 Later we take up the argument that the practice of rights is an unfortunate part of our social arrangements precisely because it encourages excessive individualism and excessive faith in one's own capacity to defend one's interests, and hence contributes to a fragmented society in which social cohesion and mutual support are dangerously lacking. See especially Chapter 9.

4 There is at least one respect in which we must qualify the contention that the role of *D* is largely indeterminate. In a number of contemporary societies and for a considerable range of questions, the role has been largely taken over by organizations that specialize in protecting certain rights. Outstanding examples would again be such organizations as the ACLU and the NAACP. Aside from immediate responses to direct face-to-face situations, large numbers of *D*s in these societies limit their personal role to financial or other forms of support of these groups. Such organizations have evolved criteria by which they decide when and how to intervene in response to encroachments upon rights. These criteria could presumably be described and such a description would be a good start toward a more detailed account of the role definition accepted by a large number of the active *D*s in the area of the practice of rights in which the organizations act.

5 We have talked of rights as held and exercised within practices but our attempt to delineate the boundaries of any example of such a practice has been limited to our discussion of the characteristics necessary for the various roles of which such practices consist. The question "Who are the *C*s (and especially the) *D*s vis-à-vis this *X*?" is in effect the question of how to draw the outer limits of the practice in which *X* is held and exercised.

6 For a particularly striking example from a context of well-established rules, see the U.S. Supreme Court case of *Screws* v. *U.S.* (325 U.S. 91) and especially the opinion of Mr. Justice Frankfurter in that case. Fundamental rights had clearly been violated and the U.S. government definitely had authority to punish the violation. Frankfurter nevertheless argued that the

matter should be left to the state government in question (Georgia). He reasoned that primary responsibility for protecting the rights in question must in any case remain with the state not the federal government, and that federal intervention in this case or that would only weaken the sense of responsibility among state officials and hence in the long run weaken the rights in question. In the terms we have used here, Frankfurter viewed the state as the locus of a distinct practice and he wanted to preserve the integrity of that practice – integrity that he thought would be threatened by outside intervention.

7 The right to petition for redress of grievances, which can be used to protect the rights of others as well as one's own rights, might be considered an exception to our last remark. The existence of such a right works like a rule granting authority in that it is, tautologically, a necessary condition of the kind of intervention called petitioning for redress of grievances. But persons who exercise this right are *A*s, not *C*s or *D*s. It is exactly the point about *D*s that the conventions and doctrines under color of which they intervene give them neither authority nor a right to do so. The conventions and doctrines may provide a justification for intervention, but it is of a different – and usually weaker – sort than the justification provided by authority or a right.

Chapter 5

1 Similar premises have led one writer to the conclusion that "all specifically human behavior . . . is *ipso facto* rule-governed." Peter Winch, *The Idea of a Social Science* (London: Routledge and Kegan Paul, 1958).

2 It is true that locutions such as "I have a right to *X*" are sometimes used in trying to win acceptance of a rule that would establish a right to that *X*. This is an important fact because it helps to put the whole notion of rule-governed practices in proper perspective. We return to it at the end of this chapter.

We should perhaps also note the argument that there is no such thing as nonlegal rights; that we use (the noun) *right* only of *X*s that are established in law. This position is argued by David Braybrooke in his *Three Tests for Democracy* (New York: Random House, 1968), pp. 31–35. But Braybrooke immensely inflates the concept *legal* in order to accommodate apparently nonlegal rights.

3 See my *Political Obligation* (New York: Atheneum, 1972), esp. Ch. 3.

4 *Ibid.*, esp. Introduction, Ch. 3, and *passim*.

5 None of these complications, we should say at once, affect the truth of the remark that many rights are created and defined by legal rules or of the generalization that the practice of rights is legalistic. But they do begin to suggest the many dimensions of legal rules and the correspondingly complex character of the modes of thought and action that have been denominated *legalism*. Such generalizations make a limited contribution to

our understanding of the practice if these dimensions and complexities have not been identified.

6 See, for example, Maurice Cranston, "Human Rights, Real and Supposed," in D. D. Raphael, ed., *Political Theory and the Rights of Man* (Bloomington: Indiana University Press, 1967), esp. pp. 43ff, and the same author's *What Are Human Rights?* (New York: Basic Books, 1962).

7 For a pertinent discussion of diverse judicial philosophies, see Wallace Mendelson, *Justices Black and Frankfurter: Conflict in the Court* (Chicago: University of Chicago Press, 1961), esp. pp. 51–60, on the question of freedom of speech.

Chapter 6

1 See Max Weber, *The Theory of Social and Economic Organization,* trans. A. M. Henderson and Talcott Parsons, ed. Talcott Parsons (New York: Free Press, 1947), pp. 328–9.

2 The degree to which the As control their rights, and hence the extent to which having rights in effect authorizes the As to act in a self-regarding and even selfish and imperious manner, has been a recurrent theme among critics of particular rights and of the practice of rights as such. The works of Charles Dickens, for example, are well supplied with rich and powerful As who hold weak and impoverished Bs to the full extent of their obligations vis-à-vis the property rights of the As. Recall also the familiar charge that such rights as freedom of speech, press, and association have provided the enemies of democratic regimes with authorizations to act to destroy the latter.

3 On this point see Richard B. Friedman, "On the Concept of Authority in Political Philosophy," in Richard E. Flathman, ed., *Concepts of Social and Political Philosophy* (New York: Macmillan, 1973), pp. 121–45.

4 On the question of the waiver of right to counsel, see *Gideon* v. *Wainwright* (372 U.S. 335, 83 S.Ct. 792 (1963), and *Powell* v. *Alabama* (287 U.S. 45, 53 S.Ct. 55 [1932]). On the issue of privileges of the accused, see especially *Miranda* v. *Arizona* (384 U.S. 436, 86 S.Ct. 1602 [1966]). Of course, the Bill of Rights enumerates a number of rights that law enforcement officials are required to respect.

5 This is one of the distinctions between rights and what, in a sense slightly different than the Hohfeldian, are often called privileges. Certain privileges, for example, holding a driver's license, can be revoked or suspended if the holder misuses them. It is also true that in some jurisdictions rights can be taken away as a punishment for certain crimes. Moreover, it is possible that one could be punished in this manner for a crime committed in the belief that the action in question was within the scope of a right. Someone who did not know the legal limits of self-help might commit a crime by using excessive force against a trespasser or assailant. But neither this nor any other case provides an example of being punished for the exercise

of a right. The latter is nonsensical except when used metaphorically.

6 See especially Alasdair MacIntyre, *Secularization and Moral Change* (London: Oxford University Press), pp. 54–7.

7 It is worth noting the parallels between the *in-authority–an authority* distinction and Max Weber's distinction between *rational-legal* and *charismatic* types of authority. Owing to the personal qualities ("gift of grace") attributed to charismatic authorities, their followers believe that their actions and decisions, substantively speaking, are good and right and should be accepted and obeyed. We might say that having authority of the charismatic type is more like having a right than having authority in the in-authority sense. But the belief in the rightness of the actions of such authorities is, according to Weber, so strong that the whole idea of rules defining and limiting their right of command is thought to be inappropriate (Weber, *op. cit.*, pp. 359–60). Because the concept of a right is dependent on the concept of rules creating and defining the right, it would be misleading to subsume pure cases of charismatic authority under this rubric.

8 John Stuart Mill, "On Liberty," in *Utilitarianism, Liberty, and Representative Government* (New York: Dutton, 1951), pp. 176–9.

9 See Article 125 of the Constitution of the Soviet Union.

Chapter 7

1 These two views seem to be combined, at least as regards so-called natural rights, in H. L. A. Hart's influential article "Are There Any Natural Rights?" *Philosophical Review*, Vol. 64 (1955), pp. 175–91. This article might be viewed as a kind of culmination of the tradition that links rights and freedom.

2 For a survey and assessment of recent treatments of this distinction, see Hanna Pitkin, *Wittgenstein and Justice* (Berkeley: University of California Press, 1972), Chs. VII, XI, and XII.

3 H. L. A. Hart, *op. cit.*, p. 178.

4 J. L. Austin, "A Plea for Excuses," in *Philosophical Papers* (London: Oxford University Press, 1961), p. 128.

5 *Ibid.*

6 See especially S. I. Benn and W. L. Weinstein, "Being Free to Act and Being a Free Man," *Mind*, Vol. 80 (1971), pp. 194–211.

7 Joel Feinberg, "Action and Responsibility," in Max Black, ed., *Philosophy in America* (London: Allen and Unwin, 1964), p. 144.

8 There is, however, another side to the coin of this point to which we return shortly. If B thinks that A's doing X is contrary to his interests, then protecting A's freedom to do X will necessarily involve restricting B's freedom to act so as to prevent A from doing X. Protecting A's freedom to do X by according a right to do it always involves interfering with B's freedom. Thus the decision to accord a right is always a decision to choose one

freedom over another. This being the case, it is evident that the decision to accord the right cannot be sufficiently defended in terms of the value of freedom *simpliciter*. Some further principle or criterion must be adduced in terms of which one can justify the choice between or among freedoms.

9 See, for example, Thomas Paine, "The Rights of Man," in Philip S. Foner, ed., *The Complete Writings of Thomas Paine* (New York: Citadel Press, 1945), esp. Vol. 1, pp. 273–9.

Chapter 8

1 See, for example, A. I. Melden, *Rights and Right Conduct* (Oxford: Blackwell, 1959).

2 See, for example, Edmond Cahn, ed., *The Great Rights* (New York: Macmillan, 1963).

3 See Edmund Burke, *Reflections on the French Revolution* (London: Dent, 1950), esp. pp. 54–60.

4 See especially T. H. Green, *Lectures on the Principles of Political Obligation* (New York: Longman, 1917), pp. 40–41.

5 This point is made by Kant in his *Metaphysical Elements of Justice*, trans. John Ladd (New York: Library of Liberal Arts, 1965), pp. 36–7, 64–5, 76–8), and is emphasized by Hegel in his *Philosophy of Right*, trans. T. M. Knox (London: Oxford University Press, 1952), pp. 103–10, 134–5, 155–60.

6 Peter Nichols' play *A Day in the Death of Joe Egg* illustrates these points in a deeply distressing way.

7 See, for example, B. F. Skinner, *Beyond Freedom and Dignity* (New York: Bantam Books, 1972).

8 See especially Norman O. Brown, *Life Against Death* (Middletown, Conn.: Wesleyan University Press, 1959), and Herbert Marcuse, *Eros and Civilization* (Boston: Beacon Press, 1966).

9 The most ingenious of a number of recent attempts along these lines has been made by Alan Gewirth. See his several recent essays, especially "The Justification of Egalitarian Justice," *American Philosophical Quarterly*, Vol. 8, No. 4 (October 1967).

10 For an elaboration of this argument, see the introduction to Part V of my *Concepts of Social and Political Philosophy* (New York; Macmillan, 1973), and my paper "Equality and Generalization: A Formal Analysis," reprinted in the same volume.

11 See Phillipa Foot, especially "Goodness and Choice," *Proceedings of the Aristotelian Society*, Suppl. Vol. XXXV (1961); "Moral Beliefs," *Proceedings of the Aristotelian Society*, Vol. 59 (1958–9), pp. 83–104; "Moral Arguments," *Mind*, Vol. LXVII (1958), pp. 102–13.

12 On this last point see especially Peter Winch, *Ethics and Action* (London: Routledge and Kegan Paul, 1972), essays 7–11.

13 I will not attempt to refine or to defend the metaethical theory implicit in the argument of this chapter. (Some elements of that theory are discussed

in Chapter 1.) As note 11 indicates, the argument is influenced by recent versions of naturalism in that it treats features of established conceptualizations as appropriate starting points for moral reasoning. Thus I attempt to derive a normative principle (the liberal principle) in part from conceptual *facts*. As indicated in the text, however, I do not view these – or any other – conceptual facts as logically, morally, or in any other way beyond question. For the reasons given, I am accepting and arguing in part from certain features of ordinary language. In the context of some other investigation it might be necessary to subject those same features to a kind of critical scrutiny not judged to be necessary here. To do so it would be necessary to accept and hold constant some other features of ordinary language, that is, those other features that are used in the course of scrutinizing the concepts here held constant. (Cf. John Searle, *Speech Acts* (London: Cambridge University Press, 1969), esp. p. 186n. I do assume that such ratiocinative activities allow of interpersonally valid results. Saying even this much about metaethical issues, however, renders inescapable one further comment on an issue about the liberal principle that is raised by concepts such as murder and cruelty. It is pretty clearly a conceptual fact that murder and cruelty are wrong. Although occasionally excused or justified, ordinary practice does treat these actions as *malum en se,* that is, holds them and reasons for taking them to be prima facie evil. Thus an account of practice that proceeds from conceptual facts must recognize a qualification of the liberal principle in respect to them.

It is tempting, and in reason not implausible, to avoid qualifying the liberal principle by arguing that these actions are condemned by the principle itself. To murder someone is certainly to deny him that consideration of his interests and desires demanded by the liberal principle. It is unlikely, however, that such reasoning is in fact behind the conceptual facts in question. Thus the preceding argument relies on the small degree of open texture that excusing, justifying, and other casuistic procedures display in *murder* and *cruelty* in order to maximize the congruence between the liberal principle and the relevant conceptual facts. But it must be admitted that the argument is a recommendation that the conceptual facts change in the respect under discussion. (Which is *not* to say that it is an argument for murder and cruelty! As stressed earlier, commitment to an unqualified liberal principle is no barrier to showing that the prima facie good of having and acting upon interests and desires is virtually always rebutted in respect to the interest or desire to murder or to be cruel. The issue is not whether murder and cruelty are wrong, it is how best to reason to that conclusion and how to coordinate that reasoning with reflection about related moral issues.)

14 It is not clear that this is more than a terminological difference with H. L. A. Hart's version of the natural rights position. Hart's argument is primarily a deduction from features of rights talk, and it is not clear that the terms *nature* and *natural* play any very definite or important role in it.

15 The present argument is importantly similar to the argument of S. I. Benn's paper, "Egalitarianism and the Equal Consideration of Interests," in Richard Flathman, ed., *Concepts in Social and Political Philosophy,* *op. cit.*

Chapter 9

1 Useful and highly sympathetic accounts of writers who have stressed community and who have been suspicious of or hostile to individualism in general and individual rights in particular are available in the works of Robert A. Nisbet. See especially his *The Sociological Tradition* (New York: Basic Books, 1966). See also W. C. McWilliams, *The Idea of Fraternity in America* (Berkeley: University of California Press, 1973). For a helpful discussion of the analytic problems in discussing community, see John Ladd, "The Concept of Community: A Logical Analysis," in Carl J. Friedrich, ed., *Community* (Nomos II) (New York: Liberal Arts Press, 1959).

2 See, for example, William Kornhauser, *The Politics of Mass Society* (New York: Free Press, 1959); Hannah Arendt, *The Origins of Totalitarianism* (New York: Harcourt Brace Jovanovich, 1968).

3 See, for example, Otto Gierke, *Political Theories of the Middle Age,* trans. Frederic William Maitland (Cambridge: Cambridge University Press, 1951); Otto Gierke, *Natural Law and the Theory of Society,* trans. Ernest Barker (Boston: Beacon Press, 1957).

4 Karl Marx, "The British Rule in India," quoted in Robert A. Nisbet, *op. cit.*, p. 68. See also the passage quoted on the following page in which, as Nisbet comments, Marx makes it clear that he had no higher regard for the guilds, corporations, and other allegedly communitarian units of medieval European societies.

5 Cited in *ibid.*, p. 36.

6 Participants in the several types of communes that have sprung up in the United States and other Western countries in the 1960s and 1970s seem to have a well-developed appreciation of the first of these two considerations. Although explicitly in quest of a greater degree of community than conventional social relationships in these societies involve, most participants in these communes insist that they enter voluntarily and have a right to leave at will. In part because they very regularly exercise the latter right, most of these communes have been short-lived.

7 See, for example, Hegel, *The Philosophy of Rights,* trans. T. M. Knox (London: Oxford University Press, 1952); Alexis de Tocqueville, *Democracy in America,* trans. George Lawrence, ed. J. P. Mayer (Garden City, N.Y.: Doubleday, 1969); Ernest Barker, *Principles of Social and Political Theory* (Oxford: Oxford University Press, 1951), esp. pp. 268–79; and *Church, State, and Education* (Ann Arbor: University of Michigan Press, 1957), esp. pp. 151–71.

8 For a very helpful discussion of the role of the family in societies that include a vigorous practice of rights, see Eli Zaretsky, *Capitalism, The*

Family and Personal Life (Santa Cruz: Loaded Press, n.d., originally published in *Socialist Revolution,* January–June 1973).

9 See Kay Scholzman, *Americans and Youth Dissent* (unpublished doctoral dissertation, University of Chicago, 1973).

Chapter 10

1 My thinking about this distinction has been influenced by the work of J. G. A. Pocock. See especially his magistral *The Machiavellian Moment: Florentine Political Thought and the Atlantic Republican Tradition* (Princeton: Princeton University Press, 1974).

2 Professor Nozick's recent statement expresses this view with unequaled insistence. See especially the "eldritch tale" spun in Ch. 9, "Demoktesis" of *Anarchy, State, and Utopia* (New York: Basic Books, 1974).

3 Nozick makes virtually the same argument. See *ibid.,* p. 272.

4 See especially Pocock, *op. cit.,* particularly the statement at pp. 66–75.

5 See especially Aristotle, *Politics,* Bk. III, 1274b 32–1275, 1277a–1278a.

6 See, for example, J. L. Talmon, *The Origins of Totalitarian Democracy* (London: Seecker and Warburg, 1952).

7 J. J. Rousseau, *The Social Contract,* trans. G. D. H. Cole (New York: Dutton, 1950), Book I, Ch. VIII, p. 18.

8 *Ibid.,* p. 106.

9 Aristotle, *Politics, op. cit.* Bk. III, 1277b.

10 Karl Marx, "Critique of the Gotha Program," in Karl Marx and Friedrich Engels, *Basic Writings on Politics and Philosophy,* ed. Lewis S. Feuer (Garden City, N.Y.: Doubleday, Anchor Books, 1959), pp. 126–29. This aspect of Marx's thinking has been strongly emphasized by recent interpretations, particularly those that stress the "humanistic" side of Marx and insist that all forms of Stalinism are totally without support from Marx's writings.

Appendix

1 See Aristotle, *Politics,* Bk. III, 1278a–1278b.

2 See *ibid.,* especially Bk. III, 1279b–1281b, Bk. IV, 1294a–1297b.

3 Legal regulation of the development and use of land presents a variety of difficult problems. The right to own and develop land has a fundamental constitutional guarantee; yet recent environmental interest has made it apparent that land use regulation is imperative for a qualitative community life. See, for example, William K. Reilly, ed., *The Use of Land: A Citizen's Policy Guide to Urban Growth* (New York: Crowell, 1973); Richard F. Babcock, *The Zoning Game* (Madison: University of Wisconsin Press, 1966); Oscar S. Gray, "Legal Issues in Environment" (Princeton: Princeton University Council on Environmental Studies, 1972); Charles A. Reich, "The New Property," *Yale Law Journal* (1973), 733.

4 R. H. Tawney's *Equality* (New York: Barnes & Noble, 1964) is a classic statement.

Index